More praise for

The Fourteenth Day

"A half century later there are still important things about the Cuban missile crisis left to explore. David Coleman is the first to use the Kennedy tapes to show that the challenges posed by the crisis did not end on the fabled thirteenth day. *The Fourteenth Day* is a brilliant reconstruction of a time of superb presidential leadership. It is essential reading for those who love presidential history or just remain fascinated by JFK." —Timothy Naftali, former director of the Richard Nixon Presidential Library and Museum and coauthor of *"One Hell of a Gamble"*

"An engrossing and revealing account. . . . Coleman has provided an excellent analysis of both short and long term results of the crisis."
—*Booklist*

"No family has been better at shaping its own mythology than the Kennedys. Using White House tapes and his own prodigious research and keen insight, David Coleman has painted a portrait of the JFK White House after the Cuban missile crisis as it really was. The picture is not damning, but it is human and revealing."
—Evan Thomas, author of *Robert Kennedy: His Life* and *Ike's Bluff: President Eisenhower's Secret Struggle to Save the World*

"[Coleman] adds nuances to our understanding. . . . He has intimate knowledge of the tapes . . . *hington Post*

"Amid shelves of books on the Kennedy era, here at last is a genuinely fresh and interesting volume about his presidency. Coleman now leads the documentary team that transcribes and explains the recordings of meetings and phone calls that JFK secretly hoarded. Armed with that evidence and an exceptionally firm grasp of the personalities, institutions, and issues of that time, Coleman skillfully shows us a pivotal year—1962 to mid-1963—the turning point of the cold war and of the Kennedy presidency." —Philip Zelikow, former counselor of the Department of State and coauthor of *The Kennedy Tapes*

"Director of the Miller Center's Presidential Recording Program, Coleman has the goods." —*Library Journal*

"Fascinating; Coleman brings this remarkable story to life, and his use of material from the Kennedy tapes is particularly impressive. This is the sort of book anyone interested in the period will enjoy reading."
—Marc Trachtenberg, author of *A Constructed Peace*

"Continues to blow holes in what we thought we knew."
—*Boston Globe*

"This is the first book to provide an insider's account based on over 260 hours of secret recordings made by Kennedy before and after the standoff, and should be in the collections of any American history holding strong in the politics of the times." —*Midwest Book Review*

"A delight to read, particularly for anyone wanting to see how America's executive branch operates under severe crisis. Simply put, *The Fourteenth Day* is a recommended read." —DCMilitary.com

The Fourteenth Day

The Fourteenth Day

JFK and the Aftermath of the Cuban Missile Crisis

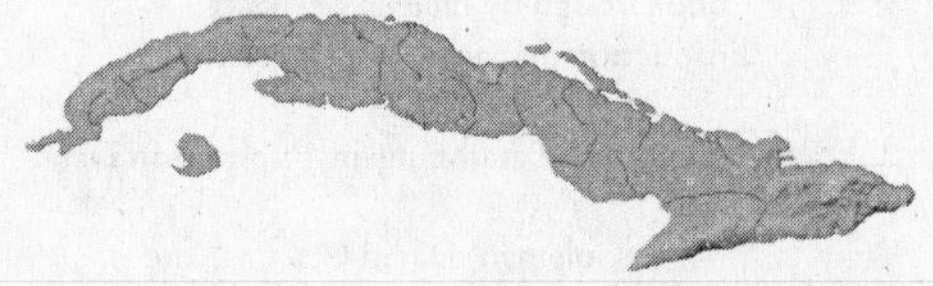

DAVID G. COLEMAN

W. W. NORTON & COMPANY
New York London

The Presidential Recordings Program is supported in part by grants from the National Historical Publications and Records Commission.

Printed in the United States of America
First published as a Norton paperback 2014

For information about permission to reproduce selections from this book, write to Permissions, W. W. Norton & Company, Inc., 500 Fifth Avenue, New York, NY 10110

For information about special discounts for bulk purchases, please contact W. W. Norton Special Sales at specialsales@wwnorton.com or 800-233-4830

Manufacturing by Courier Westford
Book design by Helene Berinsky
Production manager: Julia Druskin

Library of Congress Cataloging-in-Publication Data

Coleman, David G.
The fourteenth day : JFK and the aftermath of the Cuban Missile Crisis / David G. Coleman. — 1st ed.
p. cm.
Includes bibliographical references and index.
ISBN 978-0-393-08441-2 (hardcover)
1. Cuban Missile Crisis, 1962. 2. Kennedy, John F. (John Fitzgerald), 1917–1963. 3. Cuban Missile Crisis, 1962—Influence. 4. United States—Politics and government—1961–1963. 5. Khrushchev, Nikita Sergeevich, 1894–1971. 6. United States—Foreign relations—1961–1963. 7. United States—Foreign relations—Soviet Union. 8. Soviet Union—Foreign relations—United States. I. Title.
E841 .C567
973.922092—dc23
2012025397

ISBN 978-0-393-34680-0 pbk.

W. W. Norton & Company, Inc.
500 Fifth Avenue, New York, N.Y. 10110
www.wwnorton.com

W. W. Norton & Company Ltd.
Castle House, 75/76 Wells Street, London W1T 3QT

1 2 3 4 5 6 7 8 9 0

CONTENTS

Preface to the Paperback Edition

Despite all the scholarly attention focused on JFK's presidency and the Cuban missile crisis in the past half-century, we are still learning new things. In the relatively short time since this book was originally published, new historical evidence has been become available that sheds further light on themes and episodes discussed in this book.

The occasion of the fiftieth anniversary of the Cuban missile crisis, in October 2012, brought with it a wave of new books and conferences that explored new perspectives and added new information to our understanding of that most studied of crises. Max Holland and David Barrett drew on declassified intelligence documents to offer new information and analysis of U-2 surveillance of Cuba in the lead-up to the crisis and analyzing in depth the intelligence postmortems. Their book reveals intense political battles within the intelligence and military communities to shape the understanding of the crisis, battles that raged simultaneously with the public political ones discussed in this book.[1] Svetlana Savranskaya, a historian specializing in Soviet sources, helped bring Sergo Mikoyan's account of his father's crucial visit to Havana in November 1962. First Deputy Minister Anastas Mikoyan had been dispatched to Cuba to try to smooth things over with an irate Fidel Castro. It was largely the worrying reports Anastas Mikoyan sent back to Moscow about Castro's apocalyptic tone that persuaded Khrushchev to reclaim the tactical nuclear *Luna* missiles. The original plan had been to transfer those missiles to the Cubans, which would have effectively made Cuba the world's fifth nuclear power overnight. Kennedy and his advisers knew very little about the content of the Mikoyan-Castro discussions at the time, but we now have a much better understanding of what was going on behind the sugarcane and iron curtains at the same time that officials in Washington were searching for a way to draw a line under the crisis.[2] David Gibson, a sociologist at the University of Pennsylvania, used a range of sociological analytic tools for the first time to offer an in-depth analysis of what the talk captured on the tapes shows about how decisions were made, finding that the decision-making processes in the White House during those tense days were less systematic than one might think.[3] Echoing that finding but approaching from a very different perspective, Sheldon Stern found that the president's advisers were more erratic and inconsistent than they were subsequently portrayed. By comparing the accounts subsequently perpetuated by key advisers to Kennedy to what can be heard on the White House tapes, he found that popular understanding of the missile crisis had been willfully distorted in the decades since.[4]

A surprisingly large number of documents from fifty years ago remain classified and are still off-limits to historians. The diligent efforts of groups such as the National Security Archive and the Cold War International History Project continue to pry those classified documents loose. Coinciding with the fiftieth anniversary of the crisis, the National Security Archive published important freshly declassified details of Operation Hot Plate, the military plan developed by the U.S. Air Force in the weeks after the missile crisis to bomb the Soviet IL-28s in Cuba if diplomacy failed to convince Khrushchev to remove them. The group also published for the first time estimates of casualties in the event of a U.S. invasion of Cuba. If nuclear weapons were *not* used, the Pentagon estimated 18,500 U.S. casualties in the first ten days. Strikingly, and for the first time that has so far come to light, General Maxwell Taylor, the chairman of the Joint Chiefs of Staff, directly addressed the impact of the presence of the Soviet *Luna* tactical nuclear weapons in Cuba might have on U.S. invasion plans. If Cuban leaders were "foolhardy" enough to use nuclear weapons against a U.S. invasion force, Taylor wrote, the U.S. could respond immediately with overwhelming nuclear force. And though he could not provide a specific number, the use of tactical nuclear weapons would have led to a far higher numbers of casualties.[5] Scholars working with the National Security Archive and the Cold War International History Project also unearthed new tranches of documents internationalizing our understanding of the crisis. Among them was a remarkable document from the Czech archives describing a discussion between Nikita Khrushchev and the visiting Czech president on October 30, just two days after Khrushchev's radio message promising to remove the missiles. The Soviet premier told his Eastern European ally that "we really were on the verge of war" and he claimed victory in the confrontation. He and his Kremlin colleagues had been "aghast," Khrushchev said, when they received Fidel Castro's October 26 letter suggesting that the Soviets start a nuclear war if the Americans invaded Cuba.[6]

FIFTY YEARS after his presidency came to a violent end, John F. Kennedy basks in a mostly golden light of nostalgic popular memory. Most Americans alive today had not yet been born on that fateful day in Dallas, but his name still resonates. If JFK was alive to contest the next presidential election, he might well win; polls have repeatedly shown that if Americans could choose any president to run the country today, Kennedy comes in first by a comfortable margin.[7]

But nostalgia tends not to favor nuance, and along the way the "real" JFK has become obscured. In part, that was the way Kennedy himself wanted it. He went to considerable lengths to avoid being boxed in, publicly, privately, and politically. The pragmatism that he wore so proudly meant that he liked to keep distance between himself and a decision. He preferred to have control over when to show his hand. That presents obstacles to the historian trying to understand the "real" JFK and is part of what makes the White House tapes so important.

Despite all the scholarly attention over the years on the Cuban missile crisis and JFK's presidency, there are things we still don't know. For example, we don't yet know the full extent of the Operation Mockingbird, the secret CIA program to spy on American journalists, a program that, thanks to the secret White House tapes, we now know was authorized directly by the president himself. And historians still debate why Nikita Khrushchev decided to secretly send nuclear missiles to Cuba, a decision that pushed the two world superpowers to the brink of nuclear war. But as historians continue to study the period and new historical evidence becomes available, we continue to inch toward a better understanding of the "real" JFK, of how he avoided what British Prime Minister Harold Macmillan called in the days after the crisis "a kind of super Munich," and of what really happened when the world faced the all-too-real prospect of nuclear armageddon.[8]

PREFACE

He was almost two years into his presidency, and it had not gone as well as he had hoped. It had not been a failure—there were still impressive successes that his supporters could trumpet—but on balance his administration's record was decidedly mixed. After a remarkable flourish of oratory eloquence that characterized his inaugural address, John F. Kennedy endured bruising battles on Capitol Hill, difficult encounters with America's superpower archrival, confrontations with big business, growing restlessness about the tentative pace of progress toward civil rights, and some serious, self-inflicted foreign policy wounds. It created the impression that the president, dashing and young and inspiring as he might be, was unsure in his footing. All in all, it was an inauspicious start to a presidency.

The fall of 1962 marked a turning point. The Cuban missile crisis of late October was the cold war's most dangerous nuclear crisis. It was also a defining moment of Kennedy's presidency and a watershed of the cold war.

His handling of that most dramatic and perilous of challenges played a key part in elevating him into the pantheon of great American presidents in nearly every public poll since, putting him in the ranks of George Washington and Abraham Lincoln, although an assassin's bullet robbed him of the opportunity to build on his slender record of accomplishments. As Americans look back over their country's modern history, more than eight in ten rank Kennedy as the country's best president since World War II. It is a lead he has held comfortably; after Kennedy's 85 percent retrospective approval rating, Ronald Reagan comes in second, with 75 percent. Moreover, that mark is a significant improvement, by 27 points, over the last poll conducted while he was in office and an 18-point improvement over his average rating in polls taken throughout his presidency. For Kennedy, retrospect has been kind.[1]

Several factors have contributed to that, none more so than the tragic circumstances of his death, an event that amounted to a national trauma. The youth and grace of his young family reflected glamour. At their best, his words could be inspirational and timeless. And there is nostalgia for a pre-Vietnam, pre-Watergate generation of president. But to those factors has to be added his impressive, careful handling of the Cuban missile crisis, remembered as decision making par excellence, as a moment when, with a steady hand, Kennedy avoided the devastation of nuclear war without yielding to Soviet aggression.

Half a century later, it is easy to imagine that that is the only way the Cuban missile crisis could have been remembered. But that this became the prevailing narrative was by no means a sure thing.

The crisis itself is famously remembered as a thirteen-day crisis. Robert Kennedy chose *Thirteen Days* for the memoir of the crisis originally conceived for his 1968 presidential campaign. Much later, there was a Hollywood movie of the same name. But those thirteen days cast a long shadow. For months thereafter, new battles raged at home and abroad. At stake for Kennedy were his prospects for reelection in 1964 and ultimately his legacy.[2]

During the crisis, criticism was muted, dissent nearly nonexistent, as Americans rallied behind the president in the face of the communist threat. That would change. Once the crisis was over, that solidarity evaporated as quickly as it had formed. With the imminent peril passed, the White House's critics no longer felt compelled to hold their fire. Critics charged that the Kennedy administration had invited the crisis through neglect, had deliberately withheld information from the American people, was playing politics with the nation's security, and had allowed the Soviets and Cubans off too easily.

Kennedy spent the weeks and months after the Cuban missile crisis waging battles on multiple fronts. The nature of the crisis had changed, but the stakes for his presidency were still extraordinarily high. On the diplomatic front, the United States, Soviet Union, and Cuba embarked on months of negotiations facilitated by the United Nations to try to draw a line under the crisis, to restore the situation to a status quo ante, and to remove the issue as a nuclear flash point. On the domestic front, the White House battled a frustrated press corps upset at the administration's tight control over information that it had enforced during the crisis under the pretext of national security but that lingered long after the immediate threat had passed. On the campaign trail and on the Hill, congressional critics accused the White House of having manufactured the quintessential October surprise, lambasted its handling of the crisis, and launched congressional investigations.

KENNEDY ENJOYED the kind of public approval ratings that any other postwar president would envy. They waxed and waned, but his average Gallup poll approval rating of 70 percent measured across his whole presidency was historically high, almost 20 points above Ronald Reagan's and 25 points above that of the previous Democratic president, Harry Truman. When only first terms are considered, only Lyndon Johnson fared better in his abbreviated first term, with numbers swelled by Kennedy's assassination and before the Vietnam escalation that would drag his public approval ratings, and his presidency, down precipitously.[3]

But troubling to Kennedy was the trajectory of those ratings. At the time the Cuban missile crisis broke, his public approval rating was steadily declining. He still enjoyed a historically high average approval rating, but it was in steady decline. His 78 percent public approval rating at the start of 1962 had slipped to 73 percent by May, 67 percent in September, and 62 percent by early October.

The Cuban missile crisis sent his poll numbers soaring , temporarily. Even at their height, Kennedy was careful not to read too much into them. "These things go up and down so fast," he told the *Time* magazine reporter Hugh Sidey.[4] On more than one occasion, he spoke of an organic ebb and flow to political and international affairs. The way he saw it, some of this constant cycle was real, and some merely of the media's making. The waves of criticism were aided and abetted by the inside-the-Beltway thinking that treated politics and policy with the same kind of focused scrutiny and second-guessing that others devoted to the a baseball manager's decisions or a football quarterback's performance. With characteristic self-awareness of his person and his presidency—proudly pragmatic to a fault—Kennedy was able to put it in perspective. "I don't think the people are as mercurial out there as they are in Washington," he told Sidey, continuing, "Impressions are longer lasting out there. In Washington there is a terrific change of temperature with each issue. That is all they do here. Out there there are other things that are important."[5]

For Kennedy, the end of the Cuban missile crisis presented both a challenge and an opportunity. Many issues remained to be resolved and attacks to be repelled, foreign and domestic. But late 1962 through the first part of 1963, especially from October 1962 through February 1963, marked a new period in his presidency. To an extent that could not be known at the time, it became crucial to his legacy. The White House's resident historian, Arthur M. Schlesinger Jr., called it "the great turning," a period of transition at home and abroad, a period punctuated by fewer crises and marked by greater stability. It was a crucial, yet often overlooked, period in the making of Kennedy's legacy.

There were certainly missteps along the way. The American press bristled at what it saw as the administration's draconian information policies, the British outplayed the Americans in the Skybolt episode, and the conflict in Vietnam continued to fester. But by the summer of 1963, important progress had been made. The first agreement limiting nuclear testing had been signed, the dangerous cold war confrontation over West Berlin had been neutralized as a nuclear flash point, and Kennedy had started providing real leadership on two of the most important issues of the day, global peace and civil rights.

The John F. Kennedy of January 1963 was not the same John F. Kennedy who came into office in January 1961. By early 1963, he appeared more sure-footed, more confident, more thoughtful, and more at ease with the presidency. He was older and wiser, to be sure, and starting to show the first signs of graying, but he was also more experienced. His political career, from his first campaign for the Eleventh Congressional District of Massachusetts, was characterized by learning. And he was a quick study.

By early 1963, Kennedy was ready to put what he had learned to use and to spend some of his newly won political capital. The Cuban missile crisis was uninvited, dangerous, and dramatic. But it also created a pivot point, an opportunity for Kennedy to reboot his presidency.

It would not be easy.

Thanks to Kennedy himself, we have a remarkable view of his efforts. For unstated reasons of his own—but most likely in anticipation of one day writing a memoir—Kennedy decided in late July 1962 to start secretly capturing his presidency on tape. Previous presidents had also surreptitiously recorded meetings and conversations while they were in office, but only sparingly and sporadically.

Kennedy's immediate successors, the Democrat Lyndon Johnson and the Republican Richard Nixon, also taped secretly while in the White House. Each created more recordings than Kennedy. Johnson was the only president to tape for the entire duration of his presidency, and Nixon created a vast collection of recordings for the period he taped, thanks to a sound-activated recording system. But Kennedy was the first to capture on tape in a systematic way the business of being president.

From the end of July 1962 through November 1963, JFK compiled approximately 260 hours of recordings on tape. He taped meetings, office conversations, telephone calls, and dictations. He did not intend for them to be public records.

The tapes are the antithesis of the kind of polished and vetted communiqués usually emitted by the White House communications office. They are unguarded, unrehearsed, and unscripted. They capture history in real time, not as memories.

The taping system was secret, and the circle of people with knowledge of it very small. Aside from the president himself, the Secret Service agents who installed and maintained the system and the president's secretary, Evelyn Lincoln, certainly knew as did Robert Kennedy and his secretary. One of Kennedy's closest aides, Kenneth O'Donnell, knew and may have told another close aide, Dave Powers, but there is no direct evidence of that.[6] If others had known of the taping system at the time, they almost certainly would have chosen their words differently. Some might even have been appalled. When FBI Director J. Edgar Hoover outlined for President Kennedy and other advisers a program of domestic wiretapping and surveillance, Secretary of State Dean Rusk pointedly protested, "If I ever catch anyone in our government bugging me, I will resign and make a public issue of it."[7] (Unfortunately, historians are deprived of the delicious irony of that threat, made in the Cabinet Room, being caught on Kennedy's own taping system, for it apparently was not one of the conversations the president chose to record.) But the secrecy surrounding the tapes' creation greatly enhances their value. It also means that they can be unflattering, especially to advisers unaware that their candid recommendations and observations might one day be shared with the world. They challenge any notion of executive privilege.

There is certainly no shortage of official government documentation. Indeed, unlike many other important areas of history, government policy suffers from a surfeit of historical documentation. Public statements, minutes of meetings, memoranda, and reminiscences by participants are all crucial pieces of evidence for the historian trying to unravel what, when, and why something happened, or did not happen. But the tapes add something new.

Kennedy's most prolific period of taping was during and immediately after the Cuban missile crisis. For the thirteen days of the crisis, he captured many meetings, conversations, and telephone calls. In doing so, he created a remarkable record of a remarkable episode, of crucial decisions being made under intense pressure. The meetings that he taped were not just any meetings; they were the ultra-secret discussions of his top national security experts wrestling with the problem of how to respond to the Soviet challenge against stakes that involved, without exaggeration, the very survival of the United States and indeed much of the world. The corpus of material from those thirteen days is fascinating and important, offering the ultimate insider view of the cold war's most dangerous crisis.[8]

But Kennedy did not stop taping on 28 October 1962, the thirteenth and last day of the Cuban missile crisis. In the ensuing months, as he confronted challenges at home and abroad, tried to reinvigorate his presidency, and laid the foundation for his 1964 reelection campaign, Kennedy kept the tapes rolling.

In providing a real-time, fly-on-the-wall perspective, the tapes complement things we have already known. They sometimes correct a flawed record. They add nuance and objectivity. They also provide important new information. The tapes show that Kennedy's battles with the press in late 1962 and early 1963 were more intense, and that the president was far more intimately involved, than was previously known. In the summer, Kennedy had authorized a secret campaign against Pentagon leaks, even wading into the dubious legal territory of having the CIA and FBI spy on American journalists with warrantless wiretaps. That covert campaign, still in full swing in the fall, manifested itself in the deep public controversy in the wake of the

Cuban missile crisis about "news management"—probably the most intense public debate about information secrecy since the Second World War—in which the Kennedy administration was accused of Goebbels-like news policies and taking the American government a step closer to becoming a communist dictatorship. The tapes also yield new information on the calculations and decisions in negotiating an agreement with the Soviets on Cuba, the internal debates on what constituted a threat worth fighting for, and the unexpected neutralization of the problem of West Berlin, until then the cold war's foremost flash point. Perhaps most importantly, they show how Kennedy was approaching problems, weighing alternatives, and making decisions during the crucial four to five months following the Cuban missile crisis.

This book focuses on the period from 29 October 1962 through February 1963, and on how Kennedy and his advisers grappled with the issues and challenges raised and changes wrought by the Cuban missile crisis.

There was much else happening in the world during this period that is outside the scope of this book. As examples, China and India were coming to blows in a brief, yet intense, border skirmish. The so-called special relationship between Washington and London became strained over an important, and expensive, failure of communication about their collaboration on the Skybolt nuclear missile, a disagreement that led to that project's termination. Kennedy signed an executive order prohibiting racial discrimination in housing. Internal budget debates prompted changes in the numbers of nuclear weapons; among the notable pieces of advice caught on tape was Defense Secretary Robert McNamara's recommending to Kennedy, "Take the requirement and double it and buy it. Because I don't believe we can under any circumstances run the risk of having too few, here. So I, in my own mind, I just say, 'Well, we ought to buy twice what any reasonable person would say is required for strategic forces.' I think it's money well spent."[9] And, having earlier staked his reputation on the promise that Americans would stand on the moon before the decade was out, Kennedy restated his commitment to the space race: "This is the top priority program of the agency and one of the two—except for defense—the top priority of the United States Government."[10]

But it is the aftermath of the Cuban missile crisis that this book concerns itself with. It was a crucial and often overlooked period of change in the cold war. And it provides a remarkable window into Kennedy's presidency.

The Fourteenth Day

1

The Ultimate Source of Action

"Is this tape in? Is this plugged in?" he asked his personal secretary, Evelyn Lincoln. As John F. Kennedy sat alone in his office with his Dictaphone recorder sometime in 1959 or 1960—before he was elected president but after he had decided to run—he wanted to lay out a history of his political career and explain why he found elected office so important and personally rewarding, to explain why it had become a calling and not just a career. Mrs. Lincoln confirmed that the recorder was in fact working and switched on. The junior senator from Massachusetts began to speak. He spoke for about twenty-six minutes.

Dictating memos, letters, and speech drafts with a microphone and recorder was a habit Kennedy had recently gotten into, as had many executives of the era, to free himself from always having to summon a secretary into his office to take shorthand notes to be typed up later in long form. That had been the standard procedure in offices around the world for over a century and had provided employment for generations of secretaries and typists.

But innovations in affordable consumer recording devices offered a more efficient, more flexible option, bypassing the need for shorthand notes. And it could be done after hours without asking secretaries to work late. It could even be done away from the office. With a Dictaphone recorder, Kennedy was free to do this most time-consuming yet essential of workday chores virtually when and where he liked. The tapes, or belts, in the case of a Dictaphone, could then be passed to a pool of typists to be typed up. It was, of course, only a small step toward the revolution in office communications that came in the following decades, but it marked an important initial breakthrough.

On this occasion, Kennedy was not dictating a letter or memorandum. It is not known precisely when he made this particular recording or why. It is possible—even probable—that he was making notes for what would one day be the first draft of his memoir. He was, after all, already an accomplished and Pulitzer Prize–winning author, well versed in a historian's way of thinking. He made other, similar recordings later, while in the Oval Office, that were almost certainly early notes for such a book, something for him to work on after leaving office. After all, even if he had been reelected in 1964 and lived to serve out a second term, he would not yet have been fifty-one years old when he became an ex-president.

Whatever his reasons, the recording he created during that session provides a remarkable view of his thinking about politics, policy, and public service. Speaking in a matter-of-fact tone, he laid out why he thought politics mattered and the good that politicians could do despite their negative public image. The effects of coming of age politically in the era of Franklin D. Roosevelt and having been raised in the Democratic stronghold of Boston came through strongly. And in his own words and voice, he explained why he aspired to be president. He had been a congressman and a senator. But the presidency, he said, was "the ultimate source of action."

That John F. Kennedy chose politics as his career was by no means inevitable. His father, the family patriarch, Joseph P. Kennedy, who was never accused of lacking for ambition, audacity, or, for much of his adult life, money, had made it abundantly clear that he expected political greatness from his male offspring. Those hopes and dreams had been sharply focused on John's older brother, Joe Junior. When

Joe Junior was killed in action in World War II in Europe, the mantle of expectations was not automatically handed to the next-oldest brother, John. As a sickly child and young man—he had been given the last rites twice—John had not grown up expecting to be a leader or to run for office. Before John Kennedy embarked on a political career, a shift in his thinking was therefore required.[1]

In his pre-presidential recording, he cast himself as a reluctant convert to a political career. Glossing over some of the earliest discussions of the possibility, Kennedy noted that about a year after his brother's death he decided that he would try his hand at politics. There was never an epiphany, he said; there "never was a moment of truth for me when I saw my whole political career unfold."

It was certainly not about money. He already had plenty of family money from the fortune his father had amassed. His personal trust, managed by his father's accountants in New York, provided a generous income, so much so that since first entering Congress in 1947 and continuing through his time in the Senate and the Oval Office, Kennedy routinely donated his salary to charity. As president, that amounted to $100,000 a year, a significant sum, about double the current presidential salary when adjusted for inflation.

Nor did Kennedy lack opportunities for pursuing other career paths. He could have been a wealthy lawyer or perhaps an important figure in the world of newspapers. A career in that direction had gotten an early boost. Family connections helped land him some plum assignments that took him to the sites of several great global events: the United Nations founding conference in San Francisco; the Potsdam Conference, where Winston Churchill, Harry Truman, and Joseph Stalin decided the fate of the postwar world; and the British elections in 1945, where the party of the wartime hero Churchill suffered a stunning defeat at the polls by Clement Attlee's Labour Party. But reporting lacked something for the restless young Kennedy. As he explained it, "A reporter is reporting what happens; he's not making it happen. Even the good reporters, the ones who are really fascinated by what happens and who find real stimulus in putting their noses into the center of action, even they, in a sense, are in a secondary profession. It's reporting what happened, but it isn't participating." So Kennedy decided against that profession, although for the rest of his life he maintained a good understanding of and fascination with the media business and, unlike some of his political rivals, mingled comfortably in press circles, counting several reporters among his closest friends.

By his own explanation, Kennedy felt called to participate rather than watch from the sidelines. When combined with its corollaries of action, vigor, and decision—all virtues that he would adopt to style his political career—participation became Kennedy's self-defined approach to politics and governing. It underpinned the carefully crafted public persona that became known simply as JFK.

An opportunity arose in 1946 for the young Kennedy to test the political waters: a vacancy in the Eleventh Congressional District of Massachusetts, a seat his grandfather had held half a century before. "Suddenly, the time, the occasion, and I all met," Kennedy said. As he himself described it, a steep learning curve was accompanied by building momentum and growing enthusiasm for the possibilities: "I moved into the Bellevue Hotel with my grandfather and I began to run. I have been running ever since. Fascination began to grip me and I realized how satisfactory a profession a political career could be. I saw how ideally politics filled the Greek definition of happiness: 'A full use of your powers along lines of excellence in a life affording scope.'"

Kennedy won a seat in the U.S. House of Representatives in the 1946 election. Although there were times when his work interested him, he soon became frustrated at the difficulty in distinguishing himself from 434 other members of Congress, most of whom also had a strong interest in burnishing or building their public profiles. After six years in the House, he was again restless. "I prepared to move on," he said simply. Kennedy ran for the Senate. He was successful, beating a formidable opponent with a long family lineage of Massachusetts politics: Henry Cabot Lodge Jr.

Unlike his successor, Lyndon B. Johnson, widely celebrated as a master practitioner of Senate rules, traditions, and power, Kennedy was unimpressed with that chamber. "There is," he said, "much less than meets the eye in the Senate, frequently." And the key to success in the Senate was changing as governing the nation became infinitely more complicated. A generational shift was also under way, as a post–World War II, twentieth-century mind-set edged out that of the nineteenth century. As Kennedy saw it, approvingly, politics was also becoming more of a profession, in which the "hail-fellow, well-met" extroverts were being replaced by quiet and thoughtful men.

He soon found the strict seniority system stifling. Decades-long Senate service was not unusual; by the time Kennedy was sworn in, one member, Walter George of Georgia, was beginning his fourth decade in the Senate. Even for the most senior members, years of work could be undone by a brief vote or an even briefer presidential speech. A junior member, such as Kennedy, could count on much less. That led Kennedy to a realization: "All of the things that you become interested in doing, the President can do and the Senate cannot, particularly in the area of foreign policy." In national security, defense, and foreign policy—many of the areas Kennedy was most interested in—the reality was that the legislative branch was secondary to the executive branch. Senator Kennedy lamented that "it's the President who controls and who can affect results." And as he explained it, that motivated him to seek the presidency.

Kennedy had five successful political campaigns under his belt before deciding to run for the presidency. He had also been in the mix of contenders for his party's nomination to be Adlai Stevenson's running mate in 1956, thanks to the publicity generated by his voice-over work for a film shown at the Democratic National Convention. That, and a best-selling and Pulitzer Prize–winning book, *Profiles in Courage*, gave Kennedy a national profile.

Kennedy took from these successful campaign experiences several lessons. Having money, which he had access to in abundance, could help, but it could also hurt. It was not essential to political success, he believed, and rarely decisive. A widely recognized and respected name could be a great advantage. It was something he counted himself fortunate to have. He also learned that starting with disadvantages did not necessarily doom a campaign. When he first ran for the Congress, Kennedy had spent little time in the district and did not have deep ties there. Worse, his blue-collar credentials were weak—he lived in a fancy hotel, had spent much of the previous decade in New York, "and on top of that . . . had gone to Harvard, not a particularly popular institution at that time in the Eleventh Congressional District."

But all of that could be overcome, particularly if one adhered to what he believed was the most important factor in his political success: starting a campaign early. Through his House and Senate campaigns, he had seen what a difference it could make in helping establish a beachhead in the public consciousness. Because most people had more important things to worry about than politics and politicians most of the time, only focusing on them at election time, it was essential to get an early start on building an enduring political presence, rather than expecting one to materialize as if by magic a few months before election day. Starting a campaign early was, Kennedy said, "in my opinion the most important key to political success." At the time, it was an innovation. It became a defining feature in Kennedy's political style. During 1963, he was starting to look far ahead to the next election, in 1964, just as he had for his previous campaigns.

As he wrapped up his private recording session, Kennedy turned reflective. "I would say that I have never regretted my choice of professions, even though I cannot know what the future will bring," the young senator said. He switched off the recorder and put the Dictaphone belt in the care of his trusted personal secretary, Evelyn Lincoln. The recording would remain locked away in the files for thirty years.

ON 8 NOVEMBER 1960, Kennedy won the presidency, but just barely. His victory over Vice President Richard Nixon was by the narrowest of margins—just under 120,000 votes out of a record 68.8 million votes cast, a plurality of less than two-tenths of a percent. And as so often happens in modern presidential elections where tens of millions of votes are cast in thousands of polling centers, questions lingered about local ballot irregularities. The unconvincing manner of Kennedy's victory would have important practical ramifications. With a weak mandate, not much executive experience, and a Congress that owed little loyalty to the new, young president, Kennedy transitioned from candidate on the campaign trail to occupant of the Oval Office.

He assembled a bipartisan and centrist cabinet filled with impressive résumés. He persuaded Robert McNamara to give up his new job leading the Ford Motor Company to head the sprawling bureaucracy of the Pentagon. At the urging of Democratic elder statesmen whose counsel he trusted, especially former secretary of state Dean Acheson and former secretary of defense Robert Lovett, he brought Dean Rusk in from the Rockefeller Foundation as secretary of state. From Wall Street, he secured C. Douglas Dillon to be his treasury secretary. And he recruited McGeorge Bundy, the youngest-ever dean at Harvard, to lead the White House's national security team.

On the morning of his inauguration, the air was crisp and a layer of freshly fallen snow covered the ground in Washington. For his supporters, it was a fitting symbol of a fresh new start after eight years of a Republican White House. Adlai Stevenson, with impeccable liberal credentials, had twice failed to best Dwight Eisenhower. Now a young president, full of promise and promises, radiating health and youth (having confessed to past injuries but not to his serious illness) and of a generation born in the twentieth century, laid out his vision.

Kennedy's inauguration speech, crafted in collaboration with his longtime wordsmith Ted Sorensen, was a masterpiece of prose delivered artfully. It promised an era of progress and renewal, a legislative program that would right injustices and restore basic fairness at home, and a foreign policy of resolve and modernization. They would look forward, Kennedy said, not back. The economist Walt Rostow provided the bold new agenda with a name that stuck. It would be the New Frontier.

Almost immediately, the aspirations of bringing new, modern

ideas to the governance of the country and its foreign policy ran into problems. Although Democrats controlled both houses of Congress, southern Democrats often sided with Republicans on social legislation that formed key components of the New Frontier. Civil rights legislation he had promised during the campaign was stonewalled in Congress, and by the fall of 1962, civil rights leaders were growing increasingly disillusioned with Kennedy's reluctance to push the issue.

Some problems were of the administration's own making. When the steel industry tried to defy the White House and raise prices, Kennedy forced it to back down. It was ostensibly a victory, but one that came with a price. The White House had spent considerable political capital in the battle, and its tactics were seen as heavy-handed and antibusiness. It would take some time for those early impressions to erode. An early effort siding with the legendary Speaker Sam Rayburn to remove an uncooperative Mississippi Democrat who was creating a bottleneck in the Rules Committee that was holding up legislation ended with Rayburn and the White House winning, but unconvincingly.

Before the fall of 1962, two episodes on the world stage led many voters to question Kennedy's effectiveness as president. In April of the preceding year, the administration botched what was supposed to be covert assistance for an invasion and uprising in Cuba to oust the communist leader Fidel Castro. The invasion, known for its landing site at the Bahía de Cochinos, or Bay of Pigs, failed dismally, with tragic consequences for many involved. CIA-trained Cuban émigrés storming their homeland were quickly rounded up and captured, and Castro remained in power, more determined than ever to defy the United States. Making it worse, the White House initially mishandled its public response by denying involvement and then being forced to backtrack. The Bay of Pigs misadventure amounted to a self-inflicted wound, and a serious one at that.

Less than two months later, in June 1961, Kennedy met with Nikita Khrushchev, the Soviet premier, in Vienna. The summit did not go well. Rather than leading to the kind of mutual understanding that might reduce cold war tensions, as Kennedy had hoped when agreeing to the meeting, the closely watched summit instead led to the kind of mutual misunderstanding that made the cold war more dangerous. Khrushchev renewed his threat to West Berlin, and the exchanges created the widely held public impression that the seasoned, mercurial communist leader had browbeaten the inexperienced, young president. Such reports probably exaggerated the effectiveness of Khrushchev's tactics—it was certainly not the first time Khrushchev had resorted to blunt language, after all—but the image they created less than two months after the botched Bay of Pigs invasion was of a president unsure of his footing.

Kennedy had assumed office believing that the presidency was the ultimate source of action, but by the fall of 1962 many of his initiatives seemed to lead only to new lessons on the limits of presidential power.

One does not need the benefit of hindsight to recognize that the crisis over Cuba in the fall of 1962 was no ordinary foreign policy challenge. Nikita Khrushchev's plan, to put Soviet nuclear missiles just ninety miles off the continental United States, was audacious in the extreme. That it was to be done in secret, presenting the Americans with a fait accompli, was incendiary, especially in an election season. The stakes in the ensuing showdown were extraordinarily high: nothing less than survival or global thermonuclear annihilation. That set it apart from the dozens of decision moments and crises, big and small, that came through the Oval Office doorway on any given day. Kennedy—along with his Soviet counterpart, Khrushchev, and indeed the rest of the world—knew all too well that a misstep could be fatal to millions. It could even destroy the very nation Kennedy was sworn to protect.

What had Khrushchev been up to? Why had he risked so much, taken "one hell of a gamble," in Kennedy's words? For Kennedy, trying to untangle Khrushchev's intentions and motivations was key. The answers he arrived at helped shape his own responses and policies, and helped him anticipate how his own actions might be interpreted in Moscow. Again and again during the crisis, he would ask his Soviet experts their views and try to think through the problem himself.[2]

The foundation for the crisis had been laid back in the summer, when Khrushchev decided to add nuclear weapons to the mix of military hardware that the Soviets would send by ship to their small, feeble ally in the Caribbean. What the Cuban communists led by Fidel Castro lacked in real means they made up for with revolutionary zeal. For the Soviets, struggling with communist China for the leadership role in world communism, Cuba offered more than just a beachhead very near America. It represented an opportunity for Moscow to burnish its revolutionary credentials.

Precisely why the plan to send nuclear missiles to Cuba appealed to Khrushchev is largely a matter of informed speculation. Khrushchev himself gave several reasons, none of which, on its own, entirely satisfies. In one telling, it was an effort to defend Cuba against an American invasion. In another, it was to retaliate for American-made NATO missiles deployed close to the borders of the Soviet Union.

Historians Timothy Naftali and Aleksandr Fursenko, based on their careful reading of Soviet documents, make a convincing case that Khrushchev's thinking was initially vague, that he sensed benefits that had not yet taken full form, but that when he contemplated what the new situation would look like, he saw opportunity.[3] Khrushchev could often be mercurial and stubborn, sometimes charming and persuasive. But he was always a devoted opportunist. The State Department had warned Kennedy about that on his way to his first meeting with the Soviet premier at Vienna in June of the preceding year:

> Although it is true to a degree of almost all leaders, it is especially true of Khrushchev that he attempts to relate the various pieces of policy that he envisages to each other. Periodically he seems to take inventory of his most important problems and his most

important opportunities, put them in a blender, and come up with a synthetic solution which is meant to deal with them all.[4]

For Khrushchev, one of the greatest opportunities was to force a final resolution of the Berlin problem, something that had more than once over the preceding decade and a half caused a confrontation that could have all too easily led to nuclear war. An awkward arrangement in the closing stages of World War II had left West Berlin, protected by the United States, France, and Great Britain, as an enclave buried deep in communist East Germany. Repeated attempts by the Soviets to force the Western powers from the city had failed but had made the city one of the cold war's most dangerous flash points. Now Khrushchev apparently believed he could resolve the issue in his favor once and for all.[5]

Whatever Khrushchev's real intentions, they were thwarted by miscalculation and by the responses crafted by Kennedy and his advisers. Through an intense series of meetings and feverish departmental and agency activity, they had devised a plan of action that persuaded Khrushchev to suffer the humiliation of defeat, with all the consequences that it would have for undermining the Soviet premier's leadership.

Kennedy had first been informed of the photographic reconnaissance early on the morning of 16 October. For the following thirteen days he and his advisers wrestled with the cold war's most dangerous crisis. But tension over Cuba had been building since the summer.

On 4 September, responding to an intensifying public and political debate about growing Soviet military aid to Cuba, Kennedy, through his press secretary, Pierre Salinger, had issued a clear warning: that if the military buildup crossed a threshold from defensive forces to ones that posed an offensive threat to American territory, "the gravest issues would arise."[6]

Surveillance photographs from U-2s, cutting-edge spy planes that flew at very high altitude, provided irrefutable evidence that the threshold had been crossed. Kennedy gathered his advisers to devise a response. And he recorded many of their discussions, creating a rich historical record of high-stakes diplomatic decision making.[7]

Meeting in intense secrecy for a week, from 16 through 22 October, the group digested the available intelligence information and debated how to respond. Members of a generation for which words like "Munich" and "appeasement" instantly brought to mind images of the death and destruction of World War II, those in the group never seriously questioned that something had to be done. They initially inclined toward some kind of military strike. Shortcomings of such a course became increasingly apparent. Military commanders could not guarantee that their forces could destroy all the missile sites before the Soviets might fire some of their missiles; the CIA was not even sure it had found all the missile sites (it had not). And launching surprise attacks too distastefully echoed the Pearl Harbor attacks that had drawn the United States into World War II.

By 21 October, Kennedy had settled on a middle course: the United States would institute a naval blockade of Cuba, dubbed a "quarantine" to make it more palatable to world opinion, preventing further arms shipments from arriving on the island. That would allow time for the Soviets to reach a decision to back down. If they did not do so, the American military would stand ready to launch military strikes.

At 7 p.m. on 22 October, Kennedy gave a special televised speech announcing that U.S. surveillance had gathered hard evidence of nuclear missiles in Cuba and accusing Soviet leaders of "deliberate deception."[8] It ushered in the public phase of the crisis.

On 23 October, Kennedy signed a proclamation listing the military equipment that would be targeted by the U.S naval quarantine as prohibited items. It specified surface-to-surface missiles, bomber aircraft, bombs, air-to-surface rockets and guided missiles, warheads for any of these weapons, along with the support equipment needed to operate the weapons.[9]

Tense days followed as the U.S. Navy carried out the quarantine of Cuba. It was not clear how the Soviets would respond. Some Soviet ships bound for Cuba turned back. Others stopped.

The massive American military, the most advanced in the world, went on high alert. Its nuclear forces, capable of destroying the world many times over, went to DEFCON 2, the highest alert level before missiles were fired in anger. Children as far away as Australia rehearsed their civil defense drills, ducking and covering under their school desks. And the front pages of newspapers around the world dissected every morsel of information, every White House utterance that became available.

But then, with dramatic suddenness, Khrushchev capitulated. A flurry of secret letters between Kennedy and Khrushchev, known as the pen-pal series, had led to an agreement. That formal channel was complemented by a secret channel from the White House flowing through the president's brother Robert Kennedy and key officials at the Soviet embassy in Washington, to Moscow. Khrushchev agreed to remove the missiles that had sparked the crisis and facilitate the means of assurance that they would not be reintroduced. Kennedy agreed to provide assurances that the United States would not invade Cuba. Secretly, he also agreed to remove medium-range ballistic missiles under NATO command from Turkey. And like that, the crisis was over.[10]

Or rather, one phase was over, the most dangerous and best-remembered phase. But the crisis that has gone down in history as a thirteen-day crisis cast a long shadow. For all the palpable sense of relief felt on 28 October 1962, when Khrushchev's message that he would order the removal of the missiles was transmitted around the world, many issues that had contributed to the crisis in the first place remained unresolved. Many of those unresolved issues would drag on for months in public and in behind-the-scenes negotiations. Some would fundamentally change the cold war, ushering in a new period less threatened by nuclear crises and opening new opportunities for East–West détente. Some would never be solved, producing echoes years later for future administrations to confront.

During the crisis, the White House had put many other pressing issues on hold. China and India were coming to blows along their border. At home, an election loomed. The presidential election was still two years away, but nine days after the end of the crisis, American voters would go to the polls for midterm elections. Although only House, gubernatorial, and some Senate seats were being decided, it was widely viewed as the voters' first opportunity to pass judgment on Kennedy's presidency. History and a deepening voter apathy pointed to Democratic losses.

But before Kennedy and his advisers could turn their attention to the bulging portfolio of other urgent issues—let alone devote time to shaping the future—there was important work to be done in the present. They still had important challenges to confront in regard to Cuba, remaining vigilant against a well-armed and creative adversary. Guarding against the possibility of Soviet duplicity was their first order of business.

2

The Fourteenth Day

Kennedy began the fourteenth day much as he had the preceding thirteen: meeting with his national security team. Once again, they focused on the same part of the world that had consumed so much of their time and energy, provoked so much anxiety and so many fears around the world over the previous fortnight: Cuba. Before the day was out, the group would regather around the large, wooden conference table in the Cabinet Room in the White House's West Wing for an early-evening meeting to discuss the latest, up-to-the-minute intelligence and respond to the highly fluid situation.

Kennedy sat in the middle of the long side nearest the windows opening to the Rose Garden. At his place, attached to the table, a discreet button that looked like a buzzer to summon a secretary actually allowed Kennedy to stop and start the reel-to-reel tape recorder that was downstairs in a basement room used for filed storage. Two microphones were hidden in the Cabinet Room walls, concealed by drapes, in places where wall fixtures had once been. To Kennedy's left sat Defense Secretary Robert McNamara; to his right, Secretary of State Dean Rusk. The thirteen other principals in the meeting sat in heavy leather and wood chairs around the table, memoranda and other papers and ashtrays covering much of the table's surface. Near the fireplace to Kennedy's right, wooden easels were still set up, ready for intelligence briefers to display large blowup images of the latest intelligence photos taken over Cuba.

For some of the ExComm members meeting with Kennedy that morning, the night before had been the first for some time that they had not been forced to find whatever sleep they could catch on cots set up in the offices and corridors of the White House, State Department, and Pentagon. As the crisis peaked, their family members at home had been handed large envelopes stamped "top secret" with instructions to keep a packed overnight bag near the door and to be ready in the event that soldiers came to whisk them away to a nuclear bunker. The overnight bags would no longer be needed.

The group had been given a formal name about a week earlier: the Executive Committee of the National Security Council, often shortened to ExComm. The special designation was to distinguish it from the regular National Security Council (NSC), a body created by Congress in the National Security Act of 1947, whose membership was legislated. On the morning of 16 October, when Kennedy was first briefed by CIA photo reconnaissance analysts that the Soviets were indeed setting up nuclear missile bases in Cuba, he asked several people not normally part of the National Security Council to sit in. Having the ExComm during the thirteen-day crisis allowed Kennedy to bring in advisers on a more ad hoc basis; finding it useful, he kept the new group. Its regular members were drawn mostly from the White House, CIA, Defense Department, State Department, and Treasury Department. National Security Adviser McGeorge Bundy had taken on the role of the main coordinator, and Secretary of Defense Robert McNamara, Secretary of State Dean Rusk, and Chairman of the Joint Chiefs of Staff Maxwell Taylor had consistently taken leading roles in their meetings. Others, like Attorney General Robert F. Kennedy and Ambassador-at-Large Llewellyn Thompson, often remained relatively quiet during the formal meetings, but their opinions and advice carried much weight with the president. Robert Kennedy, in particular, preferred to offer his advice privately. Vice President Lyndon Johnson was usually present but rarely spoke up. Some deputies who were actively involved in implementing the policies, such as Under Secretary of State George Ball, Deputy Undersecretary of State for Political Affairs U. Alexis Johnson, and Deputy Secretary of Defense Roswell Gilpatric, were the details men, frequently called on to provide the latest information and coordinate any actions that needed to be taken. From time to time, Kennedy brought others into the group on an ad hoc basis, including the outspoken former secretary of state Dean Acheson.

As had become customary, the meeting began with an intelligence briefing from the CIA's top official. At the outset of the crisis, Director of Central Intelligence John McCone was out of town, honeymooning in the south of France, so his deputy, General Marshall Carter, stood in for him, taking the lead in convincing the president and his advisers that the small markings on the black-and-white photos so unidentifiable to the untrained eye were in fact precisely the kinds of buildings and equipment that one would expect to find at a Soviet missile base. When the crisis broke, McCone rushed back, ready to brief and advise the president on a topic that had been a particular concern of his for months. He had guessed that the Soviets might be up to something, but it had taken time to find hard evidence of what that might be.

The crisis unfolded quickly. Like the military, the intelligence community had been on maximum alert. A flood of information was pouring through the analysts of the more than a dozen intelligence bodies operating under the auspices of the U.S. government. Far too much intelligence was coming in to be consumed in raw form by the members of the ExComm, so intelligence analysts worked through the night, drew from aerial reconnaissance, communications intercepts, refugee reports, and reporting from human intelligence sources to prepare a 6 a.m. digest that was distributed to key policymakers, or "customers," as the CIA called them. ExComm meetings typically began with McCone summarizing that report and any other items of particular interest that had arrived since.

The meetings on the fourteenth day were part of a long series; the ExComm would keep on meeting and discussing and planning for weeks and even months to come. Khrushchev's capitulation had not brought the finality to the crisis that many had hoped for. A year after the crisis, just days before his assassination, Kennedy was still referring publicly to "unfinished business" from the Cuban missile crisis.[1]

As he opened the meeting, Kennedy likely had many things on his mind. The missiles were still in Cuba. So were nuclear bombers, short-range nuclear missiles, tens of thousands of Soviet troops, and nuclear submarines. An election loomed, one in which Democrats were expected to lose seats. And the press was clamoring for information.

One issue stood out as the most urgent: verifying that Khrushchev was following through in having the missiles removed. It was not an easy problem. It hinged on a fundamental issue notably lacking in the U.S.-Soviet relationship: trust. How could Americans be sure that they weren't being duped? Might it all be some kind of devilish trick, buying time for the Soviet nuclear forces in Cuba to be readied for action?

Khrushchev had agreed to remove "the arms which you described as offensive."[2] It had brought the crisis to a close, but it was not at all clear what that actually meant. The careful phrasing was clearly more than a translation issue, and a misunderstanding on so fundamental a point might well result in other kinds of nuclear weapons and troops remaining in Cuba, just ninety miles off the coast of the United States. Kennedy had already said publicly that such a situation would be intolerable. It could pose a threat to the United States and other nations in the hemisphere and become a political liability at home, developments that Kennedy and the ExComm were determined to avoid. And if the Soviets did start moving the weapons out, how could Americans be sure that they were moving *all* of the missiles out and not spiriting some away to hiding places on the island? Cuba was pockmarked with an extensive network of natural limestone caves that provided underground hiding places safe from American spy planes.

Among the members of the ExComm, the mild-mannered secretary of state, Dean Rusk, was the most vocal in his skepticism of the Soviets' trustworthiness. Numerous times in the ensuing meetings caught on tape, he staked out a cautious position. It was not clear what the Soviets were up to, he said, but he strongly suspected they were up to something. Until they figured out what it was, Washington should keep its options open. If United States too easily gave up control of the means of verification, he told his colleagues, "we may be subject to a massive trick here."[3] A few days later, he put it more colorfully, suggesting that it was possible that the Soviets were orchestrating "a gigantic hoax of which history has had no parallel."[4]

Military leaders were also skeptical. As Marine Corps Commandant General David Shoup put it a couple of weeks later with his characteristic brusqueness, the proposals seemed "to rest very largely upon the questionable honor of the Soviets and Castro and all their ilk. And it's hard for me to believe that their philosophy of lying would be subject to any sudden reversal to a philosophy of telling the truth."[5]

It was a theme Rusk returned to in the ensuing days. Again and again he urged caution in dealing with the Soviets. He was not, however, blind to the indications that Khrushchev was going to follow through as he said he would. Some of the indications that intelligence analysts had picked up were unusual. The U.S. embassy in Moscow had reported that the entire Politburo had gone out to the theater the preceding night, a show of public solidarity that would have been unlikely if they had still been hunkered down executing a plan. Moreover, intercepted signals intelligence showed clearly that both Castro and the Chinese were becoming increasingly frustrated with the Soviets' understanding of what it meant to be allies. That suggested that the Soviets were constrained in their options. "So I'm not discouraged yet about the possibility this may be real," Rusk said. In the same breath, he warned that if photographic intelligence came back showing continued work on the missile sites or launchers with nose cones, "we've got a heck of a decision to make." It was still possible, he said, that Khrushchev's deal turned out to be "a gigantic fraud." So emphatic was Rusk's skepticism that Bundy teased him about it. "Mr. Secretary, you are a missionary of cheer," he joked.[6]

Kennedy was less openly skeptical. The CIA, State Department, and Defense Department mostly limited their evaluations to hard evidence, but one can hear Kennedy on the tapes adding another interpretive layer to help himself understand the situation and anticipate how it might develop, something only he, as the leader of a superpower, was in a position to do. It was his own version of the mix of art and science that had come to be known as Kremlinology. With actionable intelligence about the USSR scarce, Western experts on the Soviet Union—often known as Kremlinologists or, as Kennedy, with his typical dry sense of humor, liked to call them, demonologists—relied on a mix of experience, scraps of hard evidence, gossip, and linking seemingly unrelated clues in order to divine leadership struggles or impending shifts in policy. Half a world away, the U.S. ambassador to the Soviet Union, Foy Kohler, did his best to provide on-the-ground information about goings-on in Moscow. But official telegrams were not Kennedy's preferred means of gleaning insight; instead, he relied heavily on practitioners of the mysterious art of Kremlinology closer at hand, especially Llewellyn "Tommy" Thompson, a veteran Soviet expert recently returned from a stint as U.S. ambassador to Moscow, and Charles "Chip" Bohlen, the recently appointed U.S. ambassador to France. Kennedy repeatedly talked through the logic of Khrushchev's options and likely actions. He had done that many times during the crisis, trying to decode what Khrushchev was up to by projecting what would make logical sense if Kennedy were in Khrushchev's position. With Thompson's help—Bohlen's duties in Paris kept him across the Atlantic through much of the period—Kennedy routinely tried to build on the available evidence by adding likely outcomes in an effort to understand Khrushchev's motives and anticipate his probable reactions.[7]

Kennedy used that approach in attempting to understand whether or not Khrushchev's deal was genuine. It simply did not make sense, Kennedy held, for Khrushchev to try to renege on the deal. "I think they're going to dismantle these things now," he said. Given that the United Nations Acting Secretary-General U Thant was on his way to Havana to negotiate with Anastas Mikoyan and Castro, Kennedy argued, such a blatant display of bad faith would greatly diminish Khrushchev's options, a narrowing that any world leader would probably instinctively try to avoid. "With the mobile ones [missiles], they may be hiding some in the woods; we're not going to be able to tell that. But I don't think there's any doubt . . . just that there's no logic to their going ahead now with construction with U Thant arriving Tuesday and Wednesday," he said.

These projections were about understanding and quite distinct from the trust issue. Kennedy had recently had his own experiences that led him to question the possibility of dealing with the Soviets. At the beginning of the crisis, while it was still a secret that the United States had discovered the missile sites, Kennedy met with the Soviet foreign minister, Andrei Gromyko. It was 18 October, still four days before Kennedy's televised speech. Kennedy asked Gromyko directly whether there was any truth to rumors that the Soviets were installing long-range missiles in Cuba. About six weeks earlier, on 4 September, the White House had issued a sharp warning to Moscow of "the gravest consequences" if long-range missiles were found to be in Cuba. The issue had become highly political at home, with Senator Kenneth Keating, a New York Republican, claiming that he had received reliable information that the Soviets were indeed building missile bases in Cuba. Kennedy knew that Gromyko was well versed in that 4 September statement—how could he not be?—but during their meeting he read it aloud again to reinforce the point. Gromyko's response was both disingenuous and enormously consequential. Sticking to the party line, he said that there were no such Soviet weapons in Cuba. The USSR's aid to Cuba was purely defensive, he said.

What Gromyko did not know was that as they sat on the couches near the Oval Office fireplace, just a few feet away in a drawer of Kennedy's heavy wooden desk, made from timbers salvaged from the *HMS Resolute*, was a stack of black-and-white glossy prints of Soviet missile sites in Cuba photographed by American U-2 spy planes days earlier. Kennedy chose not to confront Gromyko with the evidence; he left the photos in his desk drawer. But for him Gromyko's false assurance provided firsthand confirmation of what many American policymakers had come to regard as a truism: the Soviets—and especially those sent abroad to lie for their country—simply could not be trusted.

In the wake of the crisis, Kennedy referred back to that instructive experience a number of times. The problem was not just Gromyko, he said, but also the Soviet ambassador to the United States, Anatoly Dobrynin. Attorney General Robert Kennedy, with the president's full knowledge, had been meeting secretly with Dobrynin to establish a private communication channel to Moscow by bypassing the formal diplomatic channels, and bureaucracy, of the State Department. But the president expressed skepticism of Dobrynin's reliability. In one 29 October exchange captured on his tapes, he complained at length to military chiefs about Soviet duplicity.

> You know, with the Russians, it just shows the last two months that whole operation they've run which was, you know, complete. . . .
>
> They had their ambassador telling us—I mean it just shows how they're willing to liquidate—this [Anatoly] Dobrynin is regarded very well in Russia, supposedly, is over here and has some reputation. He's around telling—he told the attorney general, he told [Dean] Rusk that they would never send missiles there. That was two weeks ago. So now he's liquidated as a source because nobody believes him anymore. . . . And the chances are he probably didn't know! He looked so *shocked* that day. When Rusk showed him [the surveillance photographs] he still wouldn't believe it. So it's probable they didn't even tell him.[8]

This led to the unsettling conclusion that the deal that had brought the crisis to a close might not be as final as they all hoped. As Kennedy put it, "When you're dealing under those conditions where there is no basis—we just have to assume that we're going to be back with Cuba in two or three months."[9]

With so much still unresolved, Kennedy bolstered the team negotiating directly with the Soviet delegation in New York. The team was led by Adlai Stevenson, the U.S. ambassador to the United Nations. In 1960, many political pundits had predicted that Kennedy would choose Stevenson, the Democratic presidential candidate in the 1952 and 1956 elections, to be his secretary of state. But in a move widely interpreted as a snub, especially among the left wing of the Democratic Party, Kennedy had chosen Dean Rusk and offered Stevenson the post of ambassador to the United Nations.

Stevenson's performance at the United Nations had been strong. His crowning achievement was his dramatic, televised confrontation with Valerian Zorin, the Soviet ambassador to the United Nations. Stevenson surprised the Soviets, and the rest of the world, with photographic evidence of Soviet missiles in Cuba. His performance was pitch perfect and precisely in line with the image the White House was trying to portray. It would go down not only as one of Stevenson's finest moments but as one of the finest moments of American diplomacy.

In the wake of the crisis, however, Kennedy sensed a potential problem. Though Stevenson had been tough and direct with Zorin, his liberal credentials were so well established, perhaps too well established, that Kennedy saw a need for creating political cover on such a politically charged topic. And as the phase shifted to what were sure to be blunt and difficult negotiations, it was likely that congressional hawks would charge that Stevenson was being too soft on the Soviets. There was little doubt that Stevenson could handle the Soviets, but any perception of softness would limit his freedom of action. As always, Kennedy wanted wiggle room to be able to accept reasonable negotiations without the need for political posturing or diplomatic overcompensation.

Kennedy's solution was to recall John J. McCloy from Geneva, where he had been leading the negotiations for a test ban agreement. A former assistant secretary of war and U.S. high commissioner for Germany, McCloy was known to be blunt and direct, but also well respected on both sides of the aisle as a seasoned negotiator. Not insignificantly, McCloy was also a Republican; his presence would add experience and depth, as well as an air of bipartisanship and preempt attacks from the right that Stevenson, a liberal Democrat, might be too willing to make concessions to the Soviets. Kennedy told an aide, "I want the Republican senators to see this. Got ten days before an election and I know what the charge is going to be: he's [Adlai's] inadequate and all the rest. Therefore, we're protecting ourselves and protecting Adlai, whose status has never been higher."[10]

But handling the announcement of McCloy's appointment was tricky. Kennedy did not want to create the impression that Stevenson, who had many loyal supporters in the liberal wing of the Democratic Party, was being slighted. After talking with the administration's resident card-carrying liberal, Arthur M. Schlesinger Jr., Kennedy agreed to choreograph the announcement in such a way as to head off, as much as possible, any charge that he was undermining Stevenson. "We ought to make it look like this McCloy proposal is Adlai's proposal, so it doesn't look like he's being superseded in any way," he instructed. The official line would be that the idea had sprung from a conversation between Kennedy and Stevenson the preceding day.[11]

For his part, Khrushchev had dispatched Vasily V. Kuznetsov, the deputy foreign minister of the USSR, to New York to lead the Soviet negotiating team and assist the Soviet ambassador to the United Nations, Valerian Zorin. Kuznetsov arrived in New York on 29 October, the day after Khrushchev pledged to remove the missiles. Khrushchev also sent his deputy, Anastas Mikoyan, to Cuba to smooth over a potential rupture with an irate Fidel Castro.

While the American and Soviet teams readied themselves for negotiations in New York, the acting secretary-general of the United Nations, U Thant, announced that he would go to Havana to meet with Mikoyan. He had sent a request to Washington via Adlai Stevenson: would it be possible for the Americans to suspend surveillance flights over the island while he was there? It would be a signal of good faith and also reduce the risk that an unfortunate incident would mar the negotiations. No one wanted to risk having a trigger-happy Cuban air defense soldier shoot down another American surveillance plane, an action that could quickly derail the whole agreement. It was a reasonable request, and one that Kennedy was inclined to grant.

U Thant's visit, however, complicated the issue of verification. For Kennedy, the verification problem was made all the more difficult because it was one thing to convince himself, but quite another to convince the American people, especially in an election season.

Leaning too heavily on the untrustworthiness of the Soviets could be useful in generating support for his positions. But it was a fine line, and making too much of Soviet duplicity could prove counterproductive. To bring the Cuba matter to a close would require dealing with the Soviets, and Kennedy needed to balance healthy skepticism to protect American security interests while fending off the most extreme elements on the political right calling for taking a very hard line with the Soviets. Furthermore, Kennedy was privy to highly classified intelligence information. In many cases, simply revealing publicly where the information was coming from would compromise sources and methods. If Kennedy was to convince the vocal and influential skeptics who were calling for no compromise in dealing with the Soviets, he would have to do so without compromising national secrets.

The problem Kennedy confronted came down to deciding what constituted long-term reasonable assurance. It was a benchmark he referred to repeatedly in the days following the crisis. Whether the issue was American surveillance overflights, sending weapons inspectors to Cuba to conduct on-the-ground inspections, or having the Red Cross inspect Soviet ships leaving Cuba, it reverted to the same basic problem. As he put it, "how many do you have to—as a practical matter—after the first week, how many do you have to check, under what circumstances, to give you reasonable assurance."[12] Since they could not have trust, they must have proof. But how much proof was enough? And how were they going to get it?

The best option from the American perspective would be physical inspection of the missile sites by trained weapons inspectors. But there were important difficulties with that.

First, there was the problem of access. Cuba refused to budge on allowing foreign nationals, especially Americans, unfettered access to restricted military sites. For the Cubans, it was a fundamental matter of sovereignty. As Rusk noted, "they don't want other people going around rubbing their fingers on Russian missiles."[13] For their part, the Soviets were willing to allow on-site inspections of the missile sites but only after the sites had been dismantled. The problem with that, as Rusk put it, is that "the Soviets are ready to inspect disarmament, but you can't inspect arms." The weapons inspectors would see only an empty site without knowing for sure what had been there before or where it had gone. "If you don't watch the equipment going out," Rusk said, "then you've got to inspect all of Cuba."[14] That would be both logistically unfeasible and completely unacceptable to the Cubans. And without Cuban agreement, the Soviet offer was meaningless anyway.

Kennedy was sensitive to these difficulties, though only up to a point. "The Russians have a right not to expect that we're going to be able to get all their secrets," he said, but it was not unreasonable to expect that they would allow some kind of inspection, especially since they so proudly displayed them in military parades; indeed, such parades through the heart of Moscow were one of the primary sources of military intelligence on Soviet military technology. "After all, they show them in Red Square," Kennedy said. "They ought to be able to at least show putting them on the dock and going into the boat."[15]

Second, there was the decision regarding what to do about surveillance in the long term. When Khrushchev pledged to remove from Cuba "the arms which you described as offensive," American officials hoped that he meant all of the systems listed in the quarantine proclamation of 23 October.[16] But it was not clear that Khrushchev understood his pledge that broadly; many worried that the Soviet leader was indulging in word games and that he understood their obligation to extend only to the long-range missiles and not to the other nuclear-capable weapons systems, the IL-28 bombers in particular. And even if he was agreeing to the broad interpretation, many U.S. officials were disinclined to take Khrushchev at his word, especially after Andrei Gromyko had so blatantly lied to the president in the Oval Office just a couple of weeks earlier. It would be a political impossibility for Kennedy to claim to now trust the Soviets, just days before the midterm election, especially when Republicans were charging the Democrats with being soft on communism.

Ideally, there would be a permanent verification system to make sure that the offensive weapons were gone and then to ensure that they were not reintroduced. But establishing an independent verification system would not be easy. One of the most difficult aspects was finding a way to internationalize the verification process while also maintaining enough of a U.S. presence that Americans could feel confident in the regime.

The most palatable compromise for all parties was for the United Nations to provide on-the-ground inspection of the missile sites to verify that the weapons had gone. That option was still far from perfect. Along with the Cubans' vehement refusal to allow on-site inspection, the Americans were worried that the United Nations did not have the kind of expert, trained weapons inspectors who would give Washington confidence that it was not being duped or simply mistaken.

It was all very well for U Thant to be able to offer his assurances that the Soviets had stopped, Kennedy said, but "he doesn't know what the hell to look for, any more than I would." And there was no indication that U Thant had any technical experts with him. That made it essential for American overflights to continue. "So, unless we know that there are technical people on this mission in whom we have confidence, we really need a photograph of our own Wednesday," Kennedy said. But U Thant's mission could still be useful. "You ought to make sure he's got five decent photographers with him," Kennedy instructed Roswell Gilpatric.

The International Red Cross also volunteered its services. Operating as arms inspectors was well outside its typical mandate and carried considerable political risks for the organization, which expended so much effort in trying to avoid getting drawn into politics. But it had nevertheless offered to have its personnel serve as seaborne arms inspectors. Based on ships from neutral countries, they would inspect Soviet ships leaving Cuba. The Soviets were agreeable—and even said they would accept its being done in Cuban ports if they could get the Cubans to agree to it—as were the Americans. Ultimately, however, the proposal petered out.

3

Eyes in the Sky

Since on-the-ground inspection was shaping up as a non-starter, that left only one kind of verification that would be acceptable to the White House and the American people and that could be viably carried out immediately. Someone, somewhere had to watch the missile sites being dismantled, crated, and shipped back to the Soviet Union. And it had to be someone who could be trusted. It was not enough to see empty missile sites; they had to see the weapons and troops leaving. The Soviets and Cubans might engage in a giant shell game, moving weapons and troops every time arms inspectors got near them. And Cuba's caves would make it all too easy. That, explained Chairman of the Joint Chiefs of Staff Maxwell Taylor, was the crux of the problem: "the uncertainty we'll be in to what has actually left," especially when they did not know precisely what was there in the first place.[1]

Failure to secure some kind of visual inspection of the outgoing missiles, Kennedy said, was unacceptable. It would leave too much doubt on too sensitive an issue. "Everybody's going to be running around next week saying in the press, 'Well, how do you know they've left?,'" he warned. He did not want to be in a situation of having to tell the American people, "We're not going to have any pictures of them being dismantled, and we're not going to have any pictures of them being put in the boat. We don't even know what boat they're on."[2] That would put him in an untenable position politically and leave him open to accusations that he was not adequately protecting American security. At the same time, there was only so much that the Soviets would accommodate. Kennedy was forced to weigh the political risks of sparking a new, dangerous phase of the crisis, and the military's forceful lobbying for getting detailed low-level surveillance photos of Cuba's military installations.

The nascent Corona spy satellite program had recently been launched, but the first generation of spy satellites, code-named Keyhole, were not suited to the kinds of rapid-fire intelligence needs of a crisis. Their lenses were pointed at the Soviet Union, and the collection of the photographic film was cumbersome. A new generation of surveillance drones had been built and were ready for action, but the Air Force was reluctant to put them over hostile territory, lest one be shot down and the cutting-edge technology fall into unfriendly hands.[3]

That left only one good option: American spy planes. Kennedy had two main aerial surveillance options before him as the ExComm met on 29 October; he would face the same choice many times over the coming weeks. One was safer but less effective. The other was more effective but much riskier. Both carried risks. Both meant potentially putting American pilots in harm's way.

Flying planes uninvited over hostile territory was a dangerous business. The Cubans said they would treat any intrusion of their airspace as hostile, and Cuba's air defenses, thanks to Soviet help, were now formidable. Just days earlier, an American U-2 plane piloted by Major Rudolph Anderson had been shot down over Cuba. It happened on 27 October, the first day that the SA-2 network in Cuba came fully online. It made an already extraordinarily tense day even more so. It was not a considered, deliberate act of the Soviet government—a local Soviet commander, faced with the urgent need for a decision whether to fire or not and unable to locate his superiors in time was forced to make his own decision on the spot—but that was unknowable to Washington.[4] The incident served as an all-too-effective reminder of just how dangerous the Soviet-supplied surface-to-air missiles could be. If the Soviets decided to force the Americans to cease making surveillance flights, they could. Since then, American intelligence had intercepted radio communications suggesting that Cuban military forces had been ordered not to fire on American planes. But that was contradicted publicly by Fidel Castro himself.

The missile sites had originally been discovered by photos taken from U-2s. Flying at over 60,000 feet, higher than any other manned plane yet in service, these fragile, long-winged jets looked much like large gliders, and their pilots were outfitted more like astronauts than like regular pilots. First deployed in the late 1950s to photograph defense installations and airfields inside the Soviet Union's borders, they had provided photographic evidence of the state of Soviet nuclear strike capacity. Photos from then top secret U-2s had given President Dwight Eisenhower the confidence to dismiss heated political rhetoric accusing the administration of letting the Soviets leap ahead of the United States in the missile race.

U-2s had played a starring role in the missile crisis, but as a means of getting proof that the Soviets were withdrawing from Cuba, they had drawbacks and carried risks. The days that U-2s could operate with impunity, undetected over Soviet territory, were over. The Soviets had quickly adapted their warning systems and had since deployed a new generation of advanced surface-to-air missiles that could knock U-2s from the sky. One of those missiles, known to Western defense analysts as an SA-2 Guideline, had downed Francis Gary Powers in 1960, leading to a diplomatic crisis that scuttled the Eisenhower-Khrushchev summit scheduled for soon thereafter. Another had downed Major Anderson's plane.

The entire island of Cuba was now protected by a strategically placed web of SA-2 sites. The Soviets had sent and sold SA-2 systems to a number of its allies, including Iraq, Indonesia, and Cuba. It was their presence that had tipped off CIA Director John McCone in the summer of 1962 that the Soviets must be planning something unusual for Cuba. Moscow simply didn't need to send a web of SA-2s for a run-of-the-mill military deployment, he reasoned. An individual SA-2 site consisted not just of missiles but also of sophisticated radar and communications facilities. It was cutting-edge technology, and its operators were required to undergo at least six months to a year of intensive training. Because of that, American intelligence analysts concluded that they must still be under Soviet control; there had not yet been time for Cubans to go through the required training, even if some of them had been trained in the Soviet Union. American officials were somewhat reassured by this. They hoped that Soviet operators might be more rational and restrained than their Cuban colleagues. They did not, after all, take orders directly from Fidel Castro.

U-2s were outfitted with specially designed high-resolution cameras the size of a small car that were able to capture images of large swaths of territory. Once the pilot turned the camera on, thousands of feet of film at a time could run through it. As soon as the plane landed back on home soil, the exposed film would be rushed to the CIA's special processing lab, the newly created National Photographic Interpretation Center, or NPIC. There, intelligence and military experts trained in interpreting photos would decide which of the buildings and equipment was of particular interest.

U-2 photos were taken from eleven miles up. That height enhanced safety but posed problems for getting a detailed look at what was happening on the ground. Kennedy had another option for getting more detailed photos that his military and intelligence chiefs were pushing for. It was riskier, but it offered a much closer look.

Low-level surveillance flights closed the distance dramatically between camera and subject. The low-level flights swept in fast at an altitude of only 500 to 1,000 feet, ideally catching those on the ground by surprise. The resulting photos were much more detailed, enabling the NPIC analysts to distinguish between models of weapons, count individual soldiers, and even pick out the telephone cables running between the weapons and command bunkers that would be used to communicate firing orders. But the flights were especially risky because they were well within the range of Cuba's conventional anti-aircraft defenses. Those guns were operated by Cubans, not Soviets.

The first low-level flights over Cuba occurred on 23 October. They immediately proved their worth by revealing important new information. Those missions, code-named Blue Moon, were conducted by specially outfitted Air Force RF-101 Voodoos and Navy F-8U jets. To minimize risks, pilots relied on surprise, flying over their targets at maximum speed and minimum altitude. By the time the crews on the ground could scramble, the plane had already passed, its cameras having captured ground crew members running to their weapons. Each flight was above Cuban territory for only between four and seven minutes. Because it flew so low, the field of vision was limited; the plane's cameras could capture only narrow swaths of territory at a time. But the photographs they took were much more detailed than those from the U-2s. They were ideal for focusing on encampments and sites that NPIC analysts had seen on the U-2 photos but needed a closer look at. A few weeks later, Kennedy had the chance to experience firsthand just how low and fast these planes flew. He was visibly impressed. A *Time* magazine reporter on the scene recorded his reaction:

> They were gone the instant they came—a brace of Air Force RF-101 jets screeching 200 ft. above Florida's Homestead Air Force Base. On the reviewing stand, President Kennedy turned to General Walter Sweeney, commander of the Tactical Air Command, and asked: "They wouldn't have been able to shoot down those ships at that speed and altitude would they?" The general said no. Said Kennedy: "I'd like to see them again." And so the reconnaissance jets once more simulated the flights that had helped document the presence of Soviet missiles in Cuba.[5]

Minimized or not, the risks were real. On the morning of 29 October, an RF-101 Voodoo reconnaissance plane came under antiaircraft fire as it sped at low level over an IL-28 airfield in Cuba. The plane and pilot emerged unscathed and returned safely to MacDill Air Force Base in Florida, but the very fact that it had encountered hostile fire after the agreement reached the preceding day was troubling.

Kennedy did not want to publicize that incident, but he did want to send a private protest to the United Nations in New York. He instructed McCloy to pass on to Kuznetsov the message that the firing on American planes was unacceptable. He wanted it made clear to the Soviets that there had to be some means of inspection: "We've got to go back and keep doing it [aerial surveillance] unless you can provide us an alternative." The incident served as a vivid reminder of the surveillance difficulties and the unreliability of counting on Cuban restraint.[6]

Surveillance overflights, whether high-altitude or low-altitude, appealed to Washington because they could be completely under American control, with American planes, American pilots, and with the film processed in American labs. If one was shot down, however, the United States would be forced to respond. Balancing the risks with the need for detailed proof was the most important decision facing Kennedy in the days after Khrushchev's capitulation. And his advisers were split.

Wary of the diplomatic mess they would face if a plane was shot down, Secretary of State Dean Rusk favored conducting U-2 flights rather than the riskier low-level flights. He also argued that it provided the kind of overview that was needed to see whether the Soviets had stopped building. If they relied only on the low-level flights, they might see a small area in great detail, but it might well be the wrong area. As he put it to Kennedy and the ExComm, "The U-2 is more likely to discover if they're building, if they're digging a hole nearby to bury some of these damn things before the U.N. gets there. And I don't think the low-level, if it's too pinpointed, is likely to discover that as easily as the more comprehensive high-level."

Secretary of Defense Robert McNamara and Chairman of the

Joint Chiefs of Staff Maxwell Taylor disagreed. The extra detail provided by low-level, they argued, was precisely the kind of intelligence they needed to monitor the situation closely. There might be political reasons not to use low-level reconnaissance, they agreed, but from an intelligence and technical standpoint it was the better option.

But Kennedy was concerned about the political ramifications and unclear as to the benefits. "What would we be trying to find out with this?" he asked. "There isn't any doubt that it's a hazard, doing this, because it's . . . not the planes so much as politically [it's] a hazard. It would appear that, this would appear to be a somewhat backward step. But what is the advantage of it, doing it?"

There was another option that might be better in the long term but that would be difficult to put in place in the short term. The risk that a hotheaded Cuban military commander would issue orders to shoot down another plane might be lessened if the planes were clearly marked United Nations planes. U Thant's military adviser, the Indian general Indar Jit Rikhye, who had close ties with the administration and was one of the few foreigners briefed early on in the crisis, favored using an RC-130 plane outfitted with camera equipment, painted white with a UN insignia, and manned by an international crew. But the United Nations did not actually have such a plane—it would have to be donated by the United States—and only a handful of countries had crews trained in that kind of mission: Indonesia, Canada, and South Africa.

The Soviets objected strongly to the idea that the planes and cameras be operated by U.S. personnel. Failing that option, Kennedy preferred Canadians. Despite a widely publicized falling out between Kennedy and Canada's Prime Minister John Diefenbaker, ties between the continental neighbors and NATO allies were still very close. That closeness was precisely why the Soviets and Cubans would object to having Canadians operating the planes as well. Trying to find a compromise, Kennedy elaborated, "It seems to me that it would be all right if we said, 'We'll let a Russian go, but let's have an American in there.' If we can't get an American, then we shouldn't have a Russian. But we should try to get a Canadian. You don't want to put it in the hands completely of . . ."

Kennedy insisted that American-certified information was essential. But he also pushed back against the urgency expressed by his military advisers. "Say they're going ahead with the work," he told Taylor. "Well then, that means the whole deal blows. Whether it blows today or Wednesday, we're going to be faced with the same problem, General."

McNamara mostly agreed, but also emphasized the importance of providing some assurance to the American people. It was not just a matter of doing something, he said, but of being seen to be doing something. "I really think we need to show our people that we're properly protecting our interests," he said, demonstrating his political savvy, not for the first time.

The upshot of the 29 October meeting was that Kennedy agreed to a temporary halt in aerial surveillance while U Thant was in Cuba and a two-day suspension of the naval quarantine. And he wanted the message passed to the United Nations and Soviets that on-site, on-the-ground inspection was needed. "If they're not going to let us in," he added, "we've got to have the high-level and low-level photography. We're going to do it if somebody else doesn't do it. We'll do it, until somebody else does it."[7] These decisions—whether to run surveillance flights and, if so, what kind—were decisions that he would face again and again in the coming days.

4

The Postmortem Season

It was the story of the year, if not the decade. It had come suddenly, and most of the key aspects had played out in secret. Now that it was over, it seemed that everyone in Washington's press corps was clamoring for the behind-the-scenes scoop. "The post-mortem season is in full swing," is how McGeorge Bundy put it just two days after Khrushchev agreed to remove the missiles from Cuba. In the ensuring weeks, a slew of stories would try to reconstruct what had gone on behind the scenes during the crisis. Inevitably, shades of emphasis and selective omission cast some actors in poor light. In one particularly unfair example that prompted a controversy, the former Democratic presidential candidate and U.S. ambassador to the United Nations, Adlai Stevenson, was tarred with accusations that he had become the chief advocate for a soft line in dealing with the Soviets that amounted to appeasement. That one of the authors of the article that first made those claims was known to be a close friend of the president's added to the political damage to Stevenson's reputation.[1]

But the immediate problem for Kennedy became how to control the story. The press's appetite for information on what had happened behind closed doors over the preceding fortnight was voracious, and reporters squeezed their sources inside the administration hard.

Weeklies like *Newsweek*, *Time*, the *Saturday Evening Post*, and *Look* devoted multipage spreads—sometimes whole issues—to laying out the latest information. For Kennedy, the saturation press coverage could be both good and bad. Stories that set the administration's actions in a positive light were most welcome. But there was no guarantee that stories would be flattering.

In such a highly charged partisan environment, just days before an election, there was a very real risk that a different kind of picture would emerge, one more in line with his critics' views, one where the story of the Cuban missile crisis might be turned from a Kennedy victory into a Kennedy failure. Determined not to let his critics define him, Kennedy decided to tightly restrict the flow of information. That effort to control the narrative, to "manage the news," as critics called it, provoked a very public backlash that dogged the administration for months.

As the cycle inevitably shifted from reporting the facts and narrative of the thirteen days—the who and what and when—to analysis and then scrutiny, controlling the narrative was likely to get more challenging. And it certainly could not be taken for granted that the administration's actions and policies before, during, and after the crisis would be seen in a favorable light. The administration's track record on Cuba was poor. There was no reason to expect that it would be given any special breaks. For Kennedy, controlling the narrative of the missile crisis would begin with controlling the flow of information to clamoring reporters and editors.

During the crisis, with the nation directly threatened, Americans had rallied around the flag. Kennedy himself carefully avoided any talk of "winning" the crisis—and forbade his staff from talking in such terms—but in the eyes of much of the American public, and indeed the world, that was precisely what he had done. That sentiment was reflected in the polls. Kennedy's approval ratings spiked in the wake of the missile crisis, much as they had immediately following the invasion of the Bay of Pigs. It halted—albeit temporarily—a steady slide in his approval ratings that had been gaining momentum since the summer. The first Gallup poll conducted after the crisis put his approval rating at 74 percent, a 13-point bump from the preceding month.[2] But it was a fragile gain.

Although the crisis had been given saturation coverage in the press, reporters and editors had grown frustrated with the administration's tight grip on information. National security requirements were understandable and widely accepted during the crisis, but after the crisis had passed, reporters would expect the White House's grip to loosen. And with so many Washington reporters trying to get the scoop and armed with excellent sources deep inside the administration, the situation was ripe for national security leaks. Such leaks had bedeviled Kennedy before, and it was a fight that would intensify in coming months.

The *New York Times* reporter James "Scotty" Reston called his sources within the White House, State Department, and Defense Department. The *Times* was preparing special features on the crisis and hoped for White House cooperation. Kennedy felt a special obligation to cooperate with the *Times*, believing that he had personally prevented the *Times* from running a story by Reston at the outset of the crisis that would have blown the cover of secrecy. As it happened, Kennedy was mistaken; Reston did not have the story. But syndicated columnists whose work appeared in the *New York Herald Tribune*, a rival to the *Times*, Walter Lippmann and Joe Alsop, had been tipped off to the scoop. Kennedy's call to the editor of the *New York Times* was the first that that newspaper had heard of the unfolding events. Nevertheless, Kennedy intended to honor his agreement with the *Times*. But with so many other news outlets also seeking information, he recognized that showing too much favoritism to the *Times* would spark complaints. As he told the ExComm,

> We have some obligation to the *Times* because they agreed on that Sunday before not to print what Reston had, which was the story, which would have been very disastrous for us. So we said at the time that if they didn't [publish the story], we'd be cooperative

> afterward. Pierre Salinger had the conversation with them. I said that I wouldn't—in addition, Fletcher Knebel is writing a story for *Look*, and Stewart Alsop for the *Saturday Evening Post*.[3]

A *Times* front-page story on 30 October highlighted the risks of losing control of the message, prompting Kennedy to tighten his administration's press policies. The story ran under Max Frankel's byline. The headline, "Air Attack on Cuban Bases Was Seriously Considered," portrayed Kennedy and his advisers as willing to use military force if necessary, which, on its own, was favorable. But the real thrust of the article was more complicated. Frankel wrote that the reason Kennedy was considering air strikes was that he had ruled out sending in ground troops.[4]

Kennedy found Frankel's article frustrating on several levels. It implied that Kennedy favored the less forceful, perhaps weaker option. It potentially reduced Khrushchev's incentive to carry out his end of the bargain by suggesting that Kennedy would not order an invasion even if pressed. That directly contradicted the message that Washington wanted to send to Moscow. The real power of the blockade had been the implicit threat that stopping shipping was merely an interim measure preceding the use of military force. Frankel's article contended that the administration was bluffing. And that, to Kennedy, was both unhelpful and untrue.

More generally, Kennedy worried aloud that it might reduce the calculated ambiguity that formed the very foundation of the West's defense posture. To the ExComm he said, "While it did say that we decided not to because of our traditions—we don't want the Russians to ever think that we're seriously ready for a first strike, because it encourages them to do the same . . . and that it's within our capacity as a nation to do a first strike. So I think that story of Frankel's was very unfortunate."

The *Times*'s Pentagon reporter, Hanson Baldwin, who had long had a starring role in the White House's campaign against national security leaks, needled the White House once again in the *Times* the next day. This time, at least, it was buried on page 19 and not on the front page, but the implications were potentially far more serious.

Baldwin charged that the crisis was preceded by an "intelligence gap" and implied that the Kennedy administration had been both negligent and misguided. None of the several possible reasons for such an intelligence gap were flattering to the administration: the administration's increasing centralization of intelligence activities, poor intelligence gathering, intelligence analysis that may have been overly influenced by policy, or key administration officials who simply ignored the intelligence that was being gathered. To illustrate his point, Baldwin cited the obvious failure to fully detect a military buildup that had clearly been going on for months; he also suggested that there was indeed a "missile gap" after all, but that it was not in quantity, as some had charged in the 1960 presidential campaign, but rather in the quality of the technology. Specifically, he pointed to evidence that the Soviets had mastered to a greater degree than the United States the technology to make medium-range ballistic missiles mobile.[5] Probably reflecting the concerns of his sources in the Pentagon, Baldwin identified the newly created Defense Intelligence Agency, in particular, as a factor in diminishing the analytical role of the various military intelligence agencies. He wrote, "There has been worry that the centralization of intelligence facilities that has been forced in the last two years might facilitate just this mistake—that policy rather than data might dictate the answers."[6]

Another leak a few days later further frustrated Kennedy. Rowland Evans had managed to get hold of a copy of the private letter sent by Khrushchev to Kennedy on 26 October, the contents of which were classified. Evans wrote that the administration's assessment of the letter was that it was written by "an agitated and over-wrought man" and implied that the White House thought that Khrushchev was "a man deranged and . . . mentally unstable."[7]

Evans's story was not inaccurate—there had been some internal speculation that the contrast between the letter of 26 October and the one of 27 October could be explained by one letter's having been written personally by Khrushchev and the other by a group of Soviet leaders—but it was not a message Kennedy wanted to broadcast. The White House issued a public denial saying that no such view was held and requesting the return of all copies of the letter to the State Department.

"Whatever anybody's private opinion may be of the letter," Kennedy told the ExComm, "it would be a great disaster if we gave the impression the United States government was charging Khrushchev [was] unstable, because I would think it would cause him intense annoyance." "I think it's very damaging if the Russians thought we were putting that stuff out," he continued. For Kennedy, it was all the more reason to clamp down on the flow of information.

> These post-mortems are going to get worse and worse. We've just got to stop everybody talking to reporters except through the two sources that we agreed, which was Bundy and Ted [Sorensen]. I wouldn't talk to any—I mean, more and more now everybody's trying to recapitulate everything and doing it in an inaccurate way. So I think we ought to try to really . . . Ambassador [Adlai] Stevenson sent a message of his conversation with U Thant and within one hour and a half it was on the wire after we received it. So we've got to improve our procedures or we're going to find ourselves in bad shape.

Kennedy knew better than to try to blunt press curiosity. Instead, he aimed to channel it, creating a controlled flow of information through a handful of spokesmen authorized to speak to reporters on behalf of the government. Under the pretext of national security, the White House would clamp down on the information making its way to reporters. It was a significant and ongoing effort and one that Kennedy himself ordered and took a keen personal interest in.

With his secret taping system rolling at the 30 October ExComm meeting, Kennedy elaborated at some length on his instructions for dealing with the press:

President Kennedy: Now, the position that I've taken is that I would not talk to any of them. But I thought that any of them who went to see anybody could see you [Bundy], Ted Sorensen, and Pierre [Salinger]. My judgment is that probably nobody in this group probably ought to see anybody. That's at this point, at least until we see where we are going, [*Rusk agrees*] and we're out of the woods. I think if we just make it a policy that the decision of the Executive Committee is that nobody at this group will say anything.

On the other hand, I think we ought to maintain a liaison with them and have the right to go over their stories. I think we ought to say to Reston that this story this morning was very unfortunate. If we're going to cooperate, which we told him we would, and attempt to at least give an outline, with the understanding we would see it. This morning is exactly what we don't want on that air strike. I think if we permit Mac, Ted, and Pierre, working through here, to have the conversations with these people, to tell them what we want to through the line, and none of us see anybody. Because what's going to happen is [that] everybody's going to emphasize a particular point.

Later in the meeting, he continued:

President Kennedy: Yes, I think that if we have it clear that nobody in any of our departments is supposed to talk to any of these press on these projects, that's in defense, none of the generals or anybody assisting, except [Arthur] Sylvester, [Robert] Manning in state, Pierre, with you [Bundy] and Ted here, which we can then control. We will then be able to cooperate with them. It would be a mistake not to, because what happens is what we got this morning: all kinds of stories will come out, differences in view, and all the dangers. And everybody else just say, "We can't discuss this with the press."

Dean Rusk: Mr. President, I would like to urge the point that this kind of briefing is wholly premature until we get these missiles out of Cuba.

PRESIDENT KENNEDY: That's it. That's why I don't know—

RUSK: I think that we ought to put this thing off for days, not try to do it [*unclear*]—

MCGEORGE BUNDY: I agree with you.

PRESIDENT KENNEDY: We're not trying to—[what] we definitely want to do now is—we're not able to put it off for days, because somebody's obviously gone and talked to Frankel. So, now what we want to do is to have it as a solid policy that none of us will talk to these people at all personally. I think we just say that "the President has said that."

I'm not going to see any of them. I think none of us [should] see any newspapermen for a while. Anything will go through Sylvester, Manning, that's where they can go. Because they're going to go to somebody [*Bundy agrees*] and we've just had a bad situation already. Mac and Ted here. Then I think at least we'll channel it, and we have a general line on all these questions.

BUNDY: And I think the secretary's point is correct, that we ought not, even those of us who do talk to the press, to talk about this as a finished episode [*unclear*].

PRESIDENT KENNEDY: Exactly—we don't know what the hell's going on.

BUNDY: It's not [*unclear*]—

PRESIDENT KENNEDY: I think we've done it right. I think, as I say, the only unfortunate one was Frankel's this morning. We've just got to try to get control over it.

As Bundy pointed out, there were two other problems: Dean Acheson and Robert Lovett. Those elder statesmen had been brought in early on in the crisis. But neither was on the White House payroll, and both were difficult to control. The problem, Bundy said, was that "they're talkative people who know more than they should." Bundy took it upon himself to talk to both men and encourage discretion.[8]

Kennedy's biggest frustration with the flood of articles starting to appear in print was a problem he had been trying to deal with for months: leaks. Whoever he was, Frankel's anonymous source was both very well informed and not authorized to speak to the press. "I don't know where he got it, but it showed a rather detailed briefing from somebody," Kennedy surmised. Addressing the ExComm, he said, "I'm sure it wasn't anybody in this group, because this group is very secure, but I don't know who it could be." Turning pointedly to Rusk, he asked, "Anybody got any ideas over at State?"[9]

Channeling the flow of information and plugging leaks were part of a continuum of evolving press policies that his administration had been putting in place since the summer. In coming weeks, they would enter a new, public phase, sparking controversy and widespread condemnation as the administration was criticized for managing the news. The controversy amounted to open warfare with the press. But it grew out of a covert war that the administration had been waging for some time on American soil. For months before the Cuban missile crisis, Kennedy had been leading a secret war against leaks. At his direction, the FBI and CIA had engaged in legally dubious practices of spying on American journalists.

5

Mockingbird Don't Sing

Like most presidents, Kennedy was for much of his time in office frustrated with the press. It was not frustration born of a misunderstanding. To the contrary, Kennedy knew the media world well. He had spent some time as a reporter after returning from World War II service in the Pacific. And it is no exaggeration to say that some of his best friends were reporters, including, notably, Ben Bradlee of *Newsweek*, who, along with his wife, was a frequent dinner guest of the Kennedys in the White House. Bradlee and Kennedy even negotiated a deal that would allow Bradlee to use the notes of his candid discussions with the president in a publication; Bradlee eventually made them the basis for his 1975 book, *Conversations with the President*. Moreover, throughout his life, Kennedy demonstrated a strong fascination with the inner politics of the media business. But none of this experience and familiarity did anything to quell his frustrations with the press once he moved into the Oval Office.[1]

Kennedy also knew well both the value and the power of the press for someone in politics. Early in his Senate career, he had instructed his personal secretary, Evelyn Lincoln, never to discourage reporters seeking face time with the new senator. "If I know one thing," he told her, "it is that a politician can kill himself faster by playing hard-to-get with the press than he can by jumping off the Capitol dome. As long as they want to talk to me, I want to talk to them. Maybe longer."[2] He probably didn't explicitly update these standing orders once in the White House, but he didn't need to.

Kennedy had found quickly, as most presidents do, that the dynamic of his relationship with the press had irrevocably changed. It was a transition he struggled with. As a candidate, he had faced the same challenge all candidates face on campaigns: trying to get noticed by the press, to get as many inches of column space as possible in order to get his name and ideas out into the public discussion. The objective—or hope—was that with enough attention he might gain traction in the public consciousness.

But being president was different. Whether voters agreed or disagreed with him—and most had now had the opportunity to form an opinion one way or the other—he had become a household name. And members of the press also shifted their approach, greatly intensifying the level of constant scrutiny. Oftentimes, presidents yearn for less attention, not more, or at least attention on their own terms. Kennedy fell squarely into the category of those who want to control the terms.

Kennedy's relationship with the press began well. It even had an air of partnership—collusion, some critics, especially conservatives, accused. He made a point of hosting regular White House luncheons for publishers and editors from each of the states. By the summer of 1962, though, that relationship was taking a sharp turn for the worse and becoming increasingly adversarial. "It would appear that John F. Kennedy's honeymoon with the press, probably the most affectionate in the long history of Presidential politics, is on the pebbles, if not the rocks," wrote Fletcher Knebel in an August 1962 issue of *Look*.[3]

As part of his research for the article, Knebel polled about a hundred of his colleagues among the Washington correspondents. What he heard—and subsequently wrote about—amounted to a long list of grievances. Both John Kennedy and his brother Robert had personally dressed down authors of unflattering articles, as had White

House Press Secretary Pierre Salinger and Kennedy's speechwriter and counsel, Theodore Sorensen. Occasionally there were legitimate disagreements of substance, but often they dealt with petty issues. The administration threatened to sue newspapers that published critical stories that it said were inaccurate. In a fit of pique, it canceled twenty-two subscriptions to the *New York Herald Tribune*. Administration officials also put the "freeze" on reporters who had written critical articles, by denying them access to senior officials.

Of course, give-and-take between the White House and the press corps has always been a staple of Washington life. Franklin Roosevelt awarded "dunce caps" to authors of critical and, in his view, flawed articles. Harry Truman and Lyndon Johnson let fly with salty language. Reporters found themselves disinvited to events following unflattering articles. Richard Nixon even gave reporters pride of place on his notorious enemies list. But what surprised reporters covering the Kennedy White House was the intensity of its indignation that seemingly minor slights could provoke. They marveled that no slight that found its way into print, no matter how small or how far geographically removed from Pennsylvania Avenue, went unnoticed. Washington correspondents were learning that, for all its apparent self-assurance, the Kennedy White House was remarkably thin-skinned. "Never before have so few bawled out so many so often for so little," Knebel wrote, playfully adapting Winston Churchill's famous words.[4]

What no doubt contributed to the problem was the president's own voracious appetite for news. Early in his political career, Kennedy had taken speed-reading classes in order to deal with the deluge of reading material that landed on his desk. That foresight had apparently paid off; he was reportedly capable of reading at an impressive rate of 1,200 words a minute. It made for a president who, rather than avoiding things to read, actively sought them out. Kennedy personally played a leading role in digesting the press coverage of his administration, maintaining an inviolable morning ritual of uninterrupted devouring of the morning's newspapers along with his breakfast.[5]

Acute presidential interest and a low threshold for criticism made for a volatile mix. Ben Bradlee told Knebel, "It's almost impossible to write a story they like. Even if a story is quite favorable to their side, they'll find one paragraph to quibble with."[6] The comment was supposed to be off-the-record, and Bradlee quibbled with what he thought was hyperbole in Knebel's article, but he nevertheless stood by what he saw as the essential truth of his observation.[7] Kennedy and his advisers took press criticism seriously and personally, and that was always going to create problems with a press corps that saw its job as being to probe, to investigate, and to challenge.

Comfortable with reporters and publishers and familiar with how the press game was played, Kennedy frequently tried to manipulate press contacts for his own benefit, an effort that was by no means unusual in Washington.[8] Some of those efforts were successful; others were not. He had, for example, used selective leaking to preempt, and thereby minimize, the damage done to Edward Kennedy's 1962 senatorial campaign. Reporters had picked up a potentially explosive allegation that the younger Kennedy had cheated on a test while a student at Harvard.[9]

But like all presidents inevitably confronted with the problem of leaks, Kennedy adhered to a double standard: leaks you could control—and often initiated—could be useful, but leaks over which you had no control were nearly always bad.

In his *Look* article, Knebel revealed that the inner sanctum of the White House was thin-skinned when it came to press criticism, but he also hinted at what was ultimately a more serious issue: the lengths to which the administration was going to clamp down on leaks. He reported that the FBI and Pentagon security officials had interviewed at least nine newspapermen. Knebel, though, barely scratched the surface. Evidence was scarce, after all, and most of it highly classified. He heard hints but nothing strong enough to put into print. Indeed, details of the White House campaign against press leaks have emerged only fitfully over the past half century. And some of the most important evidence has come to light only in the past decade.

In the mid-1970s, while being interviewed for a series of oral history profiles, the *New York Times*'s Pentagon correspondent, Hanson Baldwin, complained that during the Kennedy years he had been the subject of a "very unusual" FBI investigation in which the bureau's agents had resorted to "outrageous measures" that included unannounced, late-night visits to his home and wiretaps on his telephone.[10] "I learned subsequently that it was done probably at the instigation of Robert Kennedy but with the President's full approval and knowledge," Baldwin said.[11] But without solid evidence, Baldwin's suspicions were unverifiable until decades later. He was certainly not the first reporter to suspect that someone might be looking over his shoulder.

At roughly the same time as Baldwin's oral history interviews, former aides to J. Edgar Hoover told congressional hearings in December 1975 that Robert Kennedy had, in 1962, personally authorized FBI wiretapping of the telephones of Baldwin and his secretary for one month. This, they said, was in addition to an earlier FBI wiretapping operation against the *Newsweek* reporter Lloyd Norman.[12] Hoover "undoubtedly" had those operations in mind, one of the aides surmised, when he told Richard Nixon and Henry Kissinger in 1969 that there were precedents for wiretapping journalists, implying that Nixon might well have interpreted that as evidence he was not doing anything his predecessors had not done when he waged his own war against members of the press.[13]

Baldwin, it turns out, was not simply succumbing to paranoia. Kennedy's secretly recorded White House tapes provide clear confirmation not only that the president knew of efforts to monitor Baldwin and other reporters but that he personally authorized them. It was part of a secret campaign to stop the flow of leaks from the Pentagon. And it evolved into policies and practices that skirted the law. The tapes show that that campaign was not limited to action by the FBI. In the summer of 1962, Kennedy secretly authorized the CIA to spy on American journalists. It was a drastic authorization and of questionable legality. Under the terms of the National Security Act of 1947, the CIA was explicitly barred by law from engaging in domestic surveillance. But it was also charged with protecting intelligence sources and methods from unauthorized disclosure. Kennedy's order fell somewhere in the unreconciled legal territory between these two mandates. The extent of the campaign remained hidden for the next forty years.

FROM THE MOMENT HE TOOK OFFICE, Kennedy confronted the problem of unauthorized leaks of military and national security information. The Pentagon, the veteran correspondent George Sokolsky pointed out, "leaked like a sieve."[14] In one of the most blatant cases, in July 1961, at the height of the Berlin crisis, the *Newsweek* reporter Lloyd Norman broke a story that exposed classified information on U.S. contingency plans in the event that the Soviets threatened West Berlin. Given the sensitivity of the Berlin issue—the cold war's premier flash point at that moment—and the reliance the United States was placing on convincing the Soviets that any action on their part could escalate uncontrollably to nuclear war, this amounted to a major security breach. The FBI opened an investigation into Norman and placed wiretaps on his telephone.[15]

But it was an episode largely forgotten that pushed national security leak investigations in a novel direction. In a front-page story in the *New York Times* on 26 July 1962, Hanson Baldwin detailed the comparative quality and size of the U.S. and the Soviet strategic missile arsenals. Baldwin revealed that U.S. intelligence agencies had learned that the Soviet military was protecting its ballistic missile sites with a process known as hardening, strengthening their missile silos with thick, reinforced concrete to make them able to withstand nuclear attack. Baldwin said that U.S. intelligence analysts had concluded that the Soviets had only about one hundred intercontinental ballistic missiles operational or in advanced stages of production. By comparison, the United States had roughly twelve hundred deployed, authorized, or planned.[16] It meant that the United States maintained a massive superiority in long-range nuclear missiles and that the missile gap was in fact strongly in America's favor.

Both sets of information—the estimate of how many missiles the Soviets had available and the methods they were using to protect them—were classified. And from the administration's standpoint, Baldwin's information was also worryingly precise; it was clear that his unnamed source was well informed. In fact, the information could be traced back to a recent, highly classified national intelligence estimate (NIE). The administration could not fault the facts, since they were taken from its own intelligence analysis. And several of the findings—such as the confirmation of the U.S. superiority both quantitatively and qualitatively in ICBMs and the evolution toward a more stable deterrent as first-strike capabilities became less feasible—could have been construed as favorable. Deputy Secretary of Defense Roswell Gilpatric had been the White House–appointed messenger of similar findings the preceding year in a public speech that dispelled the myth of the missile gap once and for all.

But it was the level of detail and Baldwin's discussion of the sources and methods the intelligence assessment was based upon that the administration and the intelligence community found most troubling. Moreover, that very level of detail might well have given readers the impression that the story had an official blessing. That was not at all the message the White House wanted Moscow to hear.[17]

Kennedy's response was initially the same as his response to Lloyd Norman's prior article about West Berlin: have the FBI investigate. But the earlier investigation had not gone well, in part because of J. Edgar Hoover's distaste for having his agents involved in what he considered a clerical task. Kennedy was persuaded that more drastic measures were needed.

He turned to the President's Foreign Intelligence Advisory Board, or PFIAB, for advice. As its name indicated, the role of the PFIAB was to advise. It had no direct power of its own. But what it lacked in operational power, PFIAB made up for in access and influence. Its purpose was to offer the president independent options for probing the intelligence community's weaknesses. The PFIAB operated in the utmost secrecy and was answerable only to the president himself. It was not subject to the same congressional oversight as other intelligence agencies such as the CIA or the Defense Intelligence Agency.

President Eisenhower had formed the group in the hope that it would help him bring the CIA under tighter control. Originally known as the President's Board of Consultants on Foreign Intelligence Activities, it was thwarted in that mission by bureaucratic maneuvering by Director of Central Intelligence Allen Dulles, who saw the oversight body as a constraint. Nevertheless, during the transition to the Kennedy administration, Eisenhower recommended the board to the incoming president as "a most useful organ of supervision." Kennedy's father had been a member under Eisenhower, but Kennedy remained unconvinced of the utility of the group. When he assumed office, and with Allen Dulles's enthusiastic support, he adjourned the group.[18]

The Bay of Pigs debacle persuaded Kennedy to reconsider, believing that he had been poorly served by the intelligence services before and during the episode. With Dulles forced out, Kennedy revived the group. The panel included Dr. James Killian of MIT as chairman; a longtime insider of Democratic administrations, the Washington lawyer Clark Clifford; the president's military adviser, General Maxwell Taylor; the former secretary of defense Robert A. Lovett; and the Harvard historian William Langer.[19] Significantly, Kennedy also appointed persons responsible for fundamental advances in technological intelligence capabilities: Edwin Land, the inventor of the Polaroid camera and a key player in the development of the photographic equipment carried by the U-2 spy planes; and William Baker, the president of Bell Labs, who would go on to serve on PFIAB until 1990, the longest term of any member. Both Land and Baker proved valuable advocates for updating the intelligence community's photographic and communications capabilities.[20]

The bulk of PFIAB's documents remain closed, without any clear path for prying them open. But a tape released by the Kennedy Library in 1997 included a remarkable August 1962 meeting of leading members of PFIAB with President Kennedy. In the course of that meeting, PFIAB recommended a drastic plan that skirted the boundary between legal and illegal surveillance of American citizens. Even more remarkably, the tape reveals Kennedy authorizing the plan to proceed.

PFIAB's chairman, James Killian, told Kennedy that the Baldwin leak was "a tragically serious breach of security" and "one of the most damaging unauthorized disclosures and leaks that we have any knowledge of in our experience." Killian forecast that it would prompt the Soviets to better conceal information about their strategic forces and lead to a reduction in the reliability of U.S. intelligence efforts on Soviet forces. That, in turn, would impact American war planning by influencing the development of the master nuclear war plan, the Single Integrated Operational Plan, or SIOP, the last-ditch effort to ensure the survival of the United States and its allies.[21]

With the information on the front page of the *New York Times*, there were few options for employing effective damage control. The White House or Pentagon could issue an official denial, but that would probably be counterproductive by seeming to authenticate the information, and it would certainly spark more unwanted attention. If the leaker could be identified, Killian said, "really drastic action" was warranted; he recommended "that such discipline be taken in a way that leaves no doubts in the minds of the offenders' associates about how disastrous their actions have been and the punishment that has been meted out."[22] The national intelligence estimate that the information came from had been widely circulated to those with the necessary security clearance, so it was not clear whether the leaker had been a top-level official or someone lower down the chain. When FBI agents investigated Baldwin's contacts, they asked whether Baldwin had met with any "Indians," by which they meant officials "low down on the totem pole."[23] Ostentatious disciplinary action against Baldwin's source was designed in large measure to deter any of these lower-level officials from leaking state secrets.

The best course, PFIAB had concluded, was to focus less on punitive action against the Baldwin leak and more on preventing future leaks. Given that hundreds, perhaps thousands, of people were involved in the preparation and circulation of even highly classified NIEs, policing that information had to rely on deterring would-be leakers. Previous timidity in addressing the problem of leaks, the PFIAB diagnosed, had led to a situation where would-be leakers had no real fear of punitive action. That, Killian told Kennedy, was "why we feel so strongly that if you could find the ways and the means appropriately to take drastic action, even though this drastic action might result in adverse criticism temporarily, after a period, that the national interest would be well served by your doing it, and taking the adverse reactions as they might come." Killian warned that if it became public, it might well stir up a political storm, but he urged the president to demonstrate political courage in the name of the nation's security.[24]

The most controversial recommendation Killian gave the president concerned chasing down future leaks. Under existing circumstances, the FBI was responsible for tracking down unauthorized disclosures of classified information. But the FBI lacked both high-level enthusiasm for that mission and the logistical infrastructure: when the FBI began its investigation into the Baldwin leak, some of its agents did not have the necessary security clearances, and getting those clearances took valuable time. Furthermore, they had to familiarize themselves with an unfamiliar subject area, learn which kinds of information were sensitive, and who needed to know what. Most damningly, the FBI's track record of successfully plugging leaks was poor.

PFIAB proposed that responsibility for investigating leaks of classified information be shifted to those better equipped to handle it, namely the defense and intelligence establishments. Rationalizing the proposal by arguing that the National Security Act of 1947 gave the director of central intelligence the responsibility for protecting the sources of intelligence information, PFIAB recommended "that the Director of Central Intelligence be encouraged to develop an expert group that would be available at all times to follow up on security leaks." It also proposed a parallel action in which the director of the Defense Intelligence Agency would be tasked with setting up a similar mechanism in the Pentagon.

Clark Clifford, a respected Washington lawyer, former adviser to Harry Truman, and secretary of defense late in Lyndon Johnson's presidency, argued,

> I think this is the most effective recommendation that the group makes: that there be a full-time, small group, devoting themselves to this all the time. I believe that that group could become knowledgeable about the pieces that these various men write, like Baldwin and [Joseph] Alsop and so forth. They can after awhile become pretty knowledgeable about who these men are seeing, these columnists, where these leaks occur. It can be done quietly, unobtrusively [so] that they have a wealth of background from which to select the information. They are at it on a full-time basis.

Clifford acknowledged that this was a sharp break from past precedent, but he continued, "Times have changed. You can't do this anymore on a hit-and-miss basis like we've done in the past because now incidents of this kind are infinitely more important and more damaging that they've ever been before."[25]

The tapes capture Kennedy green-lighting the initiative on the spot.

Meanwhile, the FBI's investigation into Baldwin was continuing. By 16 August, the FBI had determined that 761 people had access to the secret information in the leaked NIE. But Kennedy had narrowed suspicion to one Defense Department official. The name of that official remains classified, but strong circumstantial evidence points to its being Deputy Secretary of Defense Roswell Gilpatric.[26]

During an 22 August meeting with Director of Central Intelligence John McCone, Kennedy asked for an update on the Hanson Baldwin case. McCone reported,

> Well, I've got a . . . finally got a plan in which CIA is completely in agreement with. It does a number of things that were recommended, including the setting up of this task force, which would be a continuing investigative group reporting to me. We are rec-

> ommending that DIA [Defense Intelligence Agency] set up a similar group with respect to leakage of sensitive and classified information.[27]

In addition, McCone recommended a range of supplemental measures. Several of these would spark a full-blown political crisis for the administration when they became enacted and when reporters learned of them. Unknown to reporters, the CIA and the Atomic Energy Commission had long enforced a policy requiring its officers to formally report any contacts they had with members of the press. The Pentagon and the State Department had no such policy. McCone proposed that the Pentagon and State Department also require its personnel to maintain a log of any contacts with reporters and to submit memoranda outlining the content of the discussion. Chairman of the Joint Chiefs of Staff Maxwell Taylor was intrigued. Something like that was "long overdue," he said, but he was concerned about the public outcry if reporters ever got wind of the restriction.

Presciently, Kennedy predicted it would indeed set off a controversy. Members of the press would push back once they worked out what was going on. They were "the most privileged group," Kennedy said, and were quick to charge that any efforts on the part of the administration in this area were infringements on their civil rights.[28] But he said he would not shy away from it, because the stakes were too important. "Oh, well, I would think we are going to get some abuse. And, I think, [I'm] delighted to take it on this issue. If they ever get mean enough, because this—this is really . . .", he said, not finishing his thought out loud.[29]

McCone also suggested a way of shielding the president from the controversy. He, as director of central intelligence, would personally take responsibility for implementing the new information policies. The National Security Act—the same act that forbade the CIA from spying within the United States—gave him the mandate to protect classified information on sources and methods, he said. And that would, in effect, hide the president's role in the policy.[30]

Most of the information on how McCone implemented the policy remains classified. But the June 2007 release of the so-called Family Jewels, an accounting of some of the CIA's potentially illegal activities compiled in the mid-1970s, included new information on what became known as Project Mockingbird.[31]

Between mid-March and mid-June 1963, the CIA, with the active cooperation of employees of the telephone company, tapped the telephones of two journalists, Robert S. Allen and Paul Scott. They had collaborated on articles that drew upon, and sometimes quoted, classified material. According to the only two brief, declassified accounts of Project Mockingbird that have been made public, the order for warrantless wiretaps came directly from John McCone. Secretary of Defense Robert McNamara, Attorney General Robert Kennedy, and Director of the Defense Intelligence Agency Joseph Carroll were identified among a handful of top officials who knew of the operation. Walter Elder, McCone's executive assistant, later claimed that McCone agreed to the wiretaps only "under pressure" from Robert Kennedy, a claim that seems unreliable in light of McCone's enthusiasm for the project in the August 1962 Oval Office meeting with the president.[32]

Allen and Scott specialized in high-level leaks with an emphasis on national security and executive branch policy. Whether they became a target of Project Mockingbird because of a particular story or whether it was an accumulation of many leaks remains unclear. In the preceding month alone, they had published verbatim transcripts of McNamara's testimony at secret sessions of the Senate Armed Services Committee hearings, outlined internal administration debates about whether to transform the U.S. military presence in South Vietnam into an overtly combat force, revealed classified information on Cuban-based MiGs "buzzing" American surveillance planes, and reported that U.S. intelligence agencies had determined that Castro was using the ransom money paid by the United States for the Bay of Pigs prisoners on funding subversion in Latin America.[33] None of these could be regarded by the administration as helpful.

On the basis of a pre-wiretapping content analysis of the published articles, the CIA had concluded that the journalists' primary source of classified information appeared to be the Pentagon. The wiretaps provided the CIA with a valuable source of information about the journalists' sources and methods. What it found once the wiretapping operation got under way was the existence of not one individual leaker but of many. The sources were both widely dispersed and highly placed across the spectrum of government: senators, congressmen, staffers on the Hill and at the White House, members of the vice president's staff, and presumably officials of the Defense and the State Departments. As the "Family Jewels" summary put it, there was more to each individual leak than met the eye: "It was observed that through these contacts the newsmen actually received more classified and official data than they could use, and passed some of the stories to other newsmen for release, establishing that many 'leaks' appearing under other by-lines were actually from the sources of the target newsmen." It remains unclear why Project Mockingbird was terminated and what actions, if any, were taken against Allen and Scott. Whether the Allen and Scott wiretaps were the only ones conducted against American journalists by the CIA is also still unclear; the wiretapping operations against Hanson Baldwin and Lloyd Norman were apparently conducted by the FBI.

What is clear is that this highly classified effort, launched in the late summer of 1962, was the opening salvo in the Kennedy administration's campaign to clamp down on leaks of national security information to the press. That campaign would manifest itself in other controversial ways in the aftermath of the Cuban missile crisis and spark the most intense public debate about information secrecy since the Second World War.

6

The Bomber Problem

The problem of surveillance flights had still not been solved. Kennedy and his advisers were having to revisit the issue daily to decide whether to fly and, if so, how many flights to send over. But there did not appear to be any other viable option. Faced with the Cubans' unwavering refusal to allow the use of their sovereign airspace for surveillance, the United Nations had abandoned efforts to take over the job of aerial surveillance, and the prospect of on-the-ground inspection had stalled for the same reason.[1]

The principle of continuing to send U.S. surveillance flights over Cuba until the United Nations was able to implement a satisfactory alternative was one that American officials had carefully reiterated many times. But putting that principle into action involved complications.

First, there was the continuing matter of balancing the need for up-to-date information on what was happening on the ground with the risk of antagonizing the Soviets. Much to the Americans' surprise, Soviet negotiators had proved remarkably agreeable to facilitating U.S. inspections. But the Soviets were having trouble managing their relationship with the Cubans, and they could go only so far without permanently rupturing what they had declared to be an important alliance.

Second, there was the difficult question of how to respond if one of the American flights was shot down over Cuba. The latest intelligence suggested that Cubans manned the conventional antiaircraft defenses, the kind that could all too easily take down a low-level flight. The Cubans also claimed to be operating the more sophisticated SA-2 systems, the weapons that had established a potent track record of being able to take down high-level U-2 flights. Intelligence information disputed that; all indications were that the Soviets still controlled the SA-2 network. That made U-2 flights safer—the risk of the Soviets' shooting down another plane was considered less than the risk of Cuban forces' shooting down a low-level flight. In either scenario, though, Kennedy would face a very difficult decision on how to respond if a plane was lost.

It was not just that the decision would likely involve sending U.S. forces into harm's way. No good options appeared to be available. "None of us is really clear in my mind what our reprisal would be," Kennedy complained to the ExComm.[2] No contingency plan was yet drafted to cover the shooting down of a surveillance flight. And if the Soviets were indeed dismantling their sites, and thereby demonstrating that they were carrying out the agreement, it would be all the more difficult to justify a military reprisal in the court of world opinion. The United States could not simply ignore losing a plane to enemy fire, but air strikes against military installations in Cuba would almost certainly kill Soviet and Cuban troops and might escalate to war. Reinstating the naval blockade might well have been the most practical option, but it was likely to be seen as weak and could very well end up being ineffective. Faced with this paucity of options, Kennedy tasked Assistant Secretary of Defense for International Security Affairs Paul Nitze, a veteran of the Truman administration and a key architect of American cold war policy a decade earlier, with mapping out the range of reprisal options and putting forward a plan.

But the decision on whether or not to continue the surveillance flights could not wait until Nitze had finished preparing his report. It had to be resolved quickly. "We can't have this thing every morning whether we're planning to fly planes or not," Kennedy complained.[3]

By 2 November, some of the urgency in running the surveillance flights had dissipated. The Soviets—and even, on very specific issues, the Cubans—appeared to be shifting to a more accommodating stance. They said that their missiles were being crated and shipped back to the Soviet Union and that the sites were being bulldozed. All available evidence suggested that the Soviets were acting in good faith. Their nuclear submarines also appeared to be leaving the area, despite lingering suspicions that they might yet try to establish a nuclear submarine base there. Even if they could not persuade their Cuban allies, Soviet negotiators in New York seemed amenable to some kind of inspection of Soviet ships departing Cuba, either by weapons inspectors working under the auspices of the International Red Cross or by U.S. surveillance flights. Moreover, citing humanitarian grounds, Castro had agreed to return the body of Major Rudolph Anderson, the U-2 pilot shot down by a Soviet SA-2 missile over Cuba on 27 October.

But Castro flatly ruled out ground inspections anywhere in Cuba, by anyone, even the United Nations or the International Red Cross. A visit by U Thant to Cuba had been encouraging—Castro called the acting secretary-general of the United Nations a man "of great experience, competent, and inspires confidence"—but on the key issue of ground inspections Castro refused to budge. He also continued to publicly threaten to shoot down American planes over Cuba.[4]

For the Americans, that meant that they still had few options for getting reliable information about what was happening on the ground in Cuba. The issue was now not so much the missiles—they appeared to be dismantled—but trying to decipher what Khrushchev had meant when he pledged to remove "the weapons you call offensive." He presumably meant the medium-range balistic missiles (MRBMs) and intermediate-range ballistic missiles (IRBMs); there was no doubt about that. But did he also include other types of weapons? "The same forms of weapons can have different interpretations," he wrote Kennedy on 26 October. "Our conceptions are different on this score, or rather, we have different definitions for these or those military means," he said.[5]

The White House and Pentagon were particularly concerned about the IL-28 bombers. With a range of up to around 740 nautical miles, they were capable of striking a considerable portion of the southeast United States. They could be fitted with either 6,600-pound high-explosive conventional bombs or 12-kiloton nuclear bombs. Unknown to U.S. intelligence, the Soviets had in fact sent about six atomic bombs along with the fleet of forty-two bombers. In the American view, the IL-28s fell squarely in the "offensive" category, but the Soviet negotiators in New York remained steadfastly vague.

In addition, as Khrushchev and his representatives repeatedly pointed out, the IL-28s were obsolescent. They were from an earlier era, constructed in the late 1940s and powered by British Rolls-Royce engines. They were no match for modern air defense systems of the kind that the Americans had set up in Florida.[6] Their presence was more a problem of political and diplomatic appearances than an actual military threat.

Before 28 October, the presence of IL-28s in Cuba had not provoked much concern in American military and intelligence circles, even though they had been detected at the end of September, well before the missiles. In military terms, the threat they posed was not nearly so great as that posed by long-range missiles. And they did not imply the same level of terrifying imagery as the missiles, of push-button launches and near-instantaneous destruction. While not comforting, exactly—the bombers' payloads could still pack a sizable nuclear punch—bombers were old technology, which most people had become accustomed to. That these bombers were an old model further reduced the perceived urgency. Even as reports arrived in late September with the first evidence of the planes, the State Department's Bureau of Intelligence and Research calmly pointed out that "the arrival of a token number of IL-28s would not be unexpected."[7] Considered in isolation, therefore, the presence of bombers did not spark much alarm.

That changed with the end of the crisis, as they quickly became one of the central points of contention in efforts to bring the episode to a close. Kennedy himself remained skeptical that it was worth making an issue of the IL-28s. He was not convinced that they presented a serious threat to the United States or that they made any meaningful difference to the balance of power; he had said so as early as 20 October.[8] Moreover, the persuasiveness of Washington's position was undermined by the proliferation of American overseas bases, "because we've got bombers every place around him," as Kennedy put it.[9]

But it was a politically delicate issue, and Kennedy was reluctant to ignore the advice of his national security experts and come out openly as accepting the presence in Cuba of nuclear bombers that could readily reach American soil. On 28 October, he instructed Adlai Stevenson and John McCloy, the lead negotiators dealing with the Soviets in New York, to try to get the IL-28s removed. With characteristic pragmatism, he also said that he was disinclined to let the resolution of the crisis get "hung up" on the IL-28 issue.[10] Besides, he did not want to encourage too much premature, public discussion. "We don't know what is going to happen to the IL-28s," he said on 2 November. "Therefore, for very good national reasons, we don't want to get into that subject publicly."[11] When he gave a televised address later that evening from the White House's Fish Room to report that aerial surveillance showed that "the Soviet missile bases in Cuba are being dismantled, their missiles and related equipment are being crated, and the fixed installations at these sites are being destroyed," mention of the IL-28s was carefully omitted.[12]

But several of his advisers took a much harder line, and for the next few weeks there was an open debate within the ExComm on just how hard to push the point. It became the main test case for what constituted an "offensive weapon" and what was regarded as "defensive." For Kennedy, it tested how far he was willing to push before being able to draw a line under the Cuban missile crisis.

Defense Secretary Robert McNamara emerged as one of the most forceful advocates of the view that the IL-28s had to be removed. In recommending that low-level surveillance flights be resumed despite the risks of a plane's being shot down, he argued that it was essential to get more information on what was going on at the IL-28 airfields. The planes had arrived by cargo ship, which meant that they had been dismantled and the pieces shipped in crates to be reassembled once in Cuba. If the planes were still being assembled, it would provide an indication of Soviet intentions. The risk to American pilots was justified, McNamara said, and they were taking steps to minimize the risks, limiting pilots to one high-speed pass over the airfields and thereby giving Cuban antiaircraft gunners little chance to hit their target. "Curt[is] LeMay feels that the chances of losing a plane on that mission are very, very small," he said, referring to the Air Force chief of staff.[13]

CIA Director John McCone was initially skeptical that the risk was justified.

> JOHN MCCONE: I don't see why this is so important. All you're going to find is that there's some planes there and some more in boxes.
>
> ROBERT MCNAMARA: Well, you've got to find whether they have begun to dismantle or not.
>
> MCGEORGE BUNDY: You're not really going to be able to tell much, I agree.
>
> MCCONE: You're not going to be able to tell much. You'll see a fuselage. You won't know whether they haven't put the wings on it or they've taken the wings off.
>
> MCNAMARA: Oh, no, I quite disagree.
>
> DEAN RUSK: Well, they, if they were—
>
> MCNAMARA: If they've been dismantling, you'll be able to see it.

Secretary of State Dean Rusk proposed an alternative way of looking at it that put the emphasis less on the raw intelligence value and more on the strong likelihood that they were going to have to make their case in coming weeks. It was less about information than about making a statement, he suggested.

> DEAN RUSK: John, I had in mind the point that this would register our interest in the IL-28s.
>
> MCGEORGE BUNDY: I think that's a virtue.
>
> JOHN MCCONE: Well, that may be a virtue of it.[14]

Within a few days, McCone had shifted his position to be more strongly in favor. By 3 November, he was conveying the intelligence community's formal recommendation that frequent, complete aerial surveillance of the island was essential.[15]

Kennedy was in favor of sending the low-level flights over, but not strongly so. He insisted that it be done only if it was their considered judgment that they were prepared to dig in for a fight over getting the IL-28s removed. "There's no sense sending these pilots over there unless we're prepared to really make a thing about it with [Anastas] Mikoyan that these are part of the deal and have the fight," and be willing "to go to the mat with Mikoyan," he said, referring to the first deputy chairman of the Soviet Council of Ministers, whom Khrushchev had dispatched to New York as his personal representative. But it would take some doing. Up to that point, the IL-28s had not figured prominently in the negotiations, and there was much uncertainty over what was and was not part of the deal. "I don't think they think it probably is part of the deal," Kennedy said.[16]

But some of his advisers pushed the issue hard. "I think we're on pretty strong ground to make it part of the deal," argued National Security Adviser McGeorge Bundy. What's more, he said, "I think we'd be in a very difficult position if we don't try." It fell to McNamara to make the case most forcefully:

> I think it's *absolutely essential* that the IL-28s are part of the deal. I don't think we could live with the American public if they weren't. These are bombers with substantial capabilities: 750-mile range, 4,000-pound bomb load. We've just *got* to get those out of

> there. And we need to know whether there's any evidence that [the] Soviets are planning to get them out. And if they are planning to get them out, there should be at least an engine removed from a cell, or a tail assembly taken off, or a wing dismantled from a fuselage between Monday and Thursday.

With characteristic concision, McNamara summed up his recommendation the next day: "Mr. President, I recommend that until we obtain, first, a clear agreement that the IL-28s are considered offensive weapons and will be removed from Cuba, and secondly until we obtain a clear and acceptable U.N. inspection procedure, that we continue limited, daily overflights."[17]

Appealing to Kennedy's concern for political sensitivities worked. He authorized the surveillance flights. But in coming days he also continued to express skepticism about whether it was worth getting "hung up" on the IL-28s if it appeared that doing so might break the deal. It was an issue they revisited a number of times in the ensuing days.

Kennedy also remained concerned about the longer-term plan for monitoring the Soviet military presence in Cuba. If the Soviets were unable to persuade Castro to allow on-the-ground inspection or to come up with a satisfactory alternative, the United States would just have to continue its flights, he said. That would be complicated by who controlled the SA-2 sites. Although Vasily Kuznetsov had told John McCloy two days earlier in New York that Cubans were manning the antiaircraft guns and SA-2s, U.S. signals intelligence monitoring communications between Cuban and Soviet troops had picked up evidence that the SA-2s were in fact manned by Soviet personnel.[18] That gave Kennedy hope that it might be possible to reach an understanding with the Soviets.

> One of the suggestions which we ought to consider is whether—the Soviet Union will either take out the SAM sites, which is really what we ought to ask them to do. If we're unsuccessful with that over a period of negotiations, if they maintain control

> of the SAM sites and then at stated intervals, we'll run this thing [aerial surveillance] which we hope the U.N. will do. If they won't, we will do it.[19]

If the Soviets ultimately turned over the SA-2 surface-to-air-missile sites to the Cubans, as Cuban statements seemed to suggest, it would make it very difficult, perhaps impossible, for the United States to conduct aerial surveillance, especially in light of Castro's threat to shoot down American planes. Kennedy mapped out a plan for that scenario:

> the problem of the SAM sites is that if these SAM sites are going to be turned over to the Cubans, then we are going to find it impossible to do U-2 [surveillance]. And then . . . so that we ought to get—if we can't get them out of there . . . we ought to start by trying to get them out of there. That's the easiest [*unclear*]. But if they won't take them out, then we are going to do these drones and if they shoot them, then we are going to have to shoot up the SAM sites.[20]

But that should not be an excuse for taking a soft line, McNamara argued. "I don't think we ought to take surveillance off until we get a firm agreement on the removal of the IL-28s."[21]

By around 5 November, a deal on most of the important issues of the settlement seemed close. The Soviets were dismantling the missile sites, were crating and shipping the missiles back to the Soviet Union, and had promised to remove any nuclear warheads on the island. In New York, Kuznetsov even volunteered an inventory of the missile deployment, telling McCloy that as of 22 October there had been twenty-four completed missile sites and sixteen incomplete sites. Across those forty sites, they had introduced forty-two missiles in Cuba. All of those had been dismantled and rendered inoperable by 2 November. The numbers were new to American intelligence analysts. They had counted only thirty-three missiles and, on the basis of an analysis of incoming cargo ships and a study of standard

Soviet deployment patterns, had estimated that up t
might be there.[22]

It was encouraging progress, but the IL-28s remain sticking point. Even as the missile sites were being dismantled bulldozed, work on assembling the IL-28 bombers continued. Few were yet in a fully operational state—only seven of the forty-two in Cuba were ever assembled enough to be flyable—but each day U.S. surveillance planes passing over the airfields showed that new IL-28s were still being readied.[23] And the Soviets were pushing back. By insisting on the removal of these bombers, Khrushchev argued, Kennedy was adding new demands to what had been agreed in the exchanges of 26–27 October.[24] It was precisely the position that Kennedy had privately feared. It raised the prospect that the Soviets would regard removing the IL-28s as a deal breaker. When an unconfirmed, and later retracted, report came in on 5 November that another surveillance plane had been shot down, Kennedy wondered aloud if it was Khrushchev's way of pushing back on the IL-28s.[25]

That left Kennedy with a decision to make: take a quick settlement that left the IL-28s in Cuba, finally draw a line under the crisis, and move on; or hold up the settlement until the Soviets agreed to remove the IL-28s. "The problem is really whether to make a bargain on the missiles, which he's [Khrushchev] clearly ready to do," Bundy summarized, "or whether you want to keep the heat on, get the basic Soviet military presence out of Cuba, which means a small war." Bundy's sense of humor then got the better of him: "My five-second reaction is to have the small war but not today."[26]

Rusk had emerged with McNamara as strongly in favor of taking a hard line on the IL-28s, although he argued for prioritizing and compartmentalizing the public and the private tracks. "Until we get those missiles out," he said, "I don't know how much of a public fuss we want to make about the bombers. Go after it privately. But the overriding thing is to get those missiles off of Cuban soil and on their way back." On 2 November, he advised, "I don't think we ought to magnify the bombers quite yet into a major public issue." Four days later, he reiterated, "I'd like to see those wretched missiles off the island before we make an issue of the IL-28s with action. In other words, I don't think we want to play the IL-28s quite as fast as we want to play the missiles. Get those wretched things off, then we put the heat on the IL28s."[27] After having initially raised the political sensitivities of the issue, Bundy returned to a more neutral position. But in smaller gatherings he expressed agreement with the president's position. "Fundamentally, it's a political judgment," he said. "The bombers don't change the strategic balance. They're nothing like the missiles in that sense."[28]

Stevenson and McCloy told Kennedy that they were confident that the Soviets would concede the IL-28s.[29] But Vasily Kuznetsov and Anastas Mikoyan, the designated Soviet negotiators in New York, repeatedly deflected Stevenson and McCloy's efforts to address the issue head-on. The problem continued to be the understanding of what was "offensive" and what was "defensive."

McNamara did not share Stevenson's confidence. The Soviets had ignored repeated questions about the issue, he said, and they had never acknowledged that the planes fell into the category of "offensive weapons." As Stevenson himself pointed out, the Soviets continued to downplay their capabilities during the negotiations and had given no verbal indication of their thinking. McNamara said that he could interpret the continuing work on assembling the planes only as a clear sign that the Soviets intended to leave the planes in Cuba. He proposed that Stevenson and McCloy force an answer from Kuznetsov and Mikoyan. "Until we get that answer," he said, "I don't think we have a deal."[30]

That raised the issue of what pressure could be brought to bear. Removing the IL-28s was a relatively easy price to pay for an agreement, Rusk said, but there was no indication that Khrushchev was willing to pay it. One option that remained on the table was to take military action against the planes and airfields. But just as the Joint Chiefs of Staff had not been able to offer any assurance that surgical strikes could reliably take out the MRBMs and IRBMs without the possibility of considerable costs, the continued presence of the expansive network of surface-to-air missiles on the island meant that those same risks remained if the targets were the IL-28s. Military strikes against the IL-28s required taking out the SAMs. Taking out the SAMs amounted to major military action. The option remained feasible, and the Joint Chiefs maintained readiness through 20 November to implement it, but Kennedy never came close to pursuing that course.[31]

Another possibility, advanced by Llewellyn Thompson, was to offer a formal U.S. pledge not to invade Cuba as a direct quid pro quo for the removal of the IL-28s. The flaw in that course, argued Paul Nitze, was that it assumed that Khrushchev placed a high value on such a formal commitment; he had, after all, publicly said that he already had the word of the president of the United States that he would not invade Cuba and that was good enough for him. That, said Nitze, devalued a formal commitment. It "isn't very forceful trading wampum."[32]

A more drastic option was to ratchet up the quarantine, a position advocated by McNamara. He proposed tightening the blockade: "In the event we don't have a satisfactory solution to the IL-28s," he said, "I think we could very logically broaden the quarantine to cover aviation gas."[33] A weakness of that course, Kennedy knew, was that it was provocative not just to the Soviets but also to American allies; it would mean pressuring Western countries to reduce or even stop trade with Cuba.

It was also unclear what the implications of such a course might be for Khrushchev's position. Given the mystery shrouding much of internal Kremlin politics, it was easy for those in Washington to imagine that pushing strongly on the IL-28s might provide the opportunity for hard-liners within the Kremlin to exert greater influence on Soviet policy and perhaps even seize power. Although later largely debunked, such a power play was the accepted explanation at the time for Khrushchev's widely diverging letters of 26 and 27 October, therefore making for a compelling concern. And that kind of instability in Moscow would not be conducive to reducing tension. As Kennedy summarized the problem:

> I think the quarantine is the last step because it means us stopping Russian ships and it really raises things into a crisis fever again. What things can we do? After all, the major reason we wanted to get the missiles out was because of the political implications as well as the military, but the political were . . . Once you get those out, of course they've got these bombers and they can use them on a strike on us, but they're just one more hazard of life. They don't have the impact that the missiles had. So that we've accomplished a lot of what we set out to do. The question really is whether we want to, in a sense, bring the whole thing to a crisis again to get the bombers out.

Kennedy then issued instructions on how he wanted to proceed:

> If we put the quarantine back it would raise again the risk of a war, or [Soviet reprisal on] Berlin. . . . So, therefore, I'd like to have the Defense [Department] and CIA and State [Department] to be thinking about what it is that we can do to Castro on the IL-28s without formally reimposing a real quarantine. And then we have to just make a cold judgment whether it's going to be worth it to us to bring this thing back into a massive confrontation again to get the IL-28s out or whether we can just make his life miserable enough so that he'll decide it's worthwhile anyway. And just say that they haven't met their bargain, and therefore the United States is going to—can't give its formal guarantees of the kind that certainly [Yuri] Zhukov talked about and [*unclear*] agreed to about our invasion.[34]

In doing so, Kennedy reaffirmed his strong preference for pursuing a diplomatic track to persuade the Soviets to withdraw the IL-28s, without ruling out the possibility of drastically ramping up the pressure. In these private discussions, Kennedy consistently stuck to his conviction that risking a Cuban bomber crisis did not serve U.S. interests.

7

Standing in Judgment

Republicans cried foul. Cuba had been their issue, one that over the summer had underpinned some of their most potent attacks against the Democratic White House—and, by extension, the Democratic-controlled Congress—for being soft on communism.

The Republican campaign strategy all summer had been to shift the debate away from the New Frontier's domestic programs and toward national security. For all his stirring rhetoric on global peace and security, foreign policy was widely regarded as one of Kennedy's main political vulnerabilities. Congressional Republicans were better stewards of the nation's security, they argued, because they would adopt a policy of firmness, not weakness, toward the communist threat. They had accused Kennedy of playing politics with the Cuba issue in the 1960 election, and they planned to turn that issue back on the Kennedy White House and its Democratic allies.

Leading Republicans spoke out strongly against the administration's Cuba policy, their language sharpened by the campaign season. They charged that the Soviet military buildup was a much more serious threat than the White House was letting on. When Kennedy, in September, characterized the Soviet buildup in Cuba as "defensive" and the Soviets there as "technicians," critics countered that even defensive weapons could be used offensively and that "troops" was the more accurate word. They accused Kennedy of looking the other way while the Soviets built a communist beachhead just ninety miles from America's shores, of misleading the American public, and of adopting a "do-nothing" policy that abandoned the Monroe Doctrine.[1] Senator Homer Capehart, Republican of Indiana, had accused the administration of misleading the American public on the nature of the buildup and had called for an invasion of Cuba to stop the flow of Soviet troops and military equipment.[2] Campaigning to become California's governor, and still the de facto head of the Republican Party, former vice president Richard Nixon in September called on Kennedy to blockade—or, in his word, quarantine—Cuba, unilaterally if need be. "Cuba is a cancer," he said, and letting the Soviets establish a beachhead there would lead to war.[3] Governor Nelson Rockefeller of New York, considered the early front-runner for the Republican presidential nomination in 1964, also let it be known to reporters that he favored strong measures against Castro's Cuba, although he declined to go on the record.[4] They were joined by a chorus of Republicans in the summer and early fall of 1962 calling for more robust action against Cuba and the Soviet Union. "The Congressional head of steam on this is the most serious that we have had," McGeorge Bundy told the president.[5]

But the missile crisis had robbed Republicans of that line of attack. In the most sudden and unexpected way, their campaign spear had lost its point. They had been "Cubanized," as one observer put it.[6] It was a most dramatic—and, for Republicans, unwelcome—October surprise. Kennedy's 22 October speech that had first made the crisis public came just fifteen days before the midterm election. From 22 through 28 October, the White House had the floor. And the nature of the crisis made it virtually impossible for anyone to criticize the White House publicly, at least while it was ongoing.

Once the crisis was over, campaign workers from both parties scrambled. There was no question that Kennedy's personal prestige had grown, and many political operatives on campaign trails around the country believed that that would help Democrats. But until voters actually went to the polls, the effect the crisis might have on the election remained the big unknown. Would the overwhelming public approval of Kennedy's performance rub off on rank-and-file Democratic candidates around the nation? Would the national trauma sway voters to look beyond the local issues that traditionally defined a midterm election? And, of course, no one knew how it might affect voter turnout.[7]

Going into the election, Democrats held both houses of Congress. In the Senate, they held 63 seats to the Republicans' 37; in the House, they held 263 seats to Republicans' 174. But what appeared on paper to be a comfortable Democratic majority in both chambers was, in reality, often exceedingly difficult to corral into a working legislative majority.

For Kennedy, the problem was not just Republicans—although their consistent votes against his New Frontier legislation certainly created problems—but the members of his own party who often presented an even thornier problem. On some key issues there was less daylight between northern Democrats and Republicans than between northern and southern Democrats.

Southern Democrats consistently and strongly opposed many of Kennedy's most important legislative programs, especially ones that had anything to do with civil rights or that implied encroachments on states' sovereignty. The contentious and complicated issue of civil rights was a fundamental part of the political equation. A sizable core of southern Democrats remained staunchly opposed to fundamental civil rights legislation. Kennedy's leadership during the Ole Miss crisis, when he had ordered federal troops into Mississippi's flagship state university to ensure that James Meredith could enroll as the university's first African American student, won wide approval in northern industrialized states and wide disapproval in the South.

If Kennedy was going to make any meaningful progress on his ambitious legislative agenda, he would need a fundamentally different kind of Congress. Without either a stronger majority or support from across the aisle, passing any meaningful legislation was going to be difficult.

Republicans had good reason to be confident looking toward the midterm elections. For one thing, they had history on their side. Not since Franklin Roosevelt's first term, almost three decades earlier, had the party that held the White House actually made gains in Congress in a midterm election. History alone suggested that Republicans could look forward to a gain of 20 to 75 House seats and anything up to 15 Senate seats; statistically, the pattern suggested Democrats would lose around 44 House seats and 5 Senate seats.[8] Publicly, GOP party leaders expressed optimism that they could pick up the 44 seats that would give them control of the House, but their private projections were more cautious. Internal polling suggested that a more realistic target was picking up 10 to 20 House seats. That would still keep them in the minority, but it would also represent impressive gains that they could aim to build on in 1964.[9]

Even more encouraging was a Gallup poll suggesting that registered Democrats were weighed down with apathy and that Republicans were highly motivated. Forty-five percent of Republicans said they had reason to vote, while only 30 percent of Democrats said they did.[10] It seemed that the power of the protest vote would aid Republicans.

The White House was also eager to downplay expectations, not just as insulation against disappointment of losses, should they come, but also as part of the perennial Washington game of "underdoggery," a game the *Time* reporter and astute political pundit Hugh Sidey described as follows: "If one started low enough, any gain was cheering news."[11] But well before the election there were strong indications that this was not going to be a typical midterm election. Despite the historical track record, some signs suggested that the Democrats might not fare so badly after all. The glaring absence of any presidential coattails in the 1960 elections had an upside in 1962:

precisely the kind of Democrats who might normally be vulnerable in midterm elections simply were not in office—there was not going to be the traditional swing back to "normal." The Eighty-Seventh Congress, as Sidey put it, "had very little Democratic fat on it." A fifth of the electorate self-identified as independent voters, and, at that time, independent voters tended to be less likely to vote in off-year elections. And in another favorable sign for Democrats, polling through the year by George Gallup and others suggested that although support was indeed slipping for the Democrats, it was not shifting to Republicans.[12]

By early October, the pollster Lou Harris, whom the White House had hired for campaign advice, had identified civil rights, health care, and national security (framed in the rather vague terms of "war and peace") as the issues that voters were most likely to base their voting on. He suggested that if Kennedy could pound the Republicans on their partisan and divisive approach to foreign policy, he would be able to control the initiative.[13]

The race to watch, according to many political pundits, was the one in California. That state's gubernatorial campaign had been tough and bitter, both sides having gone sharply negative very early in the campaign. It had attracted much national attention not just because of the size of the electorate—California had just supplanted New York as the nation's most populous state—but because it was there that a high-profile challenger was trying to launch a political comeback: Richard Nixon. If Nixon was able to win, it would likely put him in contention for a 1964 or 1968 presidential run. Nixon, along with his fellow high-profile Republican gubernatorial candidates Nelson Rockefeller in New York and George Romney in Michigan, had promised that, if elected, he would stay in the state house in 1964 rather than campaign for the presidency. But he would not have been the first candidate to break such a promise.[14]

Particularly bitter accusations flew from both sides. Nixon accused his opponent Pat Brown of being soft on communism and lax on crime. Brown countered with similarly toned charges. The campaign featured smear tactics by supporters on both sides. One of the more notable dirty tricks used to get national attention involved a Nixon supporter who distributed at a Republican State Central Committee meeting a pamphlet with a doctored photograph of Brown bowing obsequiously before Khrushchev, implying that Brown was a "red appeaser." Nixon repudiated the pamphlet and its allegations, and it was revealed that the image of Brown bowing was actually clipped from a Laos welcoming ceremony.[15]

Thanks to the televised debates of the 1960 campaign, in which the vice president had famously failed to be as telegenic as Kennedy, Nixon is generally not remembered as someone inclined toward using television as a medium. In the 1962 campaign, however, Nixon relied on television heavily, staging seven televised telethons. The first six were three hours long, and the last one, on 3 November, was five hours long and included telephone endorsements from Dwight Eisenhower and in-person Hollywood celebrity endorsements from people like Pat Boone, Ginger Rogers, and the baseball star Jackie Robinson. And in the closing days of the campaign, fighting for his political life, Nixon once again dipped deeply into his campaign funds for a last-ditch televised effort.

Through mid-October, polls predicted a near–dead heat. But in the last two weeks of the campaign, Brown pulled ahead. On election eve, late polls showed Brown with a handy lead. While Brown wrapped up a final, marathon campaign swing by plane that took in eleven cities in eleven hours—a record for California campaigns at the time—Nixon canceled a last round of planned visits to campaign headquarters and announced an eleventh-hour exposé in the form of a special television broadcast. He said he would push back directly against the Brown campaign's allegations and implications and "take off the gloves and fight back against the personal attacks" made by Brown and his aides and reveal for the first time "the reasons behind this series of personal attacks by Mr. Brown." Nixon claimed to be the victim of a "malicious smear campaign" that was "unprecedented in the history of American politics."[16] The move was dramatic and unusual, but it did not work.[17]

The Republicans' focus on Cuba as their "number one issue" was also a calculated strategy to draw the president into the campaign by highlighting an area that was clearly under the White House's purview. And even Kennedy couldn't dispute that that issue was one of his greatest political vulnerabilities in the summer and early fall of 1962.[18]

During the summer of 1962, Kennedy faced a choice about how to approach the upcoming midterm elections. Presidents typically sat out midterm election campaigns, giving only occasional, token speeches. In the first place, that was often the most prudent course. Because the historical pattern was for the president's party to lose seats in the off-year elections, distancing the White House from the results was the safer option and offered some insulation from having the president himself be tarred with those losses. Second, the conventional wisdom held that presidents had little influence on voting in midterm elections. Predictably, most of Kennedy's advisers recommended that he sit the midterms out.

Kennedy, though, decided to ignore his advisers' recommendations, opting instead to enter the fray. He said that his prestige was already engaged, anyway, and that unless the balance of Congress was changed, none of his linchpin legislation would pass. In his calculation, that would be bad for the country and, of course, bad for his reelection chances in 1964. By deciding to insert himself into the campaign—and to have Vice President Lyndon Johnson equally engaged—Kennedy created a new political precedent.[19]

During a press conference on 23 July, he explained why he thought he should get involved. Passing legislation had been difficult, he said, and securing a working majority was essential to his legislative program:

> And that's why this election in November is a very important one. If the American people are against these programs, then of course they'll vote Republican, and we will have a state of where the President believes one thing and the Congress another for 2

> years, and we'll have inaction. There are those who believe that is what we should have. I do not. That is why I think this election is quite important. I think the choice is very clear, in other words. November 1962 presents the American people with a very clear choice between the Republican Party which is opposed to all of these measures, as it opposed the great measures of the 1930's, and the Democratic Party—the mass of the Democratic Party—the administration, two-thirds or three-fourths of the Democratic Party, which supports these measures. Fortunately, the American people will have a choice. And they will choose, as I have said, either to put anchor down or to sail. So we'll see in November.[20]

With the decision made to engage directly, Kennedy sought to move the focus of the debate away from Cuba and toward his preferred topics, particularly the signature social programs of the New Frontier. At the top of that list was Medicare. While Republicans were trying to steer the debate toward the White House's decidedly mixed record on foreign policy, the Democrats' strategy was to concentrate on Republican obstruction of key social and economic issues such as Medicare, tax cuts, prodding a sluggish economy, and unemployment.

Kennedy's campaigning in the fall of 1962 held out a number of other benefits that would likely pay off in the 1964 campaign. It provided opportunities to foster some gratitude among the Democratic members of Congress whose districts he visited, for his advisers to make or reestablish contacts with local political operatives, and for him and his campaign to dust off their campaigning skills before they were needed in earnest.

Since his last campaign in 1960, some important things had changed that would require shifts in strategy and thinking heading into 1964. In 1960, he had cast himself as the underdog, despite evidence to the contrary in the form of spending receipts and impressive staffing levels. That had been an effective tactic against Hubert Humphrey in the Wisconsin and West Virginia primaries and against Nixon in the general election, but now that he was president it was not a tactic available to him in 1964.[21] More importantly, it would be much more difficult to cast himself as the candidate of change. In 1960, he had branded himself as promising a break from what he called the staleness of the eight years of the Eisenhower-Nixon Republican administration. He would bring, he contended, a breath of fresh air, forging a new path forward. And in 1960 his own legislative record had been thin, offering few reliable clues to what he might do as president; he had the benefit of being a blank slate. He was, in short, selling a promise. That would be much harder to do in 1964. All of these changes meant that he and his political team would have to make adjustments. The 1962 campaign provided an opportunity to start that process.

Out on the hustings, Kennedy took some time to regain his campaign footing. His initial efforts were restrained and lackluster. That was partly the result of self-imposed constraints on the type of appearances he scheduled. Kennedy's political strategists tried to send him out around the country on campaign stops disguised as government business, with an emphasis on environmental issues. Doing so had a practical advantage. Arriving in *Air Force One* was convenient and prestigious; the photo opportunities of the jet decorated in presidential livery was a sure-fire hit. But the presidential plane was also expensive, costing on the order of $2,350 an hour to run. If the president's travel could be legitimately claimed as government business, the taxpayers picked up the bill. But the moment it crossed the line into explicit political campaigning, the Democratic National Committee would have to pay. And with the DNC in dire financial straits—already a million dollars in the red—that was going to be a problem.[22]

Initially, at least, Kennedy set off west and south on a tour with the twin themes of natural resources and the nation's space program. Those early appearances lacked fire, and Kennedy soon became frustrated with the constraints of trying to campaign under the guise of environmental issues. He shook off the shackles and engaged the fray directly.

Taking aim squarely at Republican opposition to his social legislative agency, he asked voters to elect Democrats, "those members of the House and Senate who support the minimum wage and medical care for the aged, and urban renewal, and cleaning our rivers, and giving security to our older people, and educating our children, and giving jobs to our workers. That is the issue of the campaign."[23] When Eisenhower went to the stump in early October to take aim at the social programs of the New Frontier, the White House politicos could not have been more delighted, because it helped the promise of the kind of political fight that might shake off voters' apathy, a development that Democrats expected to work in their favor. "We'll pay Ike's fare any day he wants to go out and make those speeches," goaded Pierre Salinger.[24]

The discovery of Soviet nuclear missiles in Cuba in mid-October brought the president's campaigning to a sudden halt.

Critics then and since have accused Kennedy of playing politics with the Cuban missile crisis. That Kennedy considered political factors in making decisions during the Cuban missile crisis does not mean that partisanship influenced those decisions. He was certainly ever mindful of politics during the missile crisis; political decision making was, after all, deeply ingrained in him, as it would be for most presidents. And the presidency is, of course, a quintessentially political position. It was only natural that he would consider the interests of the nation and how the nation would perceive actions and decisions. On the fundamental decision of whether to accept or reject the presence of Soviet missiles in Cuba, for example, his overriding concern was that it would be intolerable to the American people—even though some advisers had initially told him that, in strictly military terms, having a few dozen Soviet nuclear missiles in Cuba made little practical difference to the global balance of power.[25]

Kennedy also reached out to Dwight Eisenhower at key points, calling him personally on 22 October before his speech to the nation and again on 28 October when Khrushchev capitulated. And for the duration of the crisis he ensured that CIA Director John McCone kept Eisenhower fully briefed. There was no formal requirement that

Kennedy do so, but it was good politics. Kennedy was seeking the advice of not only an elder statesmen and an experienced military mind but also a leading Republican figure. Public criticism from Eisenhower was the very last thing Kennedy needed as he tried to devise a response to the Soviet challenge.

When Kennedy summoned legislative leaders to the White House to be briefed on the latest developments during the crisis, he had made sure that the gatherings were strictly bipartisan, providing ample opportunity for congressional leaders of both parties to express their views and ask questions in private. He was also careful to avoid partisan rhetoric in his public comments during and immediately after the crisis.

Kennedy had, for all intents and purposes, put partisan politics on hold for the fortnight of the missile crisis, and he did not record any substantive discussions he might have had with aides about the upcoming election. His first public comments after the crisis that mentioned the election came in a short radio and television broadcast on 3 November. It was an entirely nonpartisan call for Americans to exercise the strength of their democracy by voting on 6 November for the candidate of their choice. He made no further public comment on the election until 20 November, when a reporter asked him for his analysis of the results.[26]

IN CONTENTION ON ELECTION DAY were all 435 of the House seats, 39 Senate seats, and 35 governorships. All told, 1,035 candidates were on ballots across the nation.[27]

Polls conducted during the summer had suggested that voters were gripped by a deep—and deepening—apathy, even more so than was typical in an election without a presidential race on the ballot. But the predictions that voters would stay home on election day were proved wrong; turnout was unusually strong for a midterm election. The voter turnout blitzes that both parties had launched in the closing days of the campaign apparently paid off. Favorable weather across much of the nation also helped. By the time the last polling stations closed, over 53 million of the 83.5 million registered voters had cast their votes.

Exit polling gave an early indication that Democrats had fared remarkably well. Democrats lost only five seats in the House and gained two in the Senate, a result that bucked the historical trend. For Kennedy and the Democrats, it was worth celebrating, even if a closer reading suggested that the result was more likely a swing back toward the status quo after a poor performance by congressional Democrats in 1960 rather than new momentum in their favor. Extremists from both sides had done poorly. Some observers detected a tendency for young candidates to do better than older candidates, but there were no clearly detectable trends.

In historical terms, it was something new. In legislative terms, though, it failed to fundamentally change the prospects for passage of the New Frontier program. As Kennedy himself put it two weeks later, the result was comparable to the situation they had been in for the past two years. To be sure, it created a good starting position for the 1964 election. But in the interim, there was important legislative work to be done, none of it made much easier by the slimmest of working majorities that resulted from the 1962 midterms. And it would do nothing to quell press reports of a "stalemate" between the White House and the Hill.

The election results accelerated the pace of Republican gains in the South that had been building since World War II. Republicans won a record number of House seats, Kentucky elected a new Republican senator, and the Oklahoma governorship went to a Republican for the first time in over half a century. And the longtime Democratic senator from Alabama, Lister Hill, who had joined others from his state in denouncing federal intervention in the Ole Miss crisis, had only narrowly held his seat.

In broader context, though, Republicans still held relatively few southern House seats. From the nine they held in the Eighty-Seventh Congress, the recognized southern states gained another five, making a new total of fourteen when the Eighty-Eighth Congress convened in January 1963. The gains were in North Carolina, Kentucky, Tennessee, Florida, and Texas.

Democrats fared surprisingly well, and it was tempting on both sides to attribute that to Kennedy's handling of the Cuban missile crisis. In reality, that episode seems to have figured little in swaying voters one way or the other. For all of the efforts by some Republicans after the fact to paint the Cuba crisis as a White House election stunt, there is little evidence that the outcome of the crisis played any appreciable role. Despite hopes on one side and concerns on the other, any perceived viability of the Cuba issue as a decisive electoral issue, therefore, was essentially debunked. Republicans were not able to usefully exploit it to tarnish Democrats, and Democrats were not in a position to eke out any electoral benefit. The authors of the most detailed study of the issue concluded that the effects of the Cuban missile crisis were indiscriminate: "the crisis helped some Democrats and hurt some Democrats; it buoyed some Republicans and weakened some Republicans. In many cases Cuba was not even a conspicuous campaign issue." Findings of polls conducted in the weeks before the crisis were essentially identical to those where interviews were conducted in the immediate aftermath. Democrats consistently outpolled Republicans on the question of which party could do a better job confronting the country's problems.[28]

Predictably, White House spinmeisters claimed the election results as an endorsement of the president's program. Aside from Pierre Salinger's telling reporters that Kennedy was "heartened" by the result, the official White House reaction was restrained. But White House staffers made little effort to hide their jubilation that the result had defied history and their fears.

After a night of good news on 6 November, Kennedy was in high spirits a few days later when he called several Democrats around the country, including William Guy, the governor of North Dakota, and

John Reynolds, the newly elected governor of Wisconsin, a state Kennedy had lost narrowly to Nixon in 1960, to offer his congratulations.[29]

As part of his series of congratulatory calls, Kennedy compared notes with the only other person to have beaten Nixon in an election. In the closely watched California election, the first-term governor, Pat Brown, had fended off a well-funded campaign by Richard Nixon. Kennedy teased Brown that his own work in 1960 had set the stage for Brown's win: "Hell, I'd gotten them all in shape." But he credited Brown with sealing the deal: "I'll tell you this: you reduced him to the nut house."

Voter turnout in California had been high. As the returns came in overnight, it grew clear that Nixon's strategy of peaking in the final few days of the campaign had failed. Brown won more comfortably than many pundits had predicted. By ten the next morning, with Brown leading by a quarter of a million votes, Nixon appeared at a television news conference billed, dramatically, as his farewell to public life.

Unlike Kennedy's razor-thin victory over Nixon in 1960, Brown's victory was convincing. Nixon did not handle the loss gracefully, making no effort to conceal his bitterness in a tirade that amounted to a public tantrum. He charged, not for the first time, that newspaper reporters were in the pocket of the Brown campaign. He lashed out at newspapers, complaining that their reporters had unjustly given him a "going over" and listed a series of detailed grievances. "I think it's time our great newspapers have the same objectivity, the same fairness of coverage, that television has. Thank God for television and radio for keeping the newspapers a little more honest," he said. It was a somewhat odd charge given that the state's largest newspaper, the *Los Angeles Times*, had endorsed Nixon. It also stood as a marked contrast to Nixon's later war against television reporters.

In a final flourish, he declared his retirement from public life and the conclusion of his final press conference. "Just think how much you'll be missing," he said as he chastised the gathered reporters. "You won't have Nixon to kick around any more." It was not one of Nixon's finer performances, but predictions that it signaled his "almost certain political oblivion" could not have been more off the mark.[30]

Kennedy had watched Nixon's implosion from afar; Brown had been closer to the action and was not surprised. "This is a peculiar fellow," Brown told Kennedy. "I really think he's psychotic. He's an able man, but he's nuts." After chatting briefly with the governor's son, Jerry Brown, who would himself become California's governor the following decade but had at that time taken leave from Yale Law School to help his father's campaign, Kennedy and the elder Brown talked shop.[31]

Kennedy also called John Connally, the former Navy secretary who had just been elected governor of Texas. A conservative Democrat and leading supporter of Lyndon Johnson—an affiliation that had put Kennedy and Connally at odds at the 1960 Democratic National Convention—Connally had successfully fended off a challenge from the Republican Jack Cox, winning by about 125,000 votes. Democrats in Texas had done well in most of the state but had suffered in the Midland area and Dallas. Kennedy knew the difficulty of Dallas well, and he commiserated with Connally on the problem of winning the city's votes. In 1960, Kennedy had won Texas's electoral votes—albeit by only a slim margin—but had lost Dallas. In the preceding decade, Republicans had created an effective organization there, even embracing new technologies like IBM data cards recording names, telephone numbers, and street addresses, an innovation that allowed them to keep remarkably precise tabs on what votes they had where. That, in turn, gave them new tools to increase the effectiveness of their get-out-the-vote effort. Compared with their rivals, the Democrats could mount only a weak and hastily contrived organizational response.

Although he had won the state overall, Connally had been soundly defeated in Dallas. He blamed what he called Dallas's "junior executive" types and "society gals" for turning on the Democrats, "and they just got them a crusade going and they just wiped the slate clean." "I don't know why we do anything for Dallas," Kennedy complained. Just over twelve months later, Kennedy would make his own visit to the city in an effort to round up political support, a visit with a tragic end.[32]

The 1962 midterm election introduced some notable freshmen members of Congress. George McGovern, who had served as a representative for South Dakota's First Congressional District for five years and would, in 1972, become the Democratic presidential candidate against Nixon, was elected that state's junior senator. Two thirty-year-old freshmen also won election, both of whom would end up making significant marks in American political history. Donald Rumsfeld won a seat in the House of Representatives for Illinois's Thirteenth District. The other was the president's brother Edward "Ted" Kennedy, who had just passed the minimum age for election to the Senate. He won his brother's former Senate seat for Massachusetts. In doing so, he fulfilled a Kennedy family prediction. In an issue of the *Saturday Evening Post* that came out in the fall of 1957, Harold Martin had told of a future that Kennedy family and intimates were privately predicting: "they confidentially look forward to the day when Jack will be in the White House, Bobby will serve in the Cabinet as attorney general, and Teddy will be the Senator from Massachusetts." Not all had gone smoothly with Ted Kennedy's campaign, but in the end the voters of Massachusetts elected him to the Senate seat, which he held until his death in 2009.[33]

While celebrating what amounted to an electoral victory, Democrats learned that the election had a sad postscript. Thirty years to the day after celebrating with her husband his election to the presidency, Eleanor Roosevelt died, at the age of seventy-eight. Kennedy had always had a difficult relationship with the former first lady. Along with other members of the left wing of the Democratic establishment, she had staunchly supported Adlai Stevenson in the 1952 and 1956 campaigns, and during Kennedy's run for the Democratic nomination leading up to the 1960 election, she had let it be known that she regarded the young senator from Massachusetts as all style and little substance, joining Harry Truman in publicly favoring the midwestern liberal senator Hubert Humphrey for the 1960 nomination. But she had made a major contribution to American life on a national level and been a champion of the United Nations. Kennedy dutifully paid his respects. The White House issued a brief statement that read, "One of the great ladies in the history of this country has passed from the scene. Her loss will be deeply felt by all those who admired her tireless idealism or benefited from her good works and wise counsel." A few days later, Kennedy ventured to the Roosevelt home on the banks of the Hudson River in Hyde Park, New York, for her funeral.[34]

8

A Tub of Butter

THROUGHOUT HIS PRESIDENCY, Kennedy was consistently frustrated with the big, sprawling department, housed just down the road from the White House in Foggy Bottom, that was charged with managing the nation's foreign policy. His complaints with the State Department were similar to those of just about every modern president: that it was slow, bureaucratic, and unimaginative. The State Department, Kennedy said, was weighed down by bureaucracy and cautious, conservative thinking. He found the department sorely lacking in the responsiveness, initiative, and imagination that he needed in order to deal with fast-moving and complex foreign policy problems such as the recent Cuban missile crisis.

Some of Kennedy's frustration came down to style. Rusk, in particular, was pro-diplomacy, pro-negotiation, pro-protocol, pro–United Nations. His style contrasted sharply with that of Kennedy and some of White House–based national security staffers, many of whom were more inclined toward activism. As Rusk later put it, "'vigor' was the word of the day," not "discussion."[1] Inevitably recalling nostalgically the diplomatic era of his father's time at the Court of St. James when the younger Kennedy had been awed by the diplomatic style of figures like Franklin Roosevelt and Winston Churchill, not to mention his own father, Kennedy railed against what he saw as a softening of American diplomats. The new generation of diplomats, he had complained privately in the summer to a group of aides, including Dean Rusk, "don't seem to have cojones" and don't "present a very virile figure." "I think surely the defense department looks as if that's all they've got. They haven't got any brains," he said. "But when you're talking to, these days . . . when you're talking to so many people who are dictators, who sort of come off in a hard and tough way, I don't think it makes much of an impression on them if some rather languid figure . . ." By the same token, he did not want to go too far the other way: "And I know you get all this sort of virility over at the Pentagon and you get a lot of Arleigh Burkes: admirable, nice figure, without any brains. We all know that. But that, we don't want that."[2]

What he did want, though, were national security advisers he felt he could count on in each of the key foreign policy agencies, especially state, defense, and the CIA. The crisis had brought to a head his dissatisfaction on a number of fronts and exposed weaknesses in the flow of information and the coordination of foreign policy. He asked some of his closest advisers to take a new look at the makeup of his national security team. With reaction times shrinking and the stakes increasing in the nuclear age, it was more essential than ever that the president had the best possible range of options at his fingertips that harnessed, in the most effective ways possible, the cumulative wisdom, expertise, and power of the U.S. government.

One example that Kennedy cited occurred during the peak of the crisis. The ExComm discussed the possibility of trading the Jupiter missiles in Turkey for the removal of Soviet missiles in Cuba as early as 19 October, but when Khrushchev's letter of 27 October came in proposing a quid pro quo of Soviet removal of missiles in Cuba for NATO removal of missiles in Britain, Italy, and Turkey, the administration was caught flat-footed. Kennedy complained that he had asked that the issue be explored well before the Soviets had proposed it but that the State Department had not delivered. "We were not really prepared to know what we were going to say, and we weren't prepared to begin negotiations with the Turks in case this would really prove to be desirable and really gotten it so that we could do it if we wanted to do it," he noted. What he wanted was initiative and foresight: "it seems to me that some way or other the State Department ought to be about a week ahead, not be drawing plans up for six months ahead," he vented to an aide. The State Department was focused too far into the future, he complained, when what he really needed was actionable options for the here and now.

Kennedy was determined not to be caught flat-footed again. As he had in the wake of the Bay of Pigs episode, Kennedy instructed his advisers to again explore the opportunity to push through changes in his national security team. It was an effort designed to address a number of problems at once, including a recent proliferation of interdepartmental committees and dissatisfaction with the performance of some key State Department officials.

Those in Kennedy's inner circle identified the problem as a lack of organizational talent at the top. Dean Rusk was not an organizer. George Ball and Alex Johnson were both talented, but neither could tear his time away from other duties to devote to housekeeping affairs of follow-up and day-to-day operations. "So you've got—the three top officials don't have *anything* to do with organization of the place," complained Robert Kennedy. The result, Bundy added, was that the State Department was "*very* badly run as an organization."

JFK himself was even more blunt. The immediate problem was the drafting of new instructions to McCloy in New York for his discussions with Mikoyan. Although the State Department was the most logical place to undertake the task, Kennedy complained that it would take a week. "So Bobby [Kennedy] feels they're all fucked up. The Secretary [Rusk] is a fine fellow," Kennedy said, "but he doesn't run the department. George Ball is disorganized and [George] McGhee's hopeless. In fact, the department's just a tub of butter."

The key problem was one of looking ahead and not just reacting to events as they happened. As Robert Kennedy put it, "this whole thing of looking into the future is that the problems that we're going to have and the difficulties that we're going to face, to have somebody that can be doing that on a full-time basis." And the State Department culture, Bundy diagnosed, was "a kind of inwardness" that was bureaucratically cumbersome and not adequately responsive to the urgency felt in the White House. "What you really need," Bundy told Kennedy, is to install someone in the upper levels of the State Department that the White House can count on to break through that inwardness, "somebody over there who is spreading the department outlook to the government."

There was not, however, any talk of replacing Dean Rusk, who, along with Robert McNamara and McGeorge Bundy, would become one of the chief architects of American involvement in Vietnam in the following years. Reserved, soft-spoken, southern, and obsessed with confidentiality, Rusk favored quiet diplomacy and confidential counsel. He rarely made his case well in large meetings, and his marked nonassertiveness contrasted vividly with such ultra-assertive advocates as Robert McNamara and some of the New Frontiersmen in the White House. If Kennedy had wanted to replace Rusk, the secretary would not have put up much of a fight. He had effectively handed his letter of resignation to the president on his first day on the job.[3] And when, in the summer of 1963, Rusk offered to resign so that Kennedy could go into the 1964 election with a new secretary of state, Kennedy dismissed any such talk. As Rusk later wrote it, "Hell, no," Kennedy had told him, "And don't bring that up again. I like your guts, and I don't have many people around here with any guts."[4] Rusk made it abundantly clear that he knew he served at the president's pleasure. He was professional, shied away from speaking to the press, and was not given to grandstanding.

When Kennedy had first offered Rusk the job of secretary of state, in large part on the basis of the strong personal recommendations of Dean Acheson and Robert Lovett, Rusk had been emphatic that he could serve only one term, a condition based on the practical realities of supporting his family. Giving up the presidency of the Rockefeller Foundation meant taking a sizable pay cut, for the modest salary of a government official. Unlike public officials who had made their fortunes before going into government service, such as Averell Harriman and Paul Nitze, Rusk was of modest means and had not yet amassed any kind of nest egg for his family to fall back on. And there were more mundane factors for Rusk to consider, including new financial costs. The pageantry of formal diplomatic events demanded what amounted to a diplomatic costume: striped pants, a silk top hat, a long, tailed morning jacket, and a white tie and tails. None of these items had managed to find its way into Rusk's wardrobe before he had accepted the position.[5]

Like some other cabinet officers, Rusk was a stranger to Kennedy at the start of his presidency. Their relationship began awkwardly. Whereas Kennedy was disposed toward informality, appreciated diverging viewpoints, and reveled in a kind of free-flowing decision-making process that would compel him to pick up the telephone and call desk officers directly in the State Department—a practice that bucked the traditional hierarchy—Rusk was disposed toward formality, respected channels to a fault, and shied away from confrontation. Their styles, therefore, could not have been more different.

By Rusk's own admission, this contrast served the president poorly in the Bay of Pigs debacle. Focused on the interminable new challenges, with new staffers, in an unfamiliar job, and predisposed not to rock the boat, Rusk did not provide his best advice early in the new administration.[6] The most glaring error, of course, involved the Bay of Pigs. Despite stating his opposition to the invasion plan, Rusk did not argue forcefully against it. He did, however, earn Kennedy's respect and gratitude in the wake of the Bay of Pigs fiasco by never letting on that he had in fact objected to the plan all along.

Much of the awkwardness dissipated as each man became more accustomed to the style of the other, but a marked formality remained. Kennedy always addressed Rusk as "Mr. Secretary," and Rusk made no effort to prove his personal loyalty to the Kennedy clan, something that stuck in Robert Kennedy's craw and created tension between the two.[7] The younger Kennedy was critical of Rusk, complaining that because of his lack of organization skills "the whole place just bogs down." But he also recognized that Rusk was competent and offered skills and ideas that were needed. Despite the opportunity to push for Rusk's ouster, therefore, Robert Kennedy instead argued for someone to complement Rusk, not replace him.

So many of the cold war problems that confronted the administration went beyond the responsibilities of any one agency. The institutional framework created by the National Security Act of 1947 ensured that there would be much overlap. To begin with, there were multiple intelligence agencies. The Central Intelligence Agency captured imaginations with its role supervising covert activities, but its intelligence analysis role was more influential on a day-to-day basis for informing policymaking decisions. The Defense Department had recently established its own Defense Intelligence Agency to provide in-house intelligence analysis, creating tension with the CIA. The technology whizzes at the National Security Agency provided communications eavesdropping capabilities. The State Department had its Bureau of Intelligence and Research. The Army, Navy, and Air Force each had its own in-house intelligence shops. Just trying to coordinate intelligence was a major interdepartmental undertaking. And that was merely one piece of the policymaking puzzle. The State Department, the Defense Department, the CIA, and even the Treasury Department each had a stake in almost any major national security problem that came up. In addition, each was its own sprawling bureaucracy with its own culture.

Trying to corral multiple agencies into forging a coherent plan of action was not a new problem. Recent White House efforts to tame the chaos had actually made the problem worse. The White House had gone where so many had before—creating new interdepartmental committees. There had been a proliferation of them. In addition to the decades-old National Security Council (NSC), established precisely for the interdepartmental coordination of policy, Kennedy created the ExComm. There was a Special Group (CI), temporarily chaired by Robert Kennedy, focused on counterinsurgency in Southeast Asia and Latin America, a Communications Committee, a Mongoose Committee overseeing covert activity to oust Fidel Castro, a new Berlin Subcommittee chaired by Paul Nitze, and a 5412 Committee, also known as the 5412/2 Special Group, after the national security policy paper that ushered it into existence, that was mandated to oversee covert activities. A new NSC subcommittee focusing on Cuba had also been set up.

All of these new committees created new problems. Several of the people Kennedy trusted most, like Robert Kennedy, Maxwell Taylor, and McGeorge Bundy, found themselves spending so much time on committees that it was detracting from their main duties. Moreover, although many of these subcommittees had overlapping members, their reporting was each in a separate channel, and, to prevent leaks, their security clearance requirements varied.

Kennedy asked some of his closest advisers, including the beleaguered Robert Kennedy, Bundy, and Taylor, to come up with recommendations for streamlining the foreign policy–making process. They concluded that they needed a common link between all these new subcommittees. There was a specific set of requirements for such a person: it should be someone Kennedy trusted; it should be someone who came in with respect and seniority; he should be a skilled coordinator; and he should be the consummate staffer. As Robert Kennedy put it to the president, they recommended that

> it would be well if you had one person, in government, that could bring—could be your representative in all of these committees, bring all of their work together, and be responsible to see that they are being followed up and all the rest of it. That person doesn't exist at the present time. We have suggested, after our Cuba investigation, that such a man be appointed, and be working with you, and be responsible to you, and keep you advised in all of these matters, and make sure these committees met, and all the rest of it.[8]

The person in the position needed to be kind of a floating undersecretary of state, Taylor said, someone who was not going to be bogged down with the day-to-day operations of the State Department. In some measure, at least, that job description was Bundy's role. But that part of his job consumed more and more of his time, pulling him in too many directions, and his remaining duties precluded him from devoting the necessary time to being an interdepartmental coordinator. As Bundy himself put it to Kennedy, "the real trouble from my point of view, of my doing it, is that I've got other things to do."[9]

It was not just a problem of too many committees and not enough time. What Kennedy wanted was his own man. After the Bay of Pigs operation, disappointed with the advice and information he had received from the Pentagon, Kennedy had created a new White House position with direct access to him and well positioned to represent White House interests. General Maxwell Taylor had filled that position. Kennedy now entertained doing something similar with State, to bring in someone who understood what the White House was trying to do, reported directly to the president, and spoke the language of the department. The question became whether that person should be in the White House or in the State Department. There were advantages, as well as disadvantages, to each option. Creating such a position in the White House would likely provoke very real resistance from the State Department, whose senior officers might well view such a move as implicit criticism. But putting that person over at the department's Foggy Bottom headquarters might not accomplish the objective of greater White House control and influence.

There was also the problem of finding the right person. He should be a "top flight fellow," as Taylor put it, with enough gravitas and experience to be able to persuade reluctant departments. Deputy Secretary of State George Ball had already proposed having one undersecretary of state to serve as an undersecretary of interdepartmental coordination. Ball, too, emphasized the need to find someone who could command respect from the many stakeholders in carrying out American foreign policy. "If you get a big enough guy," Bundy told

Kennedy, "there's no pain in that. That's a good way of doing it. The point is to get a good guy."[10]

The impetus for such a shake-up was Kennedy's dissatisfaction with George McGhee, the number three official in the State Department. In that position, McGhee headed the U.S. efforts in the Congo, where an impossibly complex situation was deteriorating in the wake of Belgium's withdrawal from its former colony. The United States had little leverage and even less appetite for direct engagement, the United Nations was hamstrung by the competing interests of its member states, and the Soviets were actively flouting UN resolutions. Rusk put it succinctly: "The situation was a mess."[11]

In a White House briefing on 31 October, McGhee seemed overwhelmed by the problem and unable to present a clear path for moving forward. Kennedy commented, "We had a meeting the other day and I never saw a weaker presentation of the Congo. I mean, Jesus, I know it's a mess, but we didn't really seem to . . . I mean he's a good fellow, he's got good qualities. The only thing is that . . .". As he so often did, Kennedy let the thought trail off. Kennedy quickly decided that McGhee was the wrong person for the job, but he wanted to choreograph the change in such a way that a new coordinator was in place before McGhee was pushed out.

All were impressed with the work of George Ball himself, but he was not well suited to the job they had in mind. As Bundy put it, "George works very *ad hoc.* And he's got a good energy for a specific problem, but he's not a long term, continuing, follow-up guy." They all admired the work of Alexis Johnson, but he already had a full plate and there were only so many hours in the day. Dean Rusk did not have the coordinator disposition, and, Bundy said, "he always has to be at bat at whatever's coming across the plate." Dave Bell, the director of the Bureau of the Budget, was a possible candidate, but he was being considered to head the U.S. Agency for International Development after Fowler Hamilton was pushed out. Bell ultimately got the position, widely regarded as one of the most thankless jobs in Washington. It was, Bundy argued, "a matter of round peg, round hole. That's the thing Dave would do best." Sargent Shriver was another possibility, but he already had an important post and was performing well. Livingston Merchant had done a widely admired job under Christian Herter as undersecretary of state for political affairs (McGhee's predecessor in that post). But appointing him, Bundy suggested, was too conventional—Herter was deeply ingrained with the prevailing State Department bureaucratic culture. And it would also be difficult to persuade Herter to accept the job; he had already indicated that he was not interested. More importantly, in Bundy's view, it would not be enough of a shake-up to address the problems they were tackling. And that was "not really what we want," Bundy said.

Another, more radical option that Kennedy floated was to put Bundy in McGhee's place at state and move Ted Sorensen, Kennedy's longtime aide, speechwriter, and counsel, to replace Bundy as national security adviser. Pursuing that plan, though, might well have run into problems in getting Sorensen the necessary security clearance and support; Sorensen was publicly known to be a pacifist and conscientious objector. Indeed, a decade and a half later, when President Jimmy Carter nominated Sorensen to be director of the CIA in 1977, that reputation came back to haunt Sorensen and contributed to his withdrawing his nomination at the eleventh hour.

Ultimately, Kennedy settled on a more traditional response that brought Averell Harriman back onto the federal government's payroll. A former governor of New York, ambassador to the Soviet Union, ambassador to the United Kingdom, and secretary of commerce, Harriman exuded the kind of gravitas and experience Kennedy was looking for, and Kennedy had called on him from time to time. In April 1963, Harriman replaced McGhee. McGhee was moved to another important position, that of U.S. ambassador to West Germany. The appointment of Harriman did not amount to the kind of radical shake-up that Kennedy had contemplated, but within months it had profound ramifications for American involvement in Vietnam as Harriman became a leading proponent of removing the South Vietnamese president Ngo Dinh Diem from power.

9

The Military Problem

The nation's capital had a new international airport. With its distinctive, wing-shaped roof, it was a fitting modern addition to the area's efforts to accommodate the growing number of passengers looking to take advantage of that most modern of innovations: the burgeoning industry of commercial passenger aviation. And it would add a new immigration entry point to the East Coast to go along with New York.

Kennedy was on hand for the 17 November dedication ceremony. He was joined by his predecessor, Dwight Eisenhower. Eisenhower's presence was especially apt: the airport was being named for his imposing first secretary of state, John Foster Dulles, a man Winston Churchill had quipped was "the only bull I know who carries his china shop around with him." Dulles had also spent an extraordinary amount of time on the new postwar generation of passenger aircraft as part of his diplomatic shuttling around the world. And it was Eisenhower who had selected the site in what was then northern Virginia countryside, about twenty-five miles from downtown Washington, D.C.

Having played their parts in the ceremony and with the festivities winding down, Kennedy and Eisenhower slipped away from the photographers and reporters who had gathered to cover the event. They disappeared into one of the vast new terminal's back rooms, where they were joined by John McCone, the director of central intelligence.

McCone and Eisenhower knew each other well. Eisenhower had chosen McCone to chair the Atomic Energy Commission for the last two years of his administration. McCone was at the secret Dulles International Airport meeting to brief Eisenhower on the latest developments on the Cuba issue. Inviting the director of central intelligence to give the briefing was also a show of respect and of political savvy on Kennedy's part. Having a junior-level figure brief Eisenhower, especially in Kennedy's presence, simply would not do. And by making sure that Eisenhower was briefed by the nation's top intelligence official, he minimized the risk that the Republican elder statesman would criticize his administration's policies publicly, which would be far more damaging than the even more strident criticism that Richard Nixon continued to direct at the White House.

McCone's news was mixed. Progress had been made—a deal on the IL-28 bombers appeared imminent—but it was tempered by a sobering reality: some of the most fundamental issues that had sparked the recent crisis might never be fully resolved. In short, while the danger had receded, many problems remained. Ominously, McCone warned that the United States was always going to have a "missiles in Cuba" problem.

McCone was not referring to the long-range nuclear missiles capable of striking most of the continental United States, the ones that had created the crisis in the first place. Those were "the missiles we've had on our minds," McGeorge Bundy said. Khrushchev had promised to remove them, and there were indications that he was working to make good on the promise.

But the long-range missiles were not the only missiles that the Soviets had sent to Cuba. At least four kinds of short-range missiles remained. Those included hundreds of surface-to-surface, surface-to-air, and air-to-surface missiles.[1] Some were so-called dual-use missiles, capable of delivering both conventional and nuclear warheads.

Even if armed with nuclear warheads, they posed no real threat to the continental United States and could not hold American cities hostage in the same way that their long-range cousins could. But they could easily be used against the U.S. naval base at Guantánamo or American ships stationed off the coast of Cuba. Worst of all, if the president ordered an invasion of the island—which remained an option at least theoretically on the table and a scenario the military was required to remain ready for—American troops might well be entering a nuclear battlefield, which in turn could easily escalate to global nuclear war. The missiles and remaining troops also posed a political problem: as long as those military forces remained, it left an opening for the administration's critics to accuse the White House of adopting a "look-the-other-way policy" toward the establishment of a Soviet base on America's doorstep.[2] And such a charge could readily undermine the public's currently favorable view of Kennedy's performance.

A DAY EARLIER, on 16 November, the Joint Chiefs of Staff had also met with the president. This involved none of the secret choreography of the Dulles Airport meeting, but the chiefs had important news to deliver. It was almost three weeks since Khrushchev had capitulated in regard to Cuba and the crisis been declared over. When they met with Kennedy in the Oval Office, the chiefs reported that their forces were finally fully ready to take military action against Cuba if ordered to do so.

With Khrushchev's capitulation, the diplomats of the State Department had shifted gears, but the Pentagon had not. If anything, its momentum was still building. Mobilization was a slow and cumbersome business. The process had been delayed by the demand for secrecy before Kennedy's television address on 22 October. Both the Americans and the Soviets were close and skilled observers of their adversaries' military posture and alert status, and any obvious steps by the American military to move forces to the southeast United States could easily have tipped off the Soviets that their deployment in Cuba had been discovered. As a consequence, military mobilization had not begun in earnest until 22 October.

The Pentagon, therefore, was still mobilizing. It was a major operation; Defense Department accountants later estimated the department's out-of-pocket expenses for the relatively brief Cuba crisis to be north of $183 million (about $1.3 billion in 2010 dollars). It was moving thousands of troops to Florida, bolstering its air defenses, and readying its troops for a range of military actions against the island. The forces were ready for anything from air strikes on specific targets, a full-fledged amphibious invasion, or defense of U.S. airspace from incoming IL-28 nuclear bombers or even nuclear missiles.[3]

Despite his own much-celebrated World War II service as a PT-boat commander in the Pacific, Kennedy had a difficult relationship with the military brass. It was not just a matter of comparison with his five-star predecessor, Dwight Eisenhower, though that certainly did not help. Even after he left the White House, Eisenhower still preferred to be addressed as "General." Kennedy had even signed a special order in March 1961 reinstating Eisenhower to active military service and rank, both of which he had resigned for his presidential run in 1952. Eisenhower's military record was exemplary, as supreme commander of Allied forces in Europe in World War II, as leader of the D-day invasion of German-occupied Europe, and subsequently as NATO's supreme allied commander.

In fact, Eisenhower had himself been a source of much frustration in senior military circles, especially in his own branch, the U.S. Army. It was not just that he took a widely applauded parting shot at the growing power of the arms industry, part of what he called the military-industrial complex. At the heart of the frustration was fundamental disagreement over policy, a disagreement Kennedy exploited in his 1960 campaign.

In crafting and labeling his overall defense posture during his 1952 campaign for the presidency, Eisenhower had made nuclear weapons—specifically nuclear deterrence—the heart of U.S. defense policy. That pleased the Air Force, the branch that controlled the most important and visible parts of the U.S. nuclear arsenal. But it also infuriated the Army and, to a lesser extent, the Navy, for the perceived blow to their prestige and the very real blow to their funding relative to the other branches. Eager to restore their place in the most prestigious and lucrative arm of national defense, Army generals like Maxwell Taylor publicly criticized Eisenhower's emphasis on Air Force nuclear strike capabilities and offered a plan for a new strategic concept they called graduated deterrence. They argued that Eisenhower's strategy, widely known as massive retaliation, amounted to an unrealistic and dangerous reliance on an all-or-nothing approach. What was needed for the new decade and evolving threats, Taylor and like-minded strategists said, was something more flexible, something that would give the president a range of options to meet different levels of threat. Threatening nuclear annihilation in places like Korea, Laos, Vietnam, or even West Berlin, they said, would be simply ineffective; it lacked credibility. By contrast, building up conventional forces, especially having more and better-armed boots on the ground, would offer many more options. Not incidentally, that would make the Army's core strengths essential, not to mention more prestigious.

It was this shift in defense policy, couched in commonsense, everyday terms rather than the abstract strategic gymnastics required of massive retaliation, that Kennedy adopted in his 1960 presidential run as a way of marking a break from the defense policies of Eisenhower and Nixon. The stance cast Kennedy in a favorable light in the eyes of Army and Navy leaders, though the Air Force preferred a rival candidate, Senator Stuart Symington from Missouri, who put emphasis on missiles. (Missouri was a state, not coincidentally, that relied heavily on missile production for its local economy.) It was no accident, therefore, that Maxwell Taylor and his ideas found a prominent place in Kennedy's campaign and administration.

Once he was in office, however, the managerial and cultural contrasts proved too much. Kennedy's collegial approach to meetings, hosting group discussions more like a university seminar than a corporate meeting, sat poorly with the traditional military way of doing things and contrasted sharply with Eisenhower's hierarchical management style, honed in years of military service.[4] To make matters worse, Defense Secretary Robert McNamara and his so-called whiz kids—systems analysts, academics, and technocrats whom McNamara brought in to make the department more streamlined, efficient, and effective—treated the military professionals with scarcely concealed contempt. They flatly questioned the data upon which proposals and advice were based. Proud military leaders tasked with a difficult job bristled and accused McNamara and, less directly, Kennedy of micromanaging. In military circles that was a charge often ranked worse than incompetence.

For his part, Kennedy bristled at the dogmatic hawkishness of some of the military chiefs. It would have been one thing if their attitude had been accompanied by practical, actionable advice, but too often, in Kennedy's view, it amounted simply to resistance. Having worked in the White House and the Pentagon, Taylor recognized the problem, even if he did not have a solution. "We find unfortunately we're against things but we're not quite sure what we're for, at least for in the sense of within considered feasibility," he confessed.[5] That also betrayed the kind of cumbersome bureaucracy Kennedy detested.

Kennedy's view of the military brass took a sharp turn for the worse during one the darkest early days of his presidency. The word "fiasco" has become permanently affixed to the botched CIA-sponsored invasion at Cuba's Bay of Pigs in April 1961. The U.S. Navy's code name for its portion of the operation, Bumpy Road, proved an all-too-apt understatement. For a host of reasons, many of which had to do with institutionalized cultural traditions and turf tussles, the military did not take an especially active role in the planning for the invasion.[6] The White House had given the CIA the lead on the operation, and the military innately respected the notion of lead. The CIA was reluctant to invite military participation, and military leaders were disinclined to press for it. But that attitude, and its consequences, infuriated the new president. Kennedy believed he, and the nation, had been poorly served by its military leaders.

Kennedy was disappointed by Admiral Arleigh Burke, in particular, having once regarded him as something of a personal hero. The hard-charging Burke was renowned for his aggressive pursuit of the enemy. For a young PT-boat lieutenant commander operating in the same region and hearing of Burke's exploits through the military grapevine, the admiral was the epitome of decisive action and vigor.

Kennedy changed his mind about Burke during the Bay of Pigs operation. Burke should have spoken up about his reservations regarding the Bay of Pigs invasion plan, Kennedy said. Venting to his friend and aide Dave Powers, Kennedy said of the Bay of Pigs planning,

> Arleigh Burke sat right across from me, . . . I've been reading about "Thirty-knot Burke." He was terrific! I was a lieutenant on a PT boat! You should have seen how impressive it was to see the Joint Chiefs of Staff show up with all that fruit salad. . . . [a]nd they'd have colonels carrying pointers and maps.

Kennedy told Powers that he had asked Burke bluntly, "Will this plan work?," and that Burke had said, "As far as we've been able to check it out, the plan is good."[7] To Kennedy's untrained bureaucratic ear, that sounded like an endorsement. But Kennedy probably missed some of the bureaucratic nuance, assuming that the last part of the sentence was where the emphasis should fall. But Burke was evidently emphasizing "as far as we've been able to check it out," a scarcely veiled complaint that the CIA was withholding the actual invasion plan from even those military officials who were expected to carry it out.

One of the lessons that Kennedy took away from the Bay of Pigs episode was to have a personal liaison looking out for his interests with the military chiefs. To that end, he brought General Maxwell Taylor out of retirement and installed him in the White House. When an opportunity arose, Kennedy appointed Taylor chairman of the Joint Chiefs of Staff.

Kennedy was not much more impressed with the advice he received from the generals and admirals during the Cuban missile crisis. Cautious about repeating their much-criticized reticence during the Bay of Pigs operation, military chiefs overcompensated during the Cuban missile crisis, coming across—at least to Kennedy—as brash and reckless. The actions advocated by General Curtis LeMay particularly alarmed Kennedy. A hawk's hawk and famous for later threatening to bomb North Vietnam "back to the stone age," LeMay was head of the U.S. Strategic Air Command. In that capacity, he oversaw the bulk of the nation's nuclear forces, notably its long-range missile and B-52 bomber forces. Kennedy believed that LeMay did not understand the gravity of the situation and was becoming intoxicated with dangerous bravado. McNamara agreed. LeMay and his like-minded colleagues, Kennedy and McNamara worried, were too eager for war, too free with their accusations of appeasement, and not sufficiently thinking through the long-term ramifications of what they were advocating. For their part, many of the military chiefs thought Kennedy and McNamara too cautious. They were charged with a difficult job to do, they argued, and they should be allowed to do it without civilian micromanagement.

Robert Kennedy later wrote,

> President Kennedy was disturbed by this inability to look beyond the limited military field. When we talked about this later, he said we had to remember that they were trained to fight and to wage war—that was their life. Perhaps we would feel more concerned if they were always opposed to using arms or military means—for if they would not be willing, who would be? But this experience pointed out for us all the importance of civilian direction and control and the importance of raising probing questions to military recommendations.[8]

President Kennedy took from the episode a growing appreciation of and trust in Robert McNamara. That McNamara consistently infuriated the military chiefs only reinforced Kennedy's admiration.

With his sharp, analytical mind, supreme confidence, and methodical advice, he inspired Kennedy's confidence, just as he would with Kennedy's successor. Lyndon Johnson once praised McNamara's abilities by telling Sargent Shriver, "I don't think there's a man in government as valuable as McNamara."[9] Not shy about exerting his mandate as the president's delegate for managing civilian control over the military and never afraid to be perceived as meddling, McNamara did not see his role as just being a mouthpiece for the professional soldiers. Although he would be careful to present their views and advice in ExComm and other meetings, he frequently dissented from them and added his own advice.

Others were more sensitive, such as Assistant Secretary of Defense for Policy Paul Nitze. During an episode just hours before Kennedy was to go before the nation on 22 October to announce the discovery of Soviet nuclear missiles in Cuba, Nitze had resisted Kennedy's efforts to restate the standing orders for nuclear launch. Kennedy wanted to make sure that there was going to be no breakdown in command and control. "They don't know what we know and they might think a nuclear war is already on, so I don't think we should take the Chiefs' word on that," he said. A tense moment was made more so by Nitze's reluctance to reaffirm the message. They had their standing orders, Nitze said, and the implication that they somehow did not understand those orders was just going to get their back up unnecessarily. With a secretary of state unaware that American missiles in Turkey were operational and a president who had to ask what EDP was—it was the European Defense Plan, which amounted to nuclear war—the absurd, yet all-too-real, episode could easily have been lifted from the script of Stanley Kubrick's biting satirical movie *Dr. Strangelove or: How I Learned to Stop Worrying and Love the Bomb.*[10]

Despite these misgivings and experiences, finding a way to work with military chiefs was a presidential imperative. And it remained just as important in the weeks after the missile crisis as it had been during it.

THE CIA AND MILITARY CONTINUED to send spy planes over Cuba. Recent low-level surveillance photos discovered things that the high-level U-2 flights could not. The growing body of intelligence led to a more complete picture of what the Soviet military force on the island looked like. Fundamentally, that new intelligence showed that the information they had based their decision making on during the crisis was incomplete in several important ways.

One worry of the military chiefs as new information came in was that it kept turning up new surprises. That, in turn, revealed the level of uncertainty that had dogged their understanding of the crisis since the beginning.

Moscow had sent more than just a few dozen long-range nuclear missiles to Cuba. In addition to the standard support vehicles such as armored personnel carriers and antitank weapons, the buildup also included torpedo boats, submarines, short-range nuclear weapons, various types of MiG fighter jets, and long-range nuclear bombers. Sending all of this equipment, and the 42,000 Red Army troops that went with them, involved a major planning effort that dated back to mid-1960 and had gone through several iterations since.

By February 1962, several phases of Soviet military aid that began in mid-1960 had transformed Cuba into a formidable regional military power; a rapid infusion of Soviet bloc weaponry and training and a tenfold increase in size since Fulgencio Batista's ouster made the Cuban military the second largest in the region, behind Brazil. The deployment included hundreds of tanks and self-propelled guns, advanced fighter planes, ships, sophisticated radar technology, antiaircraft guns, and Soviet troops.[11]

Seeking to convince the rest of the world that the buildup was not menacing, while simultaneously trying to impress upon the United States the potential costs of sponsoring another invasion attempt, the Cubans and Soviets openly displayed their military hardware in Havana's military parades. And Cuban premier Fidel Castro boasted that the parading forces were only a small portion of the total military force Cuba could muster; there were "mountains and mountains of Communist arms in Cuba," he claimed. During the summer of 1962, hawkish critics of the Kennedy administration's Cuba policies cast the Soviet shipments to Cuba as a serious threat, but the consensus of the U.S. intelligence community was that there was nothing exceptional about the Cuban buildup in the context of earlier Soviet military aid to other third-world allies, such as Iraq, Indonesia, Egypt, and Syria, and that in the absence of the air and naval forces needed to project military power, the military forces on the island posed no imminent military threat to the United States or other countries in the hemisphere.[12]

Through the summer and fall of 1962, American intelligence on the issue remained frustratingly imprecise, a haziness that fueled public doubts about whether the administration had a good handle on what was actually going on in Cuba. The surprise outbreak of the crisis was also widely seen as the result of a devastating intelligence failure—the real possibility of another Pearl Harbor type of surprise was frequently alluded to by critical pundits and observers. Many commentators questioned the competence of U.S. intelligence agencies and of the Kennedy administration, often recalling the Bay of Pigs fiasco and suggesting a pattern. Fresh newspaper reports about new and unidentified arms shipments to Cuba and indications of around-the-clock work at Cuban military sites were unsettling. To make matters worse, the administration could not even give a firm answer to such seemingly simple questions as how many Soviet troops had been in Cuba at the height of the crisis and how many remained. Having announced that the number of Soviet troops in Cuba peaked at about 17,000 during the crisis, officials struggled to explain why that figure remained unchanged for months after the crisis even after several announcements that thousands of Soviet troops had withdrawn. The administration retrospectively increased its estimate to 22,000, but that helped little. Looking back, the discrepancy is easy enough to explain: the administration's initial counts were grossly flawed, underestimating

This is the actual Dictaphone Time-Master used by President Kennedy in the Oval Office to record telephone calls and dictation. A Dictaphone Model 117000 Type P6 made in New York, it recorded on a plastic belt that wrapped around the drum at right. For dictation, a separate handheld microphone could be plugged in, or it could be connected to the telephone line to capture telephone conversations. The recorder is now in the holdings of the John F. Kennedy Library and Museum. (*Photo by Joel Benjamen / JFK Library*)

With television cameras crammed into the Oval Office on the evening of October 22, 1962, President Kennedy revealed that U.S. intelligence had discovered Soviet nuclear missiles in Cuba despite repeated Soviet assurances to the contrary. Kennedy also announced a naval quarantine of Cuba that remained in place until November 20. (*Bettmann/Corbis / AP Images*)

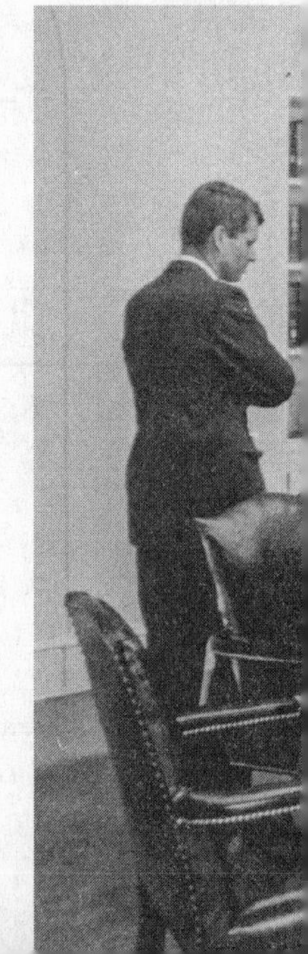

Because of the extreme secrecy surrounding ExComm meetings during the Cuban missile crisis, even White House photographers were not given access. This 29 October 1962 photo is one of the first taken of the ExComm while it met. Clockwise from left: Atty. Gen. Robert F. Kennedy (standing); Asst. Sec. of Defense Paul Nitze; USIA Dep. Dir. Donald Wilson; Special Counsel Theodore Sorensen; NSC Exec. Sec. Bromley Smith; Special Asst. McGeorge Bundy; Sec. of Treasury Douglas Dillon; Vice Pres. Lyndon B. Johnson; Amb. Llewellyn Thompson; William C. Foster; CIA Dir. John McCone (hidden); Undersec. of State George Ball (hidden); Kennedy; Sec. of State Dean Rusk; Sec. of Defense Robert McNamara; Dep. Sec. of Defense Roswell Gilpatric; JCS Chairman Gen. Maxwell Taylor. White House, Cabinet Room. *(Photo by Cecil Stoughton / JFK Library)*

When Kennedy met with the Soviet foreign minister, Andrei Gromyko, on 18 October 1962, he chose not to reveal that just a few days earlier a U-2 surveillance plane had obtained photographic proof that Soviet medium-range missile bases were being built in Cuba. Kennedy found Gromyko's denials instructive in regard to the Soviets' trustworthiness and referred to them several times in coming days. *(Photo by Abbie Rowe / NARA)*

Kennedy, Robert McNamara, and Roswell Gilpatric during the ExComm meeting of 29 October 1962. *(Photo by Cecil Stoughton / JFK Library)*

Relatively few recordings of Kennedy's phone conversations survive. He did not use the telephone as a tool of governance as religiously as his immediate successor, Lyndon B. Johnson. (12 August 1963 / *Photo by Abbie Rowe / NARA)*

Kennedy met with Adm. George Anderson, the Chief of Naval Operations, in the Oval Office on 29 October 1962. Anderson and McNamara had a series of confrontations during the crisis, and resentment simmered for months thereafter. *(Photo by Robert Knudsen / JFK Library)*

On 30 October 1962, Kennedy invited the U-2 pilots who had flown over Cuba to meet with him in the Oval Office. At left is Col. Ralph D. Steakley, who headed the team evaluating the surveillance photos of Cuba. Lt. Col. Joe M. O'Grady and Maj. Richard S. Hoyser were U-2 pilots who had flown over Cuba. Closest to Kennedy is Gen. Curtis LeMay, the Air Force Chief of Staff. Gen. Godfrey T. McHugh, an Air Force aide, is standing. A similar photo, taken by an Associated Press photographer standing behind Kennedy's left shoulder, appeared on the front page of the *New York Times* the next day. *(Photo by Cecil Stoughton / JFK Library)*

The low-level surveillance flights by Navy F-8U and Air Force RF-101 jets swept in fast at an altitude of only 500 to 1,000 feet, ideally catching those on the ground by surprise. The resulting photos, much more detailed than those taken by U-2s, enabled the NPIC analysts to distinguish between models of weapons, count individual soldiers, and even pick out the telephone cables running between the weapons and command bunkers that would be used to communicate firing orders. But the flights were especially risky because they were well within the range of Cuba's conventional antiaircraft defenses. *(Department of Defense / JFK Library)*

Missile transporters, radar installations, tanks, rocket launchers, and FROG short-range missiles are identified in this example of the low-altitude surveillance photography of one of the military camps that were discovered after low-level flights began. *(Department of Defense / JFK Library)*

Shortly after the dedication ceremony at Dulles International Airport on 17 November 1962, Kennedy, Dwight Eisenhower (speaking), and CIA Dir. John McCone (seated to right of the podium) met secretly to discuss the Cuba situation. McCone warned the current and the former presidents that the United States was always going to have a missiles-in-Cuba problem. *(Photo by Robert Knudsen / JFK Library)*

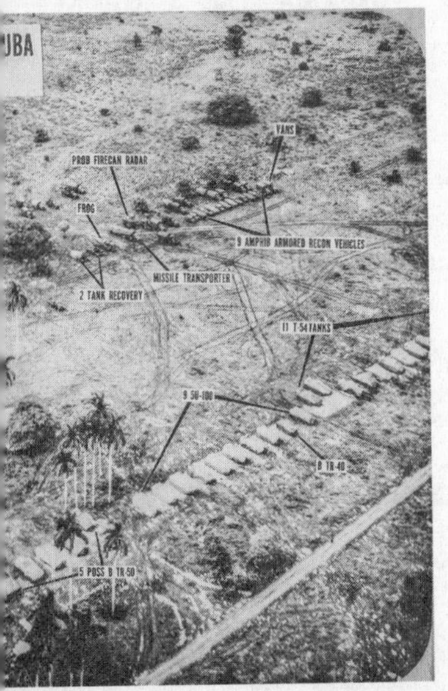

At a press conference in the State Department Auditorium on 20 November 1962, Kennedy announced a deal in which the Soviets would remove the IL-28 bombers and the Americans would lift the naval quarantine of Cuba. *(Photo by Abbie Rowe / NARA)*

The IL-28 bombers were old, obsolete, and no match for American air defenses. But they could carry nuclear bombs. Kennedy was skeptical that they were a threat, but Robert McNamara insisted, "I think it's absolutely essential that the IL-28s are part of the deal. I don't think we could live with the American public if they weren't." *(Photo by Department of Defense / JFK Library)*

Kennedy fielding questions from reporters at the 20 November 1962 press conference in the State Department Auditorium announcing that they had reached a deal to end the ongoing Cuba crisis. *(Photo by Abbie Rowe / NARA)*

Kennedy met with the Soviet deputy foreign minister, Vasily Kuznetsov (next to Kennedy), and the Soviet ambassador to the United States, Anatoly Dobrynin (next to Kuznetsov), on 9 January 1963, in the Oval Office. Kuznetsov had been dispatched from Moscow to lead the Soviet negotiating team to resolve the Cuban missile crisis. *(Photo by Robert Knudsen / JFK Library)*

A shot taken from the televised special briefing on Cuba on 6 February 1963. Proposed by Robert McNamara, the briefing played an important role in quieting persistent public rumors that offensive weapons remained in Cuba. McNamara opened the briefing with an assurance that it was "beyond reasonable doubt" that all the offensive weapons systems had been removed. *(Department of Defense)*

A low-level surveillance photo (with the shadow of the plane visible at the bottom right). At the 6 February 1963 briefing, John Hughes displayed and described this photo: “A few days later we check the port of Casilda, on 6 November. The MRBM missiles on transporters have been moved southward from that temporary storage area and six have been placed on the Soviet ship Kurchatov. Here are six missiles under canvas and loaded on this particular ship. The ship is nearing the completion of its loading cycle. The forward hatch covers are closed. The rear hatches are being closed. Here Soviet crewmen and technicians wait in line or go up the gangway in loading the ship itself.” *(Department of Defense / JFK Library)*

On 7 February 1963, a day after the Defense Department's special Cuba briefing in response to rumors that Soviet missiles remained in Cuba, President Kennedy gave his own news conference, during which he repeated Robert McNamara's assurances that offensive weapons were no longer in Cuba, but he also said, "The continued presence of Soviet military personnel is of concern to us." *(Photo by Abbie Rowe / NARA)*

Kennedy records a statement in the Oval Office on 8 February 1963, surrounded by reporters and photographers. *(Photo by Abbie Rowe / NARA)*

White House Press Sec. Pierre Salinger (center) met with reporters in his office on 12 February 1963, during the "news management" controversy, which he later described as his "most serious struggle with the press." *(Photo by Abbie Rowe / NARA)*

At a 21 February 1963 press conference, Kennedy faced pointed questions about the "news management" crisis. Kennedy responded with characteristic humor: "Let me just say we've had very limited success in managing the news, if that's what we have been trying to do." *(Photo by Abbie Rowe / NARA)*

Kennedy wraps up his fiftieth presidential press conference in the State Department Auditorium, on 21 February 1963. *(Photo by Abbie Rowe / NARA)*

At the commencement exercises at American University of 10 June 1963, Kennedy delivered one of his more significant speeches. Implicitly recalling the nuclear scare of the Cuba crisis, he said that "peace need not be impracticable and war need not be inevitable." *(Photo by Abbie Rowe / NARA)*

While Kennedy gave his "peace speech" on 10 June 1963 (on the stage in the distance at the center), audience members used their program booklets as makeshift hats in efforts to block the hot Washington sun. *(Photo by Abbie Rowe / NARA)*

During a visit to West Berlin on 26 June 1963, Kennedy delivered one of his most memorable speeches, declaring, "Ich bin ein Berliner." In this shot, he is taken to a platform overlooking the Brandenburg Gate, while a group of East German reporters watch from another small platform on the other side of the Wall at the right. *(Photo by Robert Knudsen / JFK Library)*

the number of Soviet troops by more than half. Soviet documents later confirmed that over 42,000 Soviet troops had actually been in Cuba, not the 17,000 of American estimates. The glaring inconsistencies in the figures the administration was publicizing threatened to create a credibility problem.

Even on the most basic point—missiles in Cuba—American intelligence was hazy. Surveillance and assets never accounted for more than thirty-three missiles in Cuba. On the basis of the number of missile sites, intelligence agencies estimated that up to forty-eight missiles might be in Cuba. Soviet negotiators and, more reliably, documents from Soviet archives later confirmed that the number was in fact forty-two.

Much of the problem came down to having to rely on photographs. As General Earle "Bus" Wheeler, the Army chief of staff, told Kennedy, "Now, they can't tell everything, of course, from these pictures. It's just a matter of going in and counting what you can."[13] That meant that that they were going to have to live with a disconcerting number of unknowns.

New discoveries made during and after the fortnight of crisis further highlighted how much they did not know. Recent photographs showed that the Cubans and Soviets were busy constructing defenses at the beach that were clearly designed to ward off an amphibious invasion force. The photographs also gave a much clearer view of the makeup of the Soviet ground forces in Cuba.

For intelligence analysts and military planners, one discovery in particular—and a string of derivative discoveries that it sparked—came as an unwelcome surprise: there were four Soviet combat regiments in Cuba. U.S. intelligence analysts had known during the crisis that Soviet troops were on the island, but in the wake of the crisis, as new information continued to pour in, they upgraded their assessment of the combat troops. They found them more tightly organized, more numerous, and better armed than had previously been recognized.[14]

The composition of these forces did not conform precisely to known Soviet formations, but seemed to reflect innovations observed in recent deployments in East Germany aimed at modernizing Soviet forces by creating reinforced regimental formations capable of conducting independent operations.[15] Analysts concluded that the original mission of these forces was to provide local ground defense against either American invasion or Cuban sabotage to protect the MRBM and IRBM sites. But even as bulldozers razed the MRBM and IRBM sites, construction of troop barracks continued. It suggested that the Soviets had no intention of withdrawing those troops.[16]

There was no question that these were defensive forces, for they lacked the means to operate beyond Cuba's shores, but their presence came as a new and unsettling surprise. For his part, Kennedy expressed little private concern about them, despite mentioning them repeatedly in public statements. It would be better if the Soviets removed the troops, he said, but the reality was that they were unlikely to do so unless the United States offered a formal guarantee not to invade Cuba. And that was something Kennedy was trying to avoid offering. He had already publicly denied that the United States had any intention of invading Cuba. He had also said as much in his letter to Khrushchev on 27 October. Those statements amounted to an informal pledge. That, he argued, rendered the presence of those troops unnecessary. "There's no need for them," he said, in outlining the negotiating and public position that the administration should take on the Soviet combat troops. "With our commitment on invasion, there's no need for these [Soviet troops]."[17]

But the Joint Chiefs of Staff, charged with developing contingency plans for an invasion, had to carefully account for such newly discovered defenses in their plans such as OPLAN 312 for an air attack and OPLAN 316 for a full invasion.[18] The Chiefs were particularly concerned that the number of Soviet military personnel in Cuba was larger than they had originally estimated and that they were apparently much more effectively organized than they had realized. It was causing them to revise their initial assessments. General Maxwell Taylor told Kennedy,

> We've looked very hard at these four concentrations of army-type equipment. . . . I think the evidence is getting stronger all the time that there are any tactical units involved in this, although I wouldn't say the case is entirely conclusive. But the Chiefs are very much impressed with this and the need to start pressing hard now in our negotiating to get these Soviet personnel put right in the forefront.

They did not have to start from scratch; the Pentagon had for some time thought hard about how to invade Cuba. Contingency plans had been prepared for such an eventuality, as was standard military practice in relation to a whole host of world trouble spots. When the crisis first broke, the military dusted off those plans. Drafted before the discovery of the missiles, the plans called for impressive explosive power to be used in a relatively contained geographic area: rockets, napalm, and 250-pound low-drag bombs. "We'd really make a shambles of it," said Chief of Naval Operations George Anderson. He was referring, of course, to the Soviet military presence in Cuba—at least to the extent that it was known at the time.[19]

The discovery of the missiles prompted revisions to account for a new problem. It was no longer just a matter of overpowering the ground forces on the island. For one thing, it would be important to get all the missiles and weapons. Even a single missile that escaped destruction and was fired at the United States could cause massive loss of life. For another, they did not know whether the ports had been mined; mines would pose a difficult challenge for getting the Army's armored vehicles ashore. The airfields might also be booby trapped with demolitions.[20]

Because the crisis remained unsettled—Khrushchev had still not agreed to take out the IL-28s—the invasion plans were still being actively revised. As General Curtis LeMay summed up the military situation on 16 November, "We have so far gotten the missiles out we think; we're not sure. The submarines apparently have turned around and gone back. But the rest of the whole fabric of this buildup remains there. A quarantine may get the IL-28s out, or negotiations may get them out, but it may not." If it became necessary to ramp up the naval quarantine, "we're ready to put the screws on at any time," reported Admiral George Anderson, by adding to the list of banned cargo so-called POL products, an acronym standing for petroleum, oil, and lubricants—in other words, key requirements in keeping modern military equipment in working order. "From everything we've seen, we believe they would avoid a major confrontation with us if we had to put it on again," Anderson said.

But if that failed, LeMay had a plan. "If the quarantine fails or we don't want to use it," he said, "we do have a plan for knocking out the IL-28s. [It's] very easy to do." The plan involved airstrikes by a relatively small number of Air Force and Navy jets. There were only a few airfields with IL-28s, and the close proximity of staging areas on the U.S. mainland helped. The operation would be over within minutes. There would likely be a price to pay, though, LeMay warned:

> This is not without some risk. I think if we did this we could expect our reconnaissance airplanes to be attacked from then on. And we'd probably have to follow up, if we want to continue air surveillance, by having them knock out the rest of the defenses. That small risk is there, but there's some risk in anything we undertake. We see no problems doing this. If we have to go beyond that we have plans to take out the SAM sites only, or take out the SAMs and MiGs, or go on to all of [OPLAN] 312.[21]

Reconnaissance photography had also detected new encampments in the hills near the U.S. naval base at Guantánamo Bay. It was unclear precisely what the nature of those encampments was; the photographs were not detailed enough to show specific weapons. And there did not appear to be any flurry of activity at the sites—indeed, they seemed unoccupied for the moment—but their very presence posed a potential threat to Guantánamo. American photo reconnaissance experts saw crates of missiles there and assumed that they were conventional weapons of a kind known as Sopka missiles seen elsewhere in Cuba. As it turns out, thanks to evidence from Russian archives released since the cold war, we now know that these were what were known in Soviet military jargon as FKRs (*frontovye krylatye rakety*), a type of nuclear cruise missile. They were armed with small nuclear warheads ranging from five to twelve kilotons. Khrushchev had added the FKRs to the buildup later in the process and had approved a Soviet Defense Ministry proposal on 7 September to add eighty nuclear warheads for them.[22]

The Joint Chiefs urged Kennedy to make removal of the Soviet presence in Cuba a top priority. It was not just a military problem, they argued, but also a political one. As new intelligence emerged, it was becoming increasingly clear that the military presence was not an innocuous military support group similar to the American Military Assistance Advisory Group, or MAAG; in fact, it consisted of combat units. And that was much more difficult to tolerate. Wheeler told Kennedy,

> What it amounts to is that these weapons, and the numbers of people, while they're relatively small in number, add a rather sizable dimension of Soviet influence in Cuba. They would certainly make an invasion more costly. Army equipment in there, in the hands of the Soviets, I would think would be an extra repressive force on any Cuban attempt at invasion. They've got technicians to provide know-how and expertise in using these weapons that suggests you could have in there a Soviet base for the reintroduction of [offensive] weapons at some future time. It doesn't strike me that this is a MAAG-type activity, but rather an actual introduction of Soviet army units into the Western Hemisphere.

Taylor raised the specter of a political backlash that came with growing public realization that the administration had publicly and privately underestimated the extent of the Soviet military presence in Cuba. He told Kennedy, "It would just seem to us that if and when it's apparent to our people and the rest of Latin America that really the Soviet Union have [sic] invaded our hemisphere to a degree beyond what they imagined, that's going to be a very sensitive subject."[23]

Kennedy was reassuring on that score. "I think that before we could have any sort of real slow-down of this tension they're going to have to get these forces out of there," he said.

PRESIDENT KENNEDY: Now, of course, he probably doesn't want to get them out of there until he has some assurances that we're not going to invade. So this is just a question of going back and forth.

MAXWELL TAYLOR: You wouldn't think he would want to leave his people or this equipment indefinitely.

PRESIDENT KENNEDY: That's it. Well, that's why I would think he might—I don't whether he'll—we obviously are not going to give him any assurances as long as he has this equipment in. He may not want to get this—this is even assuming he wants to. He may not want to get the equipment out. But assuming he might want to get the equipment out, I suppose he wants to know what our intentions are. So I think we're going to have to go back and forth for a period unless . . .

Again Kennedy reassured the generals: "We're not going to give away any commitment on our future freedom of action on Cuba until Cuba is very much of a changed place."[24]

10

Missiles of November

The problem with the Soviet combat troops was not just that there were more of them than U.S. officials had realized but that they were so well armed. As far as U.S. intelligence could tell, each group consisted of about 1,250 men, with its own support structure. They could operate independently, making them highly mobile. That meant they could be an effective force against an amphibious invasion. The regiments had the kind of sophisticated, battlefield military hardware one would expect: armored personnel carriers, self-propelled artillery, tanks, antitank wire-guided missiles, heavy engineering machinery, and at least three types of short-range missiles. They could put up real resistance to any ground invasion.[1] "This is first-line stuff," Wheeler told Kennedy. Taylor agreed: it was equipment "we've never seen in the hands of satellites."[2]

They had counted up to 150 cruise missiles in Cuba, although they never fully appreciated that that total included two distinct varieties, one of which was nuclear capable.[3] The first were Sopka cruise missiles designed for protecting coastlines from amphibious attack. They resembled small jet airplanes, had a range of between 40 and 110 miles, and were armed with 2,000-pound conventional warheads.[4] The second kind of cruise missiles were the FKRs. They had a range of between 90 and 110 miles and were armed with nuclear warheads of between five and twelve kilotons. Their combat role in Cuba was primarily to protect beachheads and target the U.S. naval base at Guantánamo Bay from the hills around the base. U.S. intelligence never identified the FKRs, apparently counting them as Sopka rockets.[5] The Soviets sent to Cuba eighty nuclear warheads for the FKRs.[6]

By far the most numerous of the short-range missiles were part of the sophisticated surface-to-air missile system known in the West as the SA-2. By the middle of October, there were approximately five hundred SA-2 missiles distributed over a sophisticated air defense network of twenty-four SAM sites across the island. With their state-of-the-art radar network, a lateral (or "slant") range of 25 to 30 nautical miles, an effective vertical range up to about eighty-thousand feet, and a 500-pound high-explosive warhead, these missiles posed a serious threat to aircraft but little threat to anything on the ground or at sea.[7] The technology behind the SA-2 systems was state-of-the-art, in some respects more advanced than the Hawk missiles that the United States had just recently begun supplying to Israel.[8] U.S. intelligence analysts concluded that although it was technically conceivable that the SA-2s could be armed with a nuclear warhead to turn them into a potent surface-to-surface missile with about a 100- to 150-mile range (that could be done with the American Nike Hercules missile—"Our Nike Hercules is quite a good surface-to-surface missile," Taylor said), it was also "highly improbable."[9]

There were other types of missiles, including air-to-air missiles and antiship missiles. The Soviets sent to Cuba between twelve and sixteen Komar-class guided-missile patrol boats. The Komars were similar to motor torpedo boats, but instead of torpedoes, each carried two short-range cruise missiles with a range of 10 to 15 nautical miles. The boats were small and fast, but their limited range restricted them to inshore operations; they were best used against ships and amphibious attacks. The missiles on these boats were armed with conventional warheads.[10] For air combat, the Soviets sent over one hundred MiG jets to Cuba. Of these, forty-two were advanced

MiG–21 (Fishbed) aircraft, supersonic fighters that could be used for both interception and ground attack. They had a combat radius of roughly 350 nautical miles and were typically armed with a variety of cannons, infrared homing air-to-air missiles, and air-to-surface rockets.[11] U.S. analysts concluded that MiG–21s probably were capable of carrying nuclear weapons, but that if they did so their effective range would be severely restricted to about 200 nautical miles and their navigation systems curtailed. As Kennedy's national security adviser, McGeorge Bundy, put it, such a jerry-rigged system was "not a likely configuration."[12]

Especially troubling to the Joint Chiefs was another kind of weapon, one that was armed with what the Soviets referred to as "special" warheads and that U.S. intelligence had only recently discovered in Cuba.

On 26 October, Kennedy and the ExComm had been briefed that the preceding day's low-level surveillance flights had photographed something not discernible on the less detailed U-2 photos: launchers for short-range, battlefield, nuclear-capable rockets. And where there were rocket launchers, there were of course going to be rockets. They were known in the West by the harmless-sounding acronym FROG, standing for Free Rocket Over Ground. To the Soviets, they were known as Lunas. Similar in nature and purpose to the U.S. Army's Honest John rockets, they were short-range, unguided missiles that followed a ballistic trajectory and were designed for battlefield use. Because of that, accuracy was not their strong point; over their range of ten to twenty-five miles, they might well miss their target by almost a mile. With a conventional warhead with a blast radius measured in tens of feet, that meant that Lunas fitted with conventional warheads were next to useless militarily.[13]

But fitted with a nuclear warhead of between two and twenty kilotons, the Luna became a potent battlefield weapon (for comparison, the atomic bomb dropped over Nagasaki in World War II was estimated to be a yield of about twenty kilotons). It would pose a devastating threat to an invading ground force:

Assuming that the Luna was aimed to detonate in the air, at an optimal height of 600 feet above the ground, just one of these missiles would produce a huge fireball about 31 miles from the launch site. At the epicenter of the blast, there would be 100-mile-an-hour winds and a crater 130 feet in diameter and 130 feet deep. Any tank or armored personnel carrier within 500 yards would be destroyed. Unprotected human beings 1,000 yards from the blast site would probably die immediately as a result of the dramatic increase in air pressure, but those fortunate enough to survive the explosion and the winds would suffer a painful death by radiation poisoning within two weeks.[14]

This was more than a theoretical possibility. Documents released from former Soviet archives well after the end of the cold war revealed that Khrushchev himself authorized sending the Lunas to Cuba. When he had originally authorized the secret buildup, code-named Operation Anadyr, on 24 May 1962, the plan did not include nuclear warheads for Lunas. But over the spring and summer, the plan had been modified and updated. One of those updates involved adding twelve nuclear warheads for the Luna missiles. They arrived in Cuba on 23 October, the day after Kennedy's televised address.

American military planners did not, and could not, know whether there were nuclear warheads in Cuba for the Luna missiles; finding that out was beyond the technical capabilities of intelligence gathering at the time. Missiles were generally covered or stored in hangars, large tents, or caves and were therefore hard to identify from the air. The warheads were even more difficult to spot because they were small, easily hidden in bunkers, buildings, or caves, and tightly guarded by Soviet soldiers. U.S. intelligence analysts therefore had to rely on circumstantial evidence, such as the construction of distinctive dome-shaped bunkers and unusual security measures. It complicated matters that after the low-level surveillance flights of 23 October, the Soviets began hiding and camouflaging the part of the system that was easiest to spot from the air, the launchers.

But the very real possibility, even probability, was something that the planners took seriously. It was well known that Soviet military doctrine called for the use of nuclear weapons in the battlefield. In 1957, the Soviet defense minister, Marshal Georgi Zhukov, the hero of the Soviet campaign in Eastern Europe in World War II, declared that "atomic weapons will be widely employed as organic weapons in the armies."[15]

During the crisis, military planners adjusted their plans to include the addition of surface-to-surface missiles as part of their invasion force. This was in direct response to the discovery of the FROGs. As General Maxwell Taylor explained in a postcrisis debriefing, "prudence required that we be fully prepared to retaliate promptly, should the Castro regime select to employ nuclear weapons against US forces."[16]

The original plans for possible military action against Cuba did not contemplate the use of nuclear weapons. But when intelligence confirmed the presence of Lunas, the Joint Chiefs and the commander in chief of the Atlantic theater (CINCLANT), Admiral Robert L. Dennison, recognized that their military planning now needed to anticipate the potentiality that, in the event the president ordered an invasion, American troops could confront tactical nuclear weapons. At a morning meeting on 28 October, the Joint Chiefs decided that Dennison should revisit the main military plan for the invasion of Cuba (OPLAN-316) and make recommendations on "whether tactical nuclear weapons (air and ground) should be included in the arsenal of our invasion and supporting forces."[17] As the Army later explained it in recommending language for McNamara's report to Congress, there was a direct causal link between the proposed revisions of the invasion plans and the discovery of the Luna/FROG launchers:

> when a determination was made that nuclear capable FROG (Free Rocket Over Ground) missiles were present in Cuba, CINCLANT expressed his concern, and proposed to have tactical nuclear weapons readily available in his invasion force. These weapons would be used only in retaliation for the employment of nuclear weapons against US forces.[18]

Dennison told the Joint Chiefs of Staff (JCS) that he intended to modify his plans accordingly, but the JCS and McNamara ultimately approved only part of Dennison's request: he was merely authorized to equip the invasion force with nuclear capable delivery systems such as Honest John missiles and eight-inch howitzers; he was not authorized to include nuclear warheads without explicit JCS approval. In addition, the JCS authorized the prepositioning of some tactical nuclear weapons: Honest John rockets were deployed to Florida without their nuclear warheads; batteries of Nike Hercules, nuclear surface-to-air missiles, were also sent to Florida;[19] and some sources indicate that U.S. Pershing medium-range ballistic missiles (MRBMs) were sent to Key West with nuclear warheads, although hard evidence to support that remains elusive.[20]

Precisely why Dennison's request was denied was apparently not recorded in any contemporary record.[21] Decades later, Robert McNamara said that he and President Kennedy explicitly ruled out arming the prospective invasion force with tactical nuclear weapons but that "no one should believe that, had American troops been attacked with nuclear weapons, the United States would have refrained from a nuclear response."[22] General William Y. Smith, a special assistant to Taylor who played a central role in invasion planning, said at a 1992 conference that Dennison's request was turned down "because there was no evidence any [Soviet] nuclear weapons were there."[23] It is unclear whether that decision amounted to an extraordinary order from McNamara or the White House or simply a reaffirmation of standing orders; the prevailing rules of engagement for air defense of Florida stated explicitly that nuclear weapons would not be used.[24] Whatever the specific rationale, Dennison's request was denied. To compensate, his planners tried to reduce reaction times and increase the numbers of troops in order to reduce the vulnerability of the invading force to Soviet tactical nuclear weapons.[25]

From the recording of a conversation on 29 October with Marine Corps Commandant David Shoup and Chief of Naval Operations Admiral George Anderson, it is clear that Kennedy himself had given real thought to the possibility that Cuba might turn into a nuclear battleground.

DAVID SHOUP: The question is—the $64 question is, whether they would use the tactical nuclear weapons—

PRESIDENT KENNEDY: Nuclear weapons?

SHOUP: —at that point, because they would deal bloody hell with Guantánamo, of course. If nuclear weapons start down there, I'd say we're at nuclear war. We couldn't afford to let them do that. I mean they're not [*unclear*].

PRESIDENT KENNEDY: But my guess is, well, everybody sort of figures that, in extremis, that everybody would use nuclear weapons. The decision to use any kind of a nuclear weapon, even the tactical ones, presents such a risk of it getting out of control so quickly, that there's a . . .

SHOUP: But Cuba's so small compared to the world. [*chuckles*]

PRESIDENT KENNEDY: Yeah.

SHOUP: If that joker [Castro] ever had the control [of the tactical nuclear weapons], now . . . Of course they're [the Soviets] telling us they got the keys, like we've got the keys—

PRESIDENT KENNEDY: I'm sure they do. I'm sure they do.

SHOUP: The Russians say [to the Americans]: "We got the keys and you got the keys. You trust us; we trust you" . . .

PRESIDENT KENNEDY: No, we don't *trust* each other. [*laughter*] But we figure that they're never giving them to the Cubans, anymore than we'd give them to, you know, the Turks.

GEORGE ANDERSON: No.

PRESIDENT KENNEDY: Because we know that . . . I don't think anybody wants that weapon to escape from their control. It's just too . . .[26]

The exchange is replete with the kinds of unfinished thoughts and allusions that are characteristic of this sort of free-flowing conversation, but it suggests that Kennedy and the Joint Chiefs took seriously the problem of tactical nuclear weapons in Cuba and were thinking hard about the very real risks those weapons posed.

THE PRESENCE OF THE LUNAS, which the Joint Chiefs pointedly referred to as nuclear-capable whenever they were mentioned, helped add urgency to the discussion of what they regarded as an offensive weapon and what they regarded as a defensive one. For Kennedy, it amounted to a decision about what the United States could and could not live with.

Kennedy and most of his senior advisers concluded that trying to roll back the situation to precisely as it existed before the Cuban missile crisis was unrealistic and that, even if it were possible, the price would be too high. But that did not mean that they had to accept all aspects of the Soviet military presence in Cuba. Deciding what was acceptable and unacceptable risk meant finding the right balance between assessments of military threat, domestic political considerations, and complicated international diplomacy. New materials show clearly for the first time the dynamics of those debates and shed new light on the settlement of the Cuban missile crisis.

The first MRBM transporters began leaving Cuba on 5 November. By the tenth, U.S. surveillance had counted thrity-three MRBM transporters on eight ships heading back to the Soviet Union, and the Kennedy administration had decided to take the Soviet authorities at their word that they had placed a total of forty-two MRBMs in Cuba and that all the missiles had been removed.[27]

But those early shipments leaving Cuba did not include SA-2s, cruise missiles, Lunas, or IL-28s. The flurry of letters between Kennedy and Khrushchev during the crisis had often been vague and not always consistent regarding types of weapons systems. The Kennedy administration's quarantine proclamation of 23 October had listed, "Surface-to-surface missiles; bomber aircraft; bombs, air-to-surface rockets and guided missiles; warheads for any of the above weapons; mechanical or electronic equipment to support or operate the above items; and any other classes of materiel hereafter designated by the Secretary of Defense for the purpose of effectuating this Proclamation." In his note of 28 October, Khrushchev had agreed to remove "the arms which you described as offensive,"[28] which U.S. policymakers initially interpreted rather hopefully as the list included in the quarantine proclamation of 23 October. But as the Soviets continued uncrating IL-28 bombers, constructing barracks for the combat regiments, going ahead with work on the cruise missile sites, and showing signs that they were still planning to establish submarine bases in Cuba, it became clear that Moscow and Washington interpreted the agreement differently.

On 2 November, Adlai Stevenson handed to Soviet Deputy Premier Anastas Mikoyan a list of specific weapons systems that the United States said had to be removed. At a minimum, it said, they must remove "surface-to-surface missiles, bomber or attack aircraft, other combat aircraft that can be considered as nuclear weapons carriers including the MIG–21s, Komar class PT boats, nuclear warheads of any kind, nuclear storage sites and any other nuclear delivery systems."[29] When Khrushchev objected in a note delivered to the White House three days later, Kennedy was prepared to compromise. He convened his senior advisers to come up with a revised list.

Revising that list forced U.S. policymakers to think carefully about what they considered a real threat and what they could live with, if need be. Push too hard, and they risked pushing Khrushchev beyond the breaking point, alienating allies, and reigniting the crisis; be too cautious, and they could end up with an unnecessary threat in the Caribbean, with all of the military and political consequences that would entail. Despite Kennedy's personal skepticism, a consensus had already built within the ExComm that they would insist upon removing the IL-28s. But what they would do about the other weapons was still unclear.

The short-range, surface-to-surface missiles fell within a gray area in threat assessments. Those weapons could not reach U.S. territory, but could be used against American forces at Guantánamo or, in the event of U.S. military action, against Cuba. But the primary concern was that by continuing to strengthen the defensive forces in Cuba with SAMs, Lunas, and other ground forces, the Soviets could create cover for the rapid reintroduction of strategic weapons.[30] There were also fears that warheads could be delivered even more quickly by submarine or by air, perhaps even smuggled aboard a newly established commercial passenger route from Moscow to Havana.[31] There was, in addition, the issue of appearances—allowing any nuclear-capable forces to stay in Cuba, even battlefield ones, could set a poor precedent and create political difficulties. The White House statement of 4 September had implicitly accepted that the short-range missile systems that it had publicly identified—SA-2s, Komar torpedo boats, and MiGs—were all defensive weapons systems. It said nothing about the Lunas, because they had not yet been found. But they presumably fell within the broad category of "surface-to-surface missiles."[32]

For the first couple of weeks in November, the Lunas/FROGs were an active topic of discussion in the ExComm. The discussion was informed by increasingly detailed information on the Lunas and associated forces and debate on what to do about them.

The key decisions were taken at an ExComm meeting on the evening of 7 November. The group was making final revisions to the list of prohibited weapons that Adlai Stevenson would hand to Vasily Kuznetsov in New York in an effort to bring the negotiations to a close.

ALEXIS JOHNSON: How about the FROGs? Ros?

ROSWELL GILPATRIC: Well, I think—

ALEXIS JOHNSON: I've held up this instruction to New York until we've had this discussion.

ROBERT MCNAMARA: The FROGs clearly aren't offensive weapons in the way in which we meant the term.

HARLAN CLEVELAND: No.

MCNAMARA: They've never been in our list.

NITZE: It is a ground-to-ground missile.

GILPATRIC: Well, we didn't [*unclear*]—

MCNAMARA: No, but we didn't mean FROGs.

GILPATRIC: [*Unclear.*]

BUNDY: Really, Paul . . .

DILLON: They're a kind of the missile [*unclear*] on the Komar boats.

RUSK: "Surface-to-surface missiles of a range larger than" . . .

MCNAMARA: I think we have to emphasize the IL–28s. This is . . .

NITZE: Well, that's . . .

MCNAMARA: Our objective, and it's a major one, and we ought to concentrate all [*unclear*]—

BUNDY: If we put another ratchet on these ground-to-ground missiles after our letter of last night, he really will think we're just applying the squeeze where we have [*unclear*] strong.

McNamara agreed: "Seems to me we just have to concentrate on these IL-28s and we confuse the issue by dragging in a lot of questionable items."[33] The decision that came out of the meeting was to specify long-range surface-to-surface missiles (the MRBMs and IRBMs), IL-28s, nuclear warheads, and bombs but to "let the other items go."[34] Stevenson and McCloy were instructed to convey to Kuznetsov that the administration was still concerned about the IL-28s and nuclear warheads but that it was willing to be "relaxed and flexible" about the other weapons systems.[35] Thus, the decision was made. Despite concerns expressed by the Joint Chiefs, it was decided that insisting that the Soviets remove the Lunas would be a bridge too far.

11

A Deal

THE CRAMPED QUARTERS of the White House did not yet have a properly outfitted press briefing room equipped to handle the swelling Washington press corps and the technical requirements of televised broadcast. Because of that, Eisenhower had used the Old Executive Building; Kennedy used the even larger State Department Auditorium. Reporters had been told to gather by 6 p.m. The president had an announcement to make.

Kennedy led off his 20 November news conference, his forty-fifth in the 669 days of his presidency thus far, with a prepared statement.

They had reached a deal. Khrushchev had agreed to remove all of the IL-28 bombers within thirty days and to facilitate aerial inspection of them leaving on Soviet ships. In exchange, Kennedy had ordered that the naval quarantine of Cuba be lifted. Soviet ships could once again proceed unimpeded to Havana. The United States did not offer a formal guarantee not to invade Cuba, but Kennedy repeated his September statement "We shall neither initiate nor permit aggression in this hemisphere."[1]

The core aspects of the deal had started taking shape almost two weeks earlier. On 7 November, the members of the ExComm once again convened in the Cabinet Room to discuss how to bring the crisis to a final resolution. In the situation the ExComm faced, time was of the essence. Within the next few days, the missiles that had sparked the crisis would be gone; U.S. surveillance planes had photographed them being loaded onto ships in Havana's port. If the Soviets then made a statement that all the missiles were gone and that they had therefore fulfilled their part of the 27–28 October agreement, it would become challenging to keep the pressure on IL-28 removal. It might be a hard case to make while keeping world opinion on America's side.

The options for pressuring or incentivizing were limited. There were only three major points of leverage: threatening military action, threatening to ratchet up—or promising to lift—the naval quarantine, and offering a formal noninvasion pledge.

Kennedy and his advisers therefore had to decide how hard they could realistically push on the IL-28 issue. Kennedy outlined the problem:

> I think the quarantine is the last step because it means us stopping Russian ships and it really raises things into a crisis fever again. What things can we do? After all, the major reason we wanted to get the missiles out was because of the political implications as well as the military, but the political were . . . Once you get those out, of course they've got these bombers and they can use them on a strike on us, but they're just one more hazard of life. They don't have the impact that the missiles had. So that we've accomplished a lot of what we set out to do. The question really is whether we want to, in a sense, bring the whole thing to a crisis again to get the bombers out.[2]

One potential scenario they might face was that the Soviets would respond that they had turned over the bombers to the Cubans, which may well have been their plan all along. American leverage over the Cubans was much less than over the Soviets. The quarantine was having a negligible effect on Cuba economically, and Castro had already demonstrated a willingness to defy diplomatic norms. Kennedy issued instructions to prepare a plan for that contingency.

> So, therefore, I'd like to have the Defense [Department] and CIA and State [Department] to be thinking about what it is that we can do to Castro on the IL-28s without formally reimposing a real quarantine. And then we have to just make a cold judgment whether it's going to be worth it to us to bring this thing back into a massive confrontation again to get the IL-28s out or whether we can just make his life miserable enough so that he'll decide it's worthwhile anyway.[3]

The formula to make the lifting of the quarantine a quid pro quo for a promise to remove the IL-28 bombers, without actually waiting for the bombers to be gone, had come from Llewellyn Thompson on 8 November.[4] The elegance of it appealed to Kennedy. Since they had already decided that they would insist on removal of the bombers but be more relaxed about most of the other military hardware on the island, linking these two issues provided a neat way to tie up loose ends. Maintaining the naval quarantine was expensive, draining, and becoming less crucial. But Kennedy did not want to give it up too cheaply. "The key question is going to be whether we can lift the quarantine if he doesn't take out the IL-28s," he said. "And if we don't lift the quarantine after he's taken out the missiles, whether that will cause a sort of a change in the whole atmosphere."[5]

By 12 November, the idea of trading the quarantine for the IL-28s had taken hold. They would then be in a position to trade a formal assurance not to invade Cuba for the setting up of adequate safeguards against the reintroduction of weapons.[6] Kennedy proposed the trade in a letter to Khrushchev—part of the so-called pen-pal series of diplomatic exchanges—on 15 November.[7] Five days later, they heard back. Khrushchev accepted.[8] They had a deal.

The 20 November deal accomplished the things that Kennedy and his advisers had decided were most important and most worth fighting for. But Kennedy was careful in his statement not to imply that everything was settled. Important parts of the agreement reached on 27 and 28 October remained outstanding, specifically the creation of lasting safeguards against the future introduction of offensive weapons. Those outstanding issues, Kennedy said, meant that the United States was reserving the right to continue its own surveillance of Cuba. He used the recent discovery of Soviet ground units in Cuba as an example of why continued vigilance was required, while pointing out that Khrushchev had said he would withdraw those troops "in due course."

And, significantly, the 20 November deal did not include a formal pledge that the United States would not invade Cuba. Kennedy had repeatedly said that there were no plans for such an invasion and that there would be no need to do so as long as Cuba did not pose a threat to the hemisphere—"we shall neither initiate nor permit aggression in this hemisphere," was how he put it as far back as September. But such a pledge was never codified in a formal international agreement. And Kennedy was surprised that Khrushchev did not push harder for one.[9]

12

With One Voice

As he sat in his Pentagon office skimming the pile of newspapers on his desk, Arthur Sylvester might have been forgiven for wondering how he had managed to cause so much fuss. As assistant secretary of defense for public affairs, his job was to put out press fires, not start them—to talk about the story, not become the story. And yet somehow he had managed to become just that. Through some careless honesty, he had single-handedly provoked a storm of controversy that dragged the president into a series of running battles with the press and setting the chattering classes off on the topic of "How much should the public know?" Sylvester himself came from a media background, having been the Washington bureau chief of the *Newark News*, was widely regarded as good at his job, and rarely ruffled feathers. Now he had attracted the president's attention for the wrong reasons. Kennedy had taken to teasing him as "the celebrated Mr. Sylvester," not exactly approvingly. Sylvester's job was to be a messenger, a conduit, and a troubleshooter. For a man in his job, being known as "celebrated" was not cause for celebration.[1]

A decade and a half later, after the leaking of the Pentagon Papers exposed a gaping credibility gap between what the government said in public and what it knew in private, and after Watergate took American voters' cynicism in their government to new depths, the news management crisis that Kennedy faced in late 1962 and early 1963 would seem quaint, even naive. At the time, though, it was serious. The White House campaign to stem the flow of leaks from the Pentagon developed a very public manifestation that provoked lively public debate, new press policies, and a congressional investigation.

Not clear at the time was whether Sylvester was acting upon his own inspiration or whether the policies had their origins elsewhere. Not until later did it become evident that the president supported them, if not inspired them. But the full extent of Kennedy's involvement, and the broader slate of policies that had been enacted, some secretly, had to await the release of Kennedy's White House tapes. The tapes also reveal that the news policies were not simply an ad hoc response in a crisis situation; they had in fact been discussed at the highest levels months beforehand. That, in turn, explains why Kennedy remained so unrepentant in public and defiant in private. Months earlier, Kennedy himself had privately predicted such an outcry and staked out a "bring it on" approach.

THE CONTROVERSY WAS THE RESULT of a slow, steady buildup rather than a spontaneous eruption. Tensions between the White House and the Washington press corps had been mounting for months. When the Preparedness Investigating Subcommittee of the Senate Armed Services Committee reported that speeches and writings by military commanders were subject to mandatory censorship, it touched off a series of complaints that the administration was not being straight with the American people. The conservative senators Strom Thurmond, Democrat of South Carolina, and Barry Goldwater, Republican of Arizona, accused the White House of an "insidious attack upon our military leaders" and of trying to "muzzle" military officers from taking harder lines on the topics of communism and from voicing dissent with the administration's cold war policies. It amounted to an accusation that the White House was being soft on communism and stifling valid criticism from within its own ranks.[2]

During the fortnight of peak crisis over Cuba, the administration had clamped down severely on the flow of information, engaged in deliberate misdirection, and requested that the news media exercise self-censorship, even issuing guidelines in the form of a twelve-point list.[3] But the administration had also engaged in calculated deceit: Kennedy did not in fact have a cold, the excuse Salinger used for Kennedy's premature return from Chicago on 20 October; moving Marines from California to Florida had not been part of a "normal exercise," which was the public explanation; and the cancellation of planned naval maneuvers in the Caribbean was not, in fact, due to fears of an impending hurricane.[4] Depending on where one stood on the political spectrum, these were variously regarded as forgivable untruths or blatant lies. The debate hinged on personal judgments of prudence. If Salinger had volunteered the true reason Kennedy was returning to Washington on 20 October, the administration's defenders pointed out, the president's freedom of action would have been severely compromised and the very survival of the United States placed in jeopardy. As American officials frequently pointed out during the cold war, there was no way to tell the Soviets one thing and the American people another; that was one area where totalitarian governments had an advantage over liberal democracies, they noted, a touch enviously.

So long as the two nuclear superpowers remained "eyeball to eyeball," as Dean Rusk had famously put it during the height of the missile crisis, it was hard to argue with the administration's need to hold its information closely. At that time, it was a matter of common sense. But with the crisis over, reporters expected the control to be loosened. After 28 October, however, the administration chose not to relax immediately its control over the flow of information. What really infuriated many reporters and some congressmen was that the administration brashly and publicly insisted that it was not about to. And that was a point members of the press corps were unwilling to concede; they would not be propaganda messengers.

On a number of occasions during the crisis, Sylvester had personally urged reporters on the Pentagon beat to exercise discretion. But a 29 October interview with the *Washington Star* journalist Richard Fryklund sparked the controversy. Fryklund had been a thorn in the administration's side before. He had been—and would be again—a target of FBI and Pentagon security investigations to determine leaks of national security from the Pentagon.[5]

Sylvester told Fryklund that national security interests justified the administration's managing of the news. He conceded that the flow of information during the preceding fortnight had been tighter than during World War II or the Korean War, but told Fryklund, "In the kind of world we live in, the generation of news by actions taken by the Government becomes one weapon in a strained situation. The results, in my opinion, justify the methods we used." Sometimes circumstances called for "management" of the news, Sylvester maintained, so that the nation spoke with "one voice to your adversary."[6]

Sylvester was not as out of step with public sentiment as reporters would have liked to believe and claimed. In the wake of the disastrous Bay of Pigs invasion, a Gallup poll had asked whether "the government in Washington should tell the press what news to report and what to report about situations, such as Cuba and Laos, or not." A majority said it should not, but it was a strikingly slim majority: against the 47 percent who said that the government should not tell the press what to report were 43 percent who said it should.[7]

But the press was in an unforgiving mood. Although Sylvester's comments accurately reflected administration policy—or, for that matter, the way any cold war administration approached the issue of releasing national security information—there was little to be gained in flaunting it. There was no indication that it was a premeditated statement or had been cleared in advance with the White House. Most observers inside the Beltway recognized that Sylvester was just describing business as usual; there was nothing new in the White House's selectively releasing information or even outright lying. Kennedy's predecessor had, after all, been caught red-handed lying to the American public only two years before in the U-2 affair. But in so brazenly acknowledging this truism of Washington information policy, Sylvester and the administration paid a price. In a column titled "How to Make Things Worse Than They Really Are," the *New York Times* columnist James Reston pointed out an inherent irony: "As long as the officials merely didn't tell the whole truth, very few of us complained; but as Sylvester told the truth, the editors fell on him like a fumble."[8]

It was a harbinger of what was to come, the first part of an unfolding controversy that resonated for months, provided ammunition for strident editorial attacks, and, in tandem with implementing new policies to go along with the ideas, fundamentally changed the relationship between the Kennedy administration and the press.[9]

Sylvester's comments fanned the embers of resentment among Washington reporters accustomed to espousing and shaping opinions on the news—the "most privileged group," Kennedy had called them with an edge of complaint. But the outcry managed to galvanize opposition to the Kennedy administration from its critics as well as many of its friends. A torrent of criticism spewed forth, ranging from newspeople charging that the administration's policies were imprudent, and would ultimately take a toll on public credibility in administration policies more broadly, to those who suggested that Washington was emulating totalitarian dictatorships and to those who accused the administration of politicizing the news.

Blessed with an advance copy of the article that would run in their newspaper's pages, the *Washington Star*'s editors started what quickly became a chorus of condemnation. They wrote that Sylvester had "let the ugly cat out of the bag" and described his comments as "truly sinister."[10] The editors of the *New York Times* joined in the next day. "There is no doubt that 'management' or 'control' of the news is censorship described by a sweeter term," they wrote. Recognizing that while sometimes voluntary restrictions on what editors published were warranted, "to attempt to manage the news so that a free press should speak (in Sylvester's words) in 'one voice to your adversary' could be far more dangerous to the cause of freedom than the free play of dissent, than the fullest possible publication of the facts."[11] The *Washington Post* lambasted the administration's disregard for the lessons learned in World Wars I and II and criticized the administration for treating news as a weapon of war. The system broke down in World War I, the *Post*'s editors argued, which led directly to a much better arrangement during World War II by separating out the propaganda and censorship functions into responsibilities of the Office of War Information and the Office of Censorship. Sylvester, the paper said, inappropriately "combined the functions of propaganda, censorship and military control of the news."[12] Three weeks later, when it had become clear that the administration's news policies were set from the very top, the editors of the *Chicago Daily Tribune* charged that "there have been intimations that the New Frontier regards news less as a process of imparting facts to the people than as a means of upholding policy and developing a conditioned opinion."[13] The president of the American Society of Newspaper Editors, Lee Hills, complained to Sylvester that "manipulation of the news in free societies imperils the right of the people to be fully informed under our democratic process."[14] John H. Coburn, managing editor of the *Richmond Times-Dispatch*, urged his colleagues to increase the pressure on the administration to revoke its news management policies.[15] Even Arthur Krock, a former mentor of Kennedy's who had since fallen out with the Kennedy clan, complained that "a news management policy not only exists at the White House, but in the form of direct and deliberate action has been enforced more cynically and boldly than by any previous administration in a period when the U.S. was not at war."[16] The *Chicago Daily Tribune* questioned whether anything the government said anymore could be believed: "In an atmosphere of secrecy and sham, there is an area of doubt surrounding every official pronouncement, and no one, of course, can know the extent of what the government has found fit to conceal to serve its own purposes."[17] Governor Nelson Rockefeller, at the time considered the likely Republican nominee in the 1964 presidential election, was not about to let such an easy opportunity to attack his would-be opponent slip by. "No political leader has the right to try to fool any of the people any of the time," he said.[18]

While many editors and journalists objected to "news management" and offered reasoned, cogent counterarguments that the credibility of any statement from the White House, Pentagon, or State Department was at stake, others were decidedly more strident. George Sokolsky, a hardline anticommunist whose column was syndicated in the *Washington Post* and other major newspapers, put Sylvester's news policies on a par with those of Adolf Hitler, Joseph Goebbels, and Fidel Castro. "The assumption that a government can, in a free society, manage the news is a fallacy arising from arrogance and ignorance," he wrote.[19] Some critics decried Sylvester's attitude as an assault on democracy itself.[20] The *Chicago Daily Tribune* charged that "the concept of news as weaponry takes a long step toward the managed propaganda found within a Communist dictatorship."[21]

Defenders of the administration's news policies were few and far between. The *New York Times* correspondent James Reston appealed to common sense. "The reflex action of the press is to howl like a scalded dog every time it catches the Government tinkering with the truth," he wrote. He pointed out that the practice of restricting information was certainly not new: "it is palpable nonsense to talk about these distortions as being 'unprecedented.'" Such behavior had been a part of Washington politics from the founding of the Republic. Reston noted, "Everybody remembers what happened after the U-2 plane was shot down over Russia. First the government lied about it, and then it made matters worse by telling the truth about it, thus turning the incident into the finest illustration in modern history of the difference between morality and diplomacy."[22]

Others disagreed with the policy but saw it as just another obstacle to be overcome by dedicated and talented reporters. The editor of the *Los Angeles Times*, Nick Williams, argued that it was unrealistic to expect the government to be responsible for delivering the whole truth all of the time; if it did, there would be no need for talented investigative journalists. "The truth about government must be dug out by the press—and that is the sole reason the Constitution guarantees its freedom to dig," he wrote.[23] Even the organizers of the annual Gridiron Club dinner, a black-tie event bringing together Washington's newspaper aristocracy and political newsmakers, including the president, could not resist the temptation to lampoon Salinger and Sylvester; they were greeted with the jazz hit "Little White Lies."[24]

Sylvester's efforts to clarify his comments did little to help. Although Kennedy agreed with the underlying sentiment and had put in place the press policies that restricted the flow of information, he was annoyed that Sylvester had managed to generate such public controversy.

What Sylvester could not say was that not only did "news management" have Kennedy's blessing, but it had come from the president himself. Kennedy even jokingly used the phrase. When *Newsweek* ran a cover story on managed news that had grown in part out of conversations the president had had with his friend Ben Bradlee, the *Newsweek* editor, Kennedy privately conceded that the administration had indeed "lied" to the press during the Cuban missile crisis.[25]

Nonetheless, he insisted that their motives were pure. "I think this thing on the—what's happening in Cuba is so hot though, there's so much interest in it, that we ought to try to in Arthur Sylvester's phrase, 'manage it,'" he had said. Kennedy might well have been applying his dry humor in delivery, but he was very serious about the substance. He wanted especially sensitive information about the missile sites omitted from the widely distributed intelligence summaries. And he wanted the White House to be in control of putting out information on its own terms. "We want to beat everybody," he said. "We want to get it straight in the morning before it goes, because it . . . before it would leak. And we want to get it out before anybody else has it. But I think if we can hold it as tight as possible, then we can put it out in our own way."[26]

Kennedy was deeply invested in the issue in private, but he avoided getting drawn into the public debate. Privately, he told his aide Ted Sorensen that Sylvester's comments were "unclear and unwise" and asked Sorensen to draft a letter that Sylvester could use as a partial, public retreat.[27]

Sylvester refused to sign the letter, but he did soften his language, if only slightly. He avoided using the "news as a weapon" phrasing and denied that the Pentagon had engaged in "distortion, deception, or manipulation," but he did say that national security and the safety of military personnel were factors in how and when information was shared with reporters.[28]

Sylvester denied that the administration's press policies had a chilling effect and went on to challenge journalists to look at the record, arguing that if they did so they would find that "by any measure you choose to use, the news flow has increased" since Kennedy took office.[29] Between 27 October and 3 December, he said, 129 interviews had been given by defense representatives, at a rate of about 5 a day. He also used the Bay of Pigs invasion, of which Castro had had advance notice, as the kind of "Madison Avenue operation" that was disastrous to U.S. security. But even those clarifications made things worse; the headline of the story that the *New York Times* ran was "U.S. Aide Defends Lying to Nation."[30]

Sylvester's frustration soon became apparent. His description of the controversy as "a great deal of twaddle" only served to infuriate critics further.[31] He tried framing the issue in terms of national survival: "It would seem to me basic, all through history, that it's an inherent government right, if necessary, to lie to save itself when it's going up into a nuclear war. This seems to me basic."[32] Critics, however, refused to concede that a democratically elected government had to lie to its voters.

The House Subcommittee on Government Information, headed by Congressman John Moss (Democrat of California), investigated allegations that the administration systematically and deliberately lied to reporters. Also investigating the broader issue of government news policy in a national emergency, Moss had ordered the subcommittee staff to begin their inquiry immediately after Kennedy's 22 October speech to the nation, anticipating that government information issues might arise. The following days bore out his fear that information policy was improvised in times of crisis. His stated objective was to develop a set of guidelines that could be invoked by any administration in any future international crisis. To regard public information as a "weapon," Moss charged, would lead down a slippery slope toward propaganda. Moss was no partisan hack—he had generally found himself in agreement with the Kennedy administration—and he sought to avoid the appearance of an "investigation," instead characterizing his inquiry as a "discussion." Nevertheless, the report could not help legitimizing the complaints of reporters who had accused the administration of lying.[33]

The controversy had started as one about words. It soon became one about policy. On 27 October, at the height of the missile crisis, Sylvester signed and distributed within the Pentagon a new directive governing contact with members of the press that required that a public information officer be present for any conversations with reporters or, if that was not feasible, that officials submit to the Pentagon press office a memorandum detailing the discussion. Reporters got wind of the new policy within days of Sylvester's news-as-weapons comments. On 2 November, the State Department implemented its own, less rigorous version of the policy. At a staff meeting that morning, Robert J. Manning, assistant secretary of state for information, issued an oral directive that any interviews had to be logged and reported, including information on the times and places of the meetings. The State Department had tried to institute similar controls in 1958 but had eventually been persuaded to relax those reporting requirements.[34] Challenged by reporters about the new policy, Manning insisted that the department was not trying to discourage continued interaction—that it was just trying to keep better tabs. "It is about time I got an idea of how many people are helping me do the job that I have been appointed by the President and Secretary to do," Manning joked. "I appreciate their help; it is just that I want to know how much help I am getting."[35] Weeks later, Salinger revealed that the White House had instituted a similar policy soon after the administration came into office. The Kennedy White House was more relaxed about White House officials' meeting with reporters than the Eisenhower White House had been, but Salinger still requested that all aides notify him of their contacts with reporters.[36]

When news of these policies filtered out, it set off new waves of criticism. Even moderates complained that the policies had a chilling effect on legitimate news sources. Merriman Smith, senior White House reporter of United Press International and the reporter given the charge to execute the customary "Thank you, Mr. President" that ended every presidential press conference, was one of the fiercest critics, writing, "The President had been listening to a few advisers who have the scornful idea that it is proper that the press speak only when spoken to, or reports the news with 'one-sided fairness.'"[37]

Kennedy waded into the controversy for the first time publicly at his 20 November news conference, the first since 13 September. He said that he made no apologies for the news blackout during the crisis and that it was important for the government to speak "with one voice" in times of dire crisis. He also gave the first indication that in imposing new policies on their respective agencies, Sylvester and Manning were in fact operating on instructions from the president himself. At his 22 August meeting with McCone, Kennedy had welcomed McCone's proposal to require Pentagon officials to submit detailed records of press contacts precisely because "if they begin to think they're going to have to write a report on it, it's going to have a very inhibiting effect," embracing the deterrence argument put forward by the President's Foreign Intelligence Advisory Board.[38] At the 20 November press conference, Kennedy said that he did not believe that the new measures at the Pentagon or State Department impeded the flow of information to the American people and that he would change them if he thought they did. But he was not yet convinced that the policies had "restricted the flow of essential news." He also announced that he was lifting the twelve-point request for voluntary withholding of news on certain topics that had been outlined in Salinger's memo of 24 October and said that he would be "delighted" to talk with Sylvester and press representatives to "see if we can get this straightened out so that there is a free flow of news." The primary concern, Kennedy said, was to protect sensitive intelligence information, pointing out that the CIA had for years had similar requirements for documenting any contacts between its employees and press contacts. But Kennedy also maintained that beyond the issue of protecting national security information, the news "ought to pour out." He noted, too, that the State Department policy would change because requirements there were quite different from those in the Defense Department's case.

Two weeks later, Sylvester publicly denied responsibility for the new rules at the Pentagon, but did not name names.[39] By then, "news management" had become one of several political fights raging on Capitol Hill and prompted another congressional inquiry into administration policies.

The controversy sparked by Sylvester's comments apparently did not lead the White House to change its approach, largely because the core problem of unauthorized leaks was still not solved. At a special National Security Council meeting on 22 January 1963, Kennedy gave the group his yearly *tour d'horizon* of foreign policy issues. Eerily accurate accounts of the meeting appeared in press reports the next day.[40] Those leaks prompted Bundy to raise the issue again at the following ExComm meeting, three days later. The official memorandum of that meeting credits Rusk with bringing up the issue of press contacts and making the suggestion that a triumvirate of Defense Department, State Department, and White House representatives reconstitute a group through whom current information on Soviet equipment in Cuba would flow.[41] The recording of the meeting reveals that Rusk made no such comments and that it was in fact the president himself who suggested that Arthur Sylvester delegate the issue to an information officer who could develop particular expertise on military implications of the Cuban situation. Sylvester could not be expected to keep up with all the intricacies, such as a series of recent articles by the *New York Times* reporter Tad Szulc, Kennedy said, and would be dogged by suspicion that he was simply handing out canned responses to press inquiries. Bundy added that that person should work closely with the newly appointed coordinator of Cuban affairs, Sterling J. Cottrell.[42]

The controversy dragged on for months. At a press conference on 22 February, Kennedy observed drily, "We have had very limited success in managing the news, if that is what we have been trying to do." A month later, he privately expressed his frustration to Ben Bradlee. He didn't understand what the fuss was about. "You bastards are getting more information out of the White House—the kind of information you want when you want it—than ever before," he said to Bradlee. "Except for the Cuba thing, I challenge you to give me an example of our managing the news." He also raised the Hanson Baldwin case, telling Bradlee, in nonspecific terms, that Baldwin had committed a "major security violation" that had led to a "massive FBI investigation." That, in turn, had led to Baldwin's disenchantment, he said.[43]

But Kennedy was also acutely aware that the campaign to weed out leakers could get out of hand. When he heard that civilian and military officials in the Pentagon were being subjected to lie detector tests as part of an investigation into who leaked secrets to the *Washington Star* Pentagon reporter Richard Fryklund, he personally put an immediate stop to it, complaining to Bradlee, "Boy, this is a big government. You push a button marked 'investigate,' and the whole giant machinery starts moving, and then you can't stop it."[44]

Sylvester was again in the news when he told the Air Force public relations officers that their decisions on whether to release or withhold information should be determined by the line taken by "the man who goes before the people every four years to submit his stewardship, no matter who he may be." The version of the statement translated by *Aviation Week and Space Technology* for public consumption was that Sylvester told Air Force public affairs officials that their primary job was to make the Kennedy administration look good.[45]

Controversy was still raging in early April. Not only was the issue not going away, but several associations representing news media were openly criticizing the White House's information policies and practices through the adoption of formal resolutions. In response, Salinger created an opportunity for the airing of grievances from both sides in private. He arranged for a summit with government public information officials and editors and reporters from newspapers, wire services, news magazines, and radio and television networks. This summit was held on 5 and 6 April at Airlie House, a secluded retreat in the Virginia countryside about an hour's drive outside Washington, D.C., and near Civil War battlegrounds.[46] It provided an opportunity to get outside the Beltway and essentially have it out. Whatever transpired there—and those present remained remarkably tight-lipped about what happened—it worked. The issue finally faded. But Sylvester's stumbling, along with McNamara's tendency to keep him at arm's length, did not inspire Kennedy's confidence. "Arthur's days are numbered," Kennedy told Ben Bradlee in early April 1963.[47] As it turned out, he was mistaken; Sylvester remained in his post as the Pentagon's chief press officer through some of the most important years of American involvement in Vietnam, finally leaving in February 1967.

13

The Missiles We've Had on Our Minds

A deal had been struck on the IL-28s, and Khrushchev had said that he would withdraw the Soviet combat troops in Cuba "in due course." But Kennedy recognized that the Soviets had little incentive to do so unless the United States offered a formal, UN-supervised guarantee that it would not invade the island. That, Kennedy judged, was too high a price because it would "psychologically be a source of strength to Castro and a source of difficulty for us, here."[1] America's allies also seemed reluctant to support a further ratcheting up of pressure over the lesser weapons. When Sherman Kent, chairman of the CIA's Board of National Estimates, provided a special briefing to NATO allies on 20 November, the participants pressed him to confirm that the short-range missiles still in Cuba would not be defined as offensive weapons.[2]

During a meeting on 29 November, Kennedy elaborated in detail on why he was prepared to tacitly accept the continued presence of Soviet troops. "I think without the assurance," Kennedy told his advisers,

> the chances of his [Khrushchev's] taking out those guard units and these FROGs and all the rest—which he indicated or hinted that

he'd probably be doing it in due time—I would think he wouldn't take them out. Because he'll say we haven't given the assurance, "therefore we've got to maintain our defensive strength to protect Cuba." So I would think that we have to really make a choice. My feeling would be that we would be better off to have those units in and not have the guarantee.

Bundy agreed that they were "not that important." "That would be," he continued, "a bargaining point that we don't buy." "That's what I think," Kennedy said. "I think we're all in agreement that we would much rather have all this stuff there, SAM sites, FROGs, and all the rest, than to be really locked in any kind of a guarantee that would be difficult to get out of." McNamara pointed out, "They have patrol craft missiles, the missiles on the KOMARS. And they have FROGs, surface-to-surface missiles. There are five types of missiles, and I would just guess off-hand, although we have no real basis to make such an estimate, that they have at least a thousand in total in these five categories." Interestingly, the main concern was not about the military implications of those missiles but about the lack of public understanding that the missiles were not strategic threats. In short, they saw it not as a security problem but as a public relations problem. "It really would blanket a lot of this chatter if we could get clear that there are a lot of missiles which are not the missiles we've had on our mind," Bundy said.[3]

The practical outcome of that discussion was that despite the inevitable uncertainty about the presence of warheads, Kennedy and his senior civilian advisers had decided that the United States would not pay any further price for the removal of the thousands of Soviet combat troops, the 24 to 36 Lunas that intelligence agencies estimated were in Cuba, the 500 SAMs, the MiG-21 fighters, or the 150 coastal defense missiles. Having made that decision, the administration had to defend it on several fronts, confronting tensions between diplomatic expediency, military imperatives, and domestic politics.

The Joint Chiefs remained uncomfortable with the prospect of

Soviet troops and their Lunas remaining in Cuba. They did not dispute that such short-range weapons were primarily defensive forces, but they were charged with developing contingency plans to counter Cuban and Soviet defenses in the event the president ordered military action against Cuba, something that they continued to do; the U.S. military buildup put in motion by these plans reached a maximum state of readiness on 15 November.[4] It also fell to the chiefs to provide for the defense of the U.S. naval base at Guantánamo. In particular, short-range missiles hidden in the mountains near Guantánamo and pointed at the base had attracted their attention. Subsequent information suggests that they were right to be concerned: those missiles were probably nuclear-armed FKRs.[5]

The Lunas also remained a priority for the Joint Chiefs. They repeatedly raised the issue when they met with the president during the period between November 1962 and February 1963, arguing that the weapons were a threat to Guantánamo and posed a risk that the Cubans could export them to be used in communist subversion in Latin America.[6] To improve their information on what was there, the chiefs persistently called for the resumption of low-level surveillance flights. As Maxwell Taylor argued on 15 January, "There are still very interesting, important points which we're losing touch with, particularly the heavy ground equipment, whether or not they have indeed taken out the nuclear-capable FROGs."[7] But Kennedy and most of his senior advisers (Rusk was a notable exception) considered low-level flights too risky under the circumstances; there was simply no good option if another American plane was shot down over Cuba. The request to resume low-level surveillance flights was therefore denied.

An ever-present undercurrent of all this discussion was the inevitable uncertainty on the presence of nuclear warheads. The Soviets offered assurances that all nuclear warheads had gone well before they actually were. When Sir Frank Roberts, a veteran Kremlinologist and the British ambassador to the Soviet Union, made his farewell visit with the Soviet leader at the Kremlin on 12 November, Khrushchev assured Roberts that all nuclear warheads had left Cuba, a point Roberts pressed him on.[8] During meetings in New York on 13, 15, and 18 November, Vasily Kuznetsov gave further assurances that "no nuclear weapons whatsoever were any longer on the territory of Cuba."[9] On 20 November, Khrushchev personally provided another assurance to Kennedy that "[a]ll the nuclear weapons have been taken away from Cuba."[10] None of those statements was true; the tactical nuclear warheads did not actually leave Cuba until the following month.

In fact, the Soviet commander in Cuba, General Issa Pliyev, did not receive orders to return all of the warheads until November 20. The decision not to leave tactical warheads in Cuba amounted to a reversal; the Soviet Defense Ministry was apparently operating under the assumption that the Luna rockets would be handed over to the Cubans, a move that would have instantly made Cuba a nuclear power.[11] U.S. military intelligence suspected as much; it was in keeping with the recent policy of supplying Warsaw Pact countries with tactical weapon carriers and launchers. The recently adopted standard procedure was to provide launchers and missiles for forward deployment to host countries, but to keep the missiles under tight Soviet control. In times of heightened alert, special Soviet commando units would deliver the warheads to the missiles and supervise their deployment and use. In early November, Defense Minister Rodion Malinovksy cabled General Pliyev in Havana that it was likely that the Lunas and coastal defense missiles with conventional loads would remain in Cuba, but that no final decision on the nuclear warheads for these weapons had been made.[12]

What had apparently changed Khrushchev's mind was Castro's seemingly erratic behavior in late October through mid-November. Khrushchev had dispatched First Deputy Premier Anastas Mikoyan to Havana to reason with Castro and encourage him to relax his hard line on the settlement of the crisis. Khrushchev's unilateral decision to withdraw the missiles had infuriated the Cuban leader; if Khrushchev had come to Havana instead of Mikoyan, Castro later said, "I should have boxed his ears." Even with Mikoyan, the discussions had been difficult, and Mikoyan had found that Castro's famed revolutionary passion was becoming worryingly apocalyptic. Mikoyan tried to impress upon the Cuban leader that Moscow would provide the means to defend Cuba but would not risk war with the United States. Castro's response was combative: "Cuba cannot be conquered, it can only be destroyed," he said. The fiery rhetoric of the Cuban deputy premier, Che Guevara, did not help. Talking to reporters on 28 November, in the first interview given by a Cuban leader since the crisis commenced, Guevara boasted that not only would Cubans fight to the end if the United States attacked, but "if the rockets had remained, we would have used them all and directed them against the very heart of the United States including New York." When Khrushchev learned on 15 November that Castro had issued orders to shoot down U.S. surveillance planes, he made the decision to withdraw all of the tactical nuclear warheads back to the Soviet Union, although some Luna rockets and FKRs would remain without nuclear warheads. The orders were delivered five days later. Unaware of that order, the Cubans remained hopeful that the island's defense still packed a nuclear punch. The Soviets intercepted a communication from the Cuban foreign minister, Raúl Roa, to the Cuban representative at the United Nations, Carlos Lechuga, on 20 November that "we still have tactical atomic weapons, which must be kept." Decades later, Castro claimed that he had known of the nuclear-armed Lunas in Cuba and been confident that they would be used.[13]

The warheads did not actually leave Cuba until sometime in December, although it is not clear precisely when. Some sources claim that they left Havana on 25 December; others say that they left on 4 or 1 December. Washington knew nothing of Khrushchev's order or the movement of the warheads, although U.S. aerial surveillance flights photographed ten Luna missile transporters on a pier at Mariel on 26 December. Those transporters were apparently loaded onto the *Kislovodsk* and shipped to the USSR on 5 January.[14]

As Kennedy had predicted, in the absence of either pressure or incentive, Khrushchev simply left the combat troops and some of the short-range missiles in Cuba. U.S. intelligence reports on Cuba throughout the 1960s continued to note the presence of Luna transporters and launchers at Soviet encampments on the island.[15]

For a time, critics on the Hill tried to keep the issue alive. On at least a dozen occasions through January and February, government officials testifying before congressional committees laid out detailed information about the remaining short-range missiles and the remaining Soviet combat troops, continuing with the line that they expected Moscow to withdraw the troops. Strom Thurmond cited the presence of "nuclear-tipped FROG missiles" among his many examples of what he charged were the Kennedy administration's failed Cuba policies, but relatively few in Congress showed much interest that nuclear-capable, tactical missiles were still in Cuba. Instead, committee members repeatedly focused on the possible presence of long-range strategic missiles in Cuba and the arming of MiG-21s with nuclear weapons—a less likely but more sensational scenario. That latter prospect, warned Senator Frank Lausche (Democrat of Ohio), raised the possibility that MiG jets could be used on Florida "just as we dropped atomic bombs on Hiroshima."[16]

14

Removing the Straitjacket

One of the unintended consequences of the Cuban missile crisis had profound ramifications for the cold war. In a major development that became clear only in the wake of the crisis, it turned out that, quite unintentionally, Khrushchev had given up one of the Soviet Union's most effective points of leverage against the United States: West Berlin.

It was a sharp change. In January 1962, Kennedy had ranked Berlin as "the greatest issue of all," over and above the communist insurgency in South Vietnam, nuclear proliferation, increasing ties between Cuba and the Soviet Union, or the range of other foreign policy challenges looming on the horizon.[1] A year later, he told the ExComm that the early cold war's most important flash point had finally been neutralized. "We now have a hostage in this hemisphere just as the Russians have had one in Berlin for several years," he said.[2]

Before and during the crisis in Cuba, Kennedy regarded West Berlin as a diplomatic straitjacket limiting his options. It was, he said, "paralyzing." By his own admission, the U.S. commitment to a city half a world away had constrained his options in dealing with the crisis in Cuba. But the way in which the crisis was resolved suddenly and dramatically changed the situation. Almost overnight, thanks to

Khrushchev's miscalculations, the Berlin problem, one of the most difficult and dangerous problems of the early cold war, was suddenly neutralized. Before the crisis, Khrushchev had been able to hold West Berlin hostage. But in the way that the Cuban missile crisis played out, Khrushchev effectively handed the United States its own hostage: Cuba.[3]

Although the change was abrupt, the foundation had been building for months. For a decade and a half of on-again, off-again crises, Berlin had been at the center of the cold war. Of all the cold war tinderboxes, Berlin proved the most persistent and arguably the most dangerous. It was the issue that kept presidents and secretaries of state up at night. "When I go to sleep at night, I try not to think about Berlin," Rusk confessed in 1961.[4] Dwight Eisenhower agreed.[5]

Cold war Berlin was more than a piece of conquered real estate. A combination of the peculiar bargain that had divided the city among the United States, the Soviet Union, Great Britain, and France during the closing days of World War II and deep-rooted insecurities about German power had doomed the city to become a hotbed of intrigue where cold war tensions simmered and frequently threatened to boil over in genuine nuclear crises. Successive American presidents had vowed to defend the freedom of West Berlin from communist aggression just as they would defend Washington, Chicago, or Los Angeles. So long as West Berlin remained a pivotal place in the cold war, the chances of détente were limited.

In August 1961, Soviet and East German troops had sealed the border between East and West Berlin. Over the following months, the barbed wire was replaced by a concrete wall and heavy fortifications. But the wall solved few of the underlying tensions that had so frequently arisen since the Berlin blockade. Four months after the Soviet and East German soldiers sealed the border between East and West Berlin with barbed wire, two of the foremost American experts on Soviet policy, George F. Kennan and Llewellyn Thompson, predicted that Khrushchev still intended to force a showdown with the West over Berlin.[6] The following year, another expert on the Soviet

Union, Foy Kohler, the new U.S. ambassador in Moscow, pointed out that Khrushchev had not had a good year. It would be in character, Kohler warned, for the Soviet leader to to try to compensate by plotting a diplomatic success.[7] If he did so, there was a good chance it would be something dramatic, something that would destabilize the balance of power and risk heating up the cold war. And it was West Berlin that would tempt Khrushchev the most.

During the summer of 1962, Khrushchev made Berlin a recurring theme with a stream of foreign visitors.[8] Kennedy's press secretary, Pierre Salinger, had traveled to Moscow in May 1962. He spent several days with the Soviet premier, even getting his photograph taken hunting with him, armed with a shotgun. Salinger spoke no Russian and was not noted as a keen world traveler, but he came away from the experience concluding that Khrushchev "had two fixations—Berlin and Soviet agriculture." Resorting to his typically colorful similes, Khrushchev told Salinger that the United States needed West Berlin "like a dog needs five legs." It was unreasonable for the United States to keep thwarting the "normalization" of the situation, he said, and failure to reach agreement on a German peace treaty would result in dire crisis.[9]

When U Thant, the acting secretary-general of the United Nations, ventured to the Soviet bloc in late August 1962, Khrushchev continued to insist that the Berlin problem be settled once and for all. After meeting with Khrushchev, Andrei Gromyko, and Leonid Brezhnev, U Thant came away convinced that the Soviet leaders were "very much obsessed" with the Berlin problem. U Thant shared that assessment with Kennedy and Dean Rusk.[10] Months later, at the height of the Cuban missile crisis, Rusk recalled U Thant's assessment and wondered out loud "whether maybe Mr. Khrushchev is entirely rational about Berlin."[11]

Notes of a Presidium meeting on 1 July, on the eve of the arrival in Moscow of Raúl Castro, the Cuban defense minister, reveals that Khrushchev announced his intention to force the Berlin issue. In those notes, which historians Timothy Naftali and Aleksandr Fursenko drew attention to in their 2006 book on Khrushchev, the Soviet leader outlined a schedule under which Western troops would be phased out of West Berlin over a six-year period: the USSR and German Democratic Republic (GDR) would sign a peace treaty, half of the Western troops in West Berlin would leave, and those remaining would be under UN auspices; two years after the treaty was signed, those troops would be replaced by non-Western UN forces; and six years after the signing, all UN troops would leave West Berlin. There would be no international access authority or other guarantee of Western access, something the Kennedy administration had been pushing for. It was his last offer, Khrushchev said. But he also reassured his colleagues that he was not going to saber rattle for its own sake—he intended to seek a diplomatic settlement by reaching out directly to Kennedy before escalating, if necessary, at the UN in early November. He told the Presidium that the weapons deployments in Cuba would be in place by 1 November and that he was exploring ways to protect the shipments en route from the prying eyes of American aerial surveillance. The notes of the meeting suggest that Khrushchev's plan was accepted without dissent.[12] They also suggest strongly that Khrushchev's Berlin threats in the summer and fall of 1962 amounted to far more than hollow threats or deliberate misdirection.

In November 1958 and June 1961, Khrushchev had issued his ultimatums brusquely. This time he adopted a quieter and more gradual approach less susceptible to open defiance by the West. Rather than resorting to declarations of a deadline, this time he relied on implication. Khrushchev began the process with Llewellyn Thompson. During Thompson's farewell visit with the Soviet premier in late July 1962, a customary rite for important departing diplomats, Khrushchev gave him a message to pass on to Kennedy. He offered to delay the Berlin issue until after the U.S. congressional elections scheduled for early November. But the implication of his generosity was clear: he intended to push the issue soon after the midterm election.[13]

In the ensuing weeks, Khrushchev repeated that schedule.[14] It was not immediately clear to Western diplomats what had prompted the shift, but a few days after Thompson's visit with the Soviet premier, Kennedy quietly signaled that he had received the message. During a secret back-channel meeting on 30 July, Robert Kennedy delivered to Georgi N. Bolshakov, a Soviet military intelligence officer stationed in Washington, a counteroffer of good faith from the president: if Khrushchev would put the Berlin issue "on ice," then the Americans would curtail U-2 flights over Soviet shipping. It was a proposal that fit neatly the Soviets' secret plans to ship Soviet missiles and other military equipment to Cuba. Khrushchev agreed to the deal.[15]

Although Khrushchev had said he would not act on the Berlin issue before the November elections, he had not said that he would not lay the groundwork for his plan. In the course of a series of conversations with foreign visitors in the summer of 1962, Khrushchev seeded his plan. In addition to Salinger and U Thant, Khrushchev also told U.S. Secretary of the Interior Stewart Udall, Hans Kroll, and the celebrated American poet Robert Frost of his intentions. Taken in isolation, each instance might have been dismissed as fragmented and bombastic rhetoric. Cumulatively, they amounted to a concerted diplomatic campaign with an increasingly direct message.

Senior American officials responded with repeated declarations of resolve. Three American presidents had committed the United States to defend West Berlin, and that was precisely what the United States intended to do. In the process, they played their own important part in the escalating tension.

In the public bracing for a Berlin crisis anticipated to break in November, the primary objective was to deter Soviet action there. But the administration also had other objectives: diverting political attention at home away from the increasing inflammatory campaign rhetoric regarding Cuba, cultivating domestic and world opinion, and casting Khrushchev as the aggressor. Simultaneously, hawkish Republicans ramped up their attacks on the Kennedy administration and its Democratic allies in the lead-up to the November midterm elections. Polls indicated that Cuba was Kennedy's main foreign policy vulnerability, and Republicans hoped to exploit it in the run-up to the November elections.[16] For its part, the administration and its allies countered with attempts to shift the debate to safer issues such as Medicare and Berlin.

By September, then, two cold war issues separated by half a world—Cuba and West Berlin—were becoming increasingly entangled.

One of the most dramatic episodes in Khrushchev's Berlin campaign in the fall of 1962 was a remarkably candid conversation with the West German ambassador to the USSR, Hans Kroll. Kroll developed an unusually close diplomatic relationship with Khrushchev, having earned the Soviet premier's trust by being an outspoken advocate of closer ties between Bonn and Moscow and, just as importantly, favorable toward recognition of the GDR. Both Khrushchev and Kroll used that trust for their own ends.[17]

Khrushchev rewarded Kroll with unusual access, repeatedly inviting the ambassador to his summer home for talks. By 1962, however, the outspoken Kroll had become too much of a liability for the Adenauer government, and political pressures led Adenauer to recall him back to a desk job in Bonn. Khrushchev used Kroll's farewell visit in late September to the Kremlin to issue his most explicit warning yet. In the course of the three-hour discussion, Khrushchev impressed upon his guest that action on Berlin was imminent. He would force a resolution of the Berlin problem once and for all in November, he told Kroll.[18] If it had been an isolated threat, it could have been dismissed as classic Khrushchev bluster. His proposal for Berlin was essentially the same one he had been peddling for years—an international "free city" guaranteed by the United Nations. If all went according to plan, what was going to be new in November 1962, he hoped, was a leveling of the strategic status quo on a global scale.[19] Never shy about publicity, Kroll duly reported the message in great detail to the press, handing the scoop to the right-wing Munich newspaper *Deutsche Soldaten Zeitung*. "Final Fight for Berlin in 4 Weeks," ran the paper's front-page headline on 28 September above a transcript of its exclusive interview with Kroll.[20]

A few days after his talk with U Thant, and around the same time that he was secretly asking Soviet Defense Minister Rodion Malinovsky to explore the possibility of rushing tactical nuclear weapons to Cuba, Khrushchev received another visitor at his dacha, U.S. Secretary of the Interior Stewart Udall.[21] Khrushchev repeated his tough line on Berlin, and Udall sensed that the Soviets were preparing yet another Berlin ultimatum. "We will give him [Kennedy] a choice," Udall reported Khrushchev as saying, "go to war, or sign a peace treaty. . . . It's been a long time since you could spank us like a little boy—now we can swat your ass."[22] The Soviet premier had also told the visiting American poet Robert Frost that the West was "too liberal to fight."[23]

A few days later, on 11 September, Reuters news agency in Moscow reported that in the midst of a strong reaffirmation of its intention to press for a German peace treaty and removal of Western troops from West Berlin, the Soviet government had said that it would create a "breathing space" on the West Berlin situation until after the November congressional elections.[24] It was the first time that Moscow had publicly conveyed the message Khrushchev had been delivering privately through the summer. Washington, already anticipating a crisis, interpreted the public message as a diplomatic escalation. When, on 4 September, a Soviet SA-2 brought down an American U-2 surveillance plane that had inadvertently strayed into Soviet airspace, it deepened Washington's unease. And all the while, a flood of reports and rumors was coming in about a Soviet military buildup in Cuba.[25]

Intelligence chatter on Soviet intentions remained garbled, but Bundy warned Ted Sorensen, special counsel to the president, in late August 1962 that "the Berlin crisis has warmed up a lot in recent weeks and looks as if it is getting worse." The problem, Bundy diagnosed, was that Khrushchev was becoming emboldened by the weak responses the West was making to his increasingly inflammatory rhetoric. This, he told Sorensen, "owes much to the President's own temper, and much also to the fact that the Soviets have been crying wolf since 1958," when Khrushchev had issued the first of his ultimatums, only to rescind it later. Bundy urged Sorensen to use his upcoming meeting with Soviet mmbassador to the United States, Anatoly Dobrynin, to help redress that by conveying clearly and emphatically "that it would be a most dangerous business to confuse our calmness and good manners with any weakening of determination whatsoever." Sorensen also used the opportunity to reiterate Kennedy's request of Khrushchev not to make Berlin a campaign issue and thereby strengthen the hand of Republican hawks already calling for a much tougher line with the Soviets.[26]

In an attempt to quell the political damage of the persistent rumors about Soviet offensive weapons in Cuba, Kennedy summoned the congressional leadership to the White House on 4 September to brief them on the latest intelligence. When some congressmen proposed blockading Cuba to stop the incoming arms shipments, Kennedy shot the idea down. It would be a mistake to hand the Soviets a pretext for ratcheting up the Berlin situation, he said. "I think Berlin is coming to some kind of a climax this fall, one way or another, before Christmas," he said. "I would say the biggest danger right now is for Berlin," he warned.[27]

The first days of September constituted a period of intense, high-level diplomatic chatter. During meetings with Robert Kennedy and Ted Sorensen, Dobrynin repeated Khrushchev's offer not to do anything until after the congressional elections. But he also emphasized that the German and Berlin problems would have to be settled shortly thereafter.[28] On 5 September, the Kremlin issued a statement that the time had come to "liquidate the occupation regime in West Berlin" and for Western troops to withdraw.[29] In closed session, Rusk warned the Senate Foreign Relations Committee and the Senate Armed Services Committee that the Berlin situation was "more dangerous than it has been since 1945."[30] Kennedy told Sorensen, "If we solve the Berlin problem without war, Cuba will look pretty small. And if there is a war, Cuba won't matter much either."[31]

Publicly, Washington sought to head off growing speculation that the two hot spots might be linked. By mid-September there was chatter in diplomatic circles that Khrushchev might use the excuse of U.S. military action against Cuba to gamble on military action in Berlin. The Hungarian uprising of 1956 offered an ominous precedent.[32] During a television interview broadcast on 30 September, Rusk dismissed rumors of a Berlin-for-Cuba trade because "you cannot support freedom in one place by surrendering freedom in another," a statement frequently cited in the following weeks.[33]

In the first weeks of October, the tension continued to grow. Kennedy personally gave Willy Brandt the kind of reassurance the West Berlin mayor wanted to hear. If Western access was challenged, Kennedy said, he would order an airlift to maintain the viability of the city; if the Soviets interfered with that, it would mean war. The importance of West Berlin to the United States, he declared, was that "our actions were our assurances." For this reason he was prepared to accept that the U.S. commitment to West Berlin restricted his freedom of action in other areas vital to U.S. interests, specifically Cuba. If the communists decided on a new push on Berlin, Brandt warned Kennedy, it might stir an uprising more dangerous than the ones in June 1953. Given the questionable reliability of the East German military police, the Volksarmee, the situation could become dangerously unstable.[34]

At the same time, Rusk's discussions with Brandt and Gromyko on the Berlin problem continued to be reported in the press. In the 9 October issue of the *Washington Post*, the columnist Chalmers Roberts reported that in anticipation that Khrushchev would go "close to the brink" the following month over Berlin, the administration was in a "batten-down-the-hatches" posture.[35] That same day, during a speech in Las Vegas, Robert Kennedy warned, "It is quite possible that we will face a great crisis in Berlin in the weeks ahead. But the determination and unity of this country to maintain our position in West Berlin is apparent. American military strength has increased and we face that possible crisis with confidence."[36] And when the State

Department adviser Chester Bowles lunched with Anatoly Dobrynin on 13 October, he warned the Soviet ambassador that if the Soviets planned to use Cuba to divert attention from Berlin or put even more pressure on the issue, "a global chain of events might be set in motion which could have catastrophic consequences."[37]

On the morning of 15 October, the *New York Times* broke the story that several weeks previously a high level official from a communist nation had approached some Western delegates to the United Nations claiming to be delivering an offer from Khrushchev to moderate his course with Cuba if the United States relaxed its stand on West Berlin. This, the journalist surmised, explained Rusk's statement several weeks earlier dismissing a Berlin-for-Cuba trade.[38] The next morning, the *Washington Post* carried the State Department's dismissive response on its front page. In the same issue, the veteran foreign affairs columnist Walter Lippmann forecast an imminent showdown on Berlin and warned Moscow not to misunderstand Washington's resolve. Apart from the strategic dimensions of the issue, he cautioned the politicians in the Kremlin, it was a political problem for Kennedy. Unwittingly echoing Khrushchev's private warning to Kennedy the preceding November ("You have to understand, I have no ground to retreat further, there is a precipice behind,")[39] Lippmann wrote, "President Kennedy cannot surrender Berlin even if he were the kind of man who wanted to. A surrender would destroy him."[40]

It is still unclear how Khrushchev intended the West to learn of the missiles he had sent to Cuba. Given that he had previously declared his intention of traveling across the Atlantic to raise the Berlin issue at the UN General Assembly in New York in early November around the time that the missiles in Cuba were scheduled to become operational, it is tempting to speculate that he might have planned to stop in Havana en route to New York, although no evidence of such a planned detour has so far come to light. Whatever plans he had, though, were preempted by U.S. intelligence in dramatic fashion.

Kennedy's secret tapes of White House meetings during the Cuban missile crisis capture in unusual detail the thinking of American officials. The focus was of course on the Caribbean, but West Berlin comes through strongly. In the first ExComm meeting, on 16 October, Rusk suggested that one of the most plausible explanations was that "[t]hey may be thinking that they can either bargain Berlin and Cuba against each other, or that they could provoke us into a kind of action in Cuba which would give an umbrella for them to take action with respect to Berlin."[41] This was not the first time the prospect of a Berlin-for-Cuba trade had been examined by U.S. policymakers—indeed, it had already been a subject of the informal East–West dialogue—but with the discovery that the Soviets were already transforming Cuba into a strategic base, the "trading ploy" theory, as George Ball put it, suddenly grew in significance.[42]

Moreover, the matter of timing played an influential part in the way in which policymakers perceived the problem. Kennedy's chief Soviet expert, Llewellyn Thompson, had been at a loss to explain Khrushchev's offer to delay a confrontation on the Berlin issue until after the U.S. congressional elections. The missiles in Cuba seemed to be the missing link. To Thompson, it now made sense: "Khrushchev knew what he was doing, wanted a showdown on Berlin, and believed that missiles in Cuba armed him for that confrontation."[43] The secrecy of the deployment clearly suggested that Khrushchev wanted to present the United States with a fait accompli, and on the basis of the results of the aerial surveillance, the CIA judged that the bulk of the medium-range ballistic missiles would be operational by the time of the elections.

On the afternoon of 16 October, during a previously scheduled off-the-record address before a gathering of the nation's leading press editors and correspondents, Kennedy reported that a Berlin crisis was clearly brewing and likely to erupt before Christmas. Whatever form Soviet pressure took, the president insisted, the United States would not relinquish its right to keep troops in West Berlin even in the face of nuclear war. To some extent, though, Kennedy was trying to mask his concern for the Cuba issue. "The situation in Cuba is obviously not in the same classification as yet," he said, "because the Cubans do not possess the nuclear arsenal that the Soviet Union possesses, and we are not in as direct course of collision as we are over Berlin." With the benefit of hindsight, it was a disingenuous statement, but understandably so.[44] And the ploy apparently worked. By the time the message made its way from an unknown source through Ambassador Anatoly Dobrynin back to Moscow, Cuba was not even mentioned. "Some sort of crisis relating to Berlin is clearly brewing now," Dobrynin quoted Kennedy as saying.[45]

Kennedy perceived other indications from other sources that seemed to confirm that he was facing a nexus of the Berlin and Cuba problems. On 17 October, he met with the West German foreign minister, Gerhard Schröder. Without revealing that U.S. intelligence had detected Soviet missile sites under construction, Kennedy told Schröder that he expected the Berlin confrontation to be resumed within the next two to three months. It was urgent, he said, that the Western allies reach political agreement on Berlin contingency plans in order to avoid risking military conflict on the wrong issue. Schröder countered by disputing that Khrushchev was likely to force a crisis in November.[46] The next day the president met with Gromyko. Deciding not to reveal for the moment that he knew about the construction of the missile sites, Kennedy used the opportunity to probe Soviet intentions. In a veiled effort to preempt the Soviets' linking of Berlin and Cuba, he emphasized that West Berlin was not a NATO base and that Western forces there were not equipped with nuclear weapons. Contrary to Soviet assertions, Kennedy insisted, the U.S. military presence there was wholly symbolic and not a threat to Soviet security. At the same time, he declared, the ongoing presence of U.S. military troops in the city was not something he was willing to negotiate. Gromyko, however, would not be drawn out and merely conveyed Khrushchev's hope to meet with Kennedy in late November when they could discuss "first and foremost" the German and West Berlin problems.[47] Later that evening, when Gromyko repeated Khrushchev's proposal to make West Berlin a "free city," Rusk warned Gromyko that the United States could not be driven out of West Berlin without war, and that Khrushchev therefore had to decide if he was willing to go to war.[48]

Kennedy later described Gromyko's attitude as "completely unreasonable and downright insulting." He came away from the meeting more convinced than ever that Berlin was the prize that the Soviets were after and that Cuba was simply a means to that end. Echoing what he had heard from his Kremlinologists—Thompson, Bohlen, and Kennan—Kennedy told the Joint Chiefs the next day, "What's basic to them [the Soviets] is Berlin. . . . There isn't any doubt [about that]. In every conversation we've had with the Russians, that's what . . . Even last night we [Gromyko and Kennedy] talked about Cuba for a while, but Berlin—that's what Khrushchev's committed himself to personally."[49]

There are conflicting accounts of the Kennedy-Gromyko meeting, however, suggesting that Kennedy's interpretation was influenced to some extent by his own preoccupations and expectations. American versions, probably colored by the expectation of a Berlin crisis that they themselves had played a part in escalating over the previous months, came away from the meeting believing that Berlin was the major issue discussed. Soviet reports and recollections of the meeting, on the other hand, place overwhelming emphasis on Cuba. Gromyko and Dobrynin, both present at the meeting, recalled that the problems of Germany and Berlin "took a back seat" and were mentioned "only in passing."[50]

As the ExComm continued to deliberate in secret, Kennedy repeatedly found his Cuba options constrained by the Berlin problem. He privately confessed to admiring the ingenuity of Khrushchev's linkage ploy to David Ormsby-Gore, the British ambassador to Washington and a friend of Kennedy's.[51] There were few ways in which the commitment to West Berlin could be turned to American advantage, although Robert Kennedy at one point raised the prospect of needling the Soviets by threatening to give American nuclear weapons to West Germany, West Berlin, and France.[52] Overwhelmingly, though, the commitment to West Berlin was a vulnerability.

The frustration, President Kennedy complained, was that for every U.S. action, Khrushchev had a range of strong options for his own reprisal. "One has to realize that they [decisions on Cuba] will have their effect on Berlin as well as on Cuba," Prime Minister Harold Macmillan of Britain warned Kennedy at the height of the crisis. "That is really why we have not done more than we've done up until now," Kennedy responded.[53]

The early consensus in the ExComm was that military action would be required. During the following days, however, the military option became decreasingly attractive for a range of reasons, prominent among them that Soviet troops in Cuba acted as a trip wire in much the same way as American troops in West Berlin.[54] Any U.S. military strikes would almost certainly kill Soviet troops, thereby inflaming the crisis and drawing in the Soviets directly. Reminiscing years later, Khrushchev confirmed that there was a solid basis for such fears. "If the Americans had started a war at that time we were not prepared to adequately attack the United States. In that case, we would have been forced to start a war in Europe," he wrote.[55]

Kennedy knew only too well that military action would, in all likelihood, lead inexorably to a nuclear exchange. For all of the administration's talk of flexible, gradual, and controlled responses to Soviet challenges, in practice there was nothing "flexible" about the Berlin situation. No one seriously believed that West Berlin could be defended with conventional forces. The problem, as Kennedy spelled it out for the Joint Chiefs, was that "if we attack Cuba, the missiles, or Cuba, in any way then it gives them a clear line to take Berlin." Then, he said, "we would be regarded as the trigger-happy Americans who lost Berlin." That, he complained, "leaves me only one alternative, which is to fire nuclear weapons—which is a hell of an alternative."[56]

Unconvinced that surprise air strikes on Cuba could lead to anything other than uncontrolled escalation, Kennedy began to shift toward blockading Cuba. Again the analogy to the Berlin situation was troubling. In this case, there was of course an important precedent. The Berlin blockade of 1948–49 had played a central part in shaping

U.S. policymakers' understanding of the cold war. Indeed, several of Kennedy's advisers had held key roles in devising the Truman administration's policy during that earlier crisis. These same policymakers also recognized that nothing the United States had done in 1948–49 had in any way discouraged Moscow from doing it again. It remained an important Soviet capability and, Washington believed, a policy option still open to Khrushchev. In short, past experience suggested that the Soviets could blockade West Berlin with relative impunity. Nevertheless, there was an important new element. The United States now recognized the threat and over the preceding fourteen years had developed detailed contingency planning. At least in theory, therefore, it was prepared for a new blockade. If the Soviets retaliated to the U.S. blockade of Cuba with a blockade of their own on West Berlin, then NATO would likely blame the United States for provoking the action, but at the very least there were contingency plans in place designed to buy time before the situation escalated uncontrollably.[57]

Yet American policymakers were not sure that West Berlin was as sturdy as they hoped. In an 19 October memorandum, David Klein of the NSC Staff examined the problem. Assuming that "Khrushchev would trade Berlin for Cuba any day," but that such a trade would deal a serious blow to U.S. interests, Klein argued that "the simple psychological equality of 'blockade for blockade' would be powerful" despite Washington's efforts to differentiate between the two cases. Moreover, the range of options open to Khrushchev was daunting. A blockade of Berlin "could be screwed up and down in a neat parallel to our Cuba effort," and this could be done simply to end the Cuban quarantine or taken further to effectively seize West Berlin. Whatever action the United States took, there was no way to prevent the Europeans for laying the blame for a Berlin blockade on the United States. This, coupled with British and French domestic political problems, would place the burden even more heavily on the United States to take unilateral action. "We may find ourselves in the usual position of bearing the full brunt of responsibility while our Allies stand by and watch us carry on," Klein warned. That prospect was not attractive. The result would be that "we should have to shorten our reaction times, increase the directness and force of our responses, and be prepared to confront Khrushchev at a very early stage with a bluntly nuclear choice. This is a direct reversal of our current posture in a number of ways, but without it I do not believe that Berlin can be held."[58]

Klein judged that the immediate U.S. response would be governed by prepared contingency plans, but that these were slow to implement and incomplete and depended on a degree of Allied unity that did not appear feasible under existing conditions. At best, they could protect West Berlin for a few months, but under a prolonged blockade the West Berliners' morale was likely to deteriorate rapidly, and, Klein argued, "no one would fight a nuclear war for a dying city." In sum, it was difficult to see how the United States could protect its interests if Khrushchev blockaded West Berlin: "such a confrontation could hardly lead to a lifting of the Berlin blockade without a parallel relaxation in Cuba. And then where would we be? Castro would still be there. His weapons systems would be there still, and covert supply could continue."[59]

A few days later, on 23 October, the CIA provided its own estimate of West Berlin's viability if blockaded. In economic terms, the city was prepared for a total blockade. Existing stockpiles of essential supplies were sufficient to maintain the city physically for six months. The CIA warned, however, that "the critical factor . . . is not physical or economic but psychological." Unless the United States took forthright action, it was likely that the West Berliners' morale would undermine the Western position. To complicate matters, the West Berliners were likely to "become extraordinarily sensitive to, and suspicious of any indication from either side that the Cuban crisis might lead to an accommodation at their expense."[60]

One of the most difficult challenges if the Soviets blockaded West Berlin would be maintaining NATO unity. Despite the publicity campaign conducted over the previous months, if the United States triggered an escalation of the crisis by launching air strikes or blockading Cuba, it could not be sure that it would have its NATO allies on its side. In justifying to others his decision to blockade rather than attack, Kennedy emphasized that point. Knowing that he could not prevent Soviet retaliation against Berlin, he at least hoped to face such a crisis without splitting the alliance. The compelling factor, Thompson observed during an ExComm meeting, was that "if we have to face the crunch on Berlin, then we should have some of them still with us."[61] The likely course of events, as the ExComm saw it, was that U.S. military strikes against Cuba would earn the condemnation of world opinion and alienate the NATO allies. Then, when the Soviets retaliated against Turkey or Berlin or both, there could be no escaping the impression that the Soviets were responding to American aggression. As a result, the United States would be left to defend its interests in West Berlin unilaterally, which it could not do without resorting to nuclear weapons. "The prospect of that pattern," Bundy observed wryly, "is not an appetizing one."[62] Adenauer and de Gaulle fully recognized the potential of Soviet retaliation in Berlin, but made it known that Washington had their full support in any action it took to respond to the Soviet challenge in the Caribbean.[63]

Not everyone, however, agreed that the link between Berlin and Cuba was so direct. The Joint Chiefs challenged the connection Kennedy drew between the Berlin and the Cuba situations during a meeting on 19 October, in part to counter Kennedy's objections to air strikes. Berlin and Cuba were linked, the chiefs argued, but in a far more abstract way than in Kennedy's formulation. With the missile gap having been debunked publicly, Khrushchev was trying to make up for Soviet strategic inferiority in preparation for a global challenge to the credibility of American power. "Our strength in Berlin, our strength anyplace in the world," Maxwell Taylor insisted, "is the credibility of our response under certain conditions. And if we don't respond here in Cuba, we think the credibility is sacrificed." Air Force Chief of Staff General Curtis LeMay, who had directed the Berlin airlift of 1948–49, put it even more bluntly: "I don't share your view that if we knock off Cuba, they're going to knock off Berlin. We've got the Berlin problem staring us in the face anyway. If we don't do anything in Cuba, then they're going to push hard in Berlin and push *real hard* because they've got us *on the run*." In short, LeMay warned, "if you lose Cuba, you're going to get more and more pressure right on Berlin."[64]

Separately, former President Eisenhower agreed. Kennedy called Eisenhower twice during the crisis to personally inform him of developments, on the morning of 22 October and again on 28 October. During each call, Kennedy said that he anticipated correlated action in Berlin. Each time, Eisenhower disagreed. When Kennedy said, during the 28 October call, that although the immediate crisis had passed, he expected to be "toe-to-toe on Berlin" by the end of November, Eisenhower told Kennedy, "These people [the Soviets] do not equate, and I think it's a mistake to equate, Berlin with Cuba or anything else. They take *any* spot in the world. They don't care where it is. It's just a question [of] 'Are you in such a place that you either can't or won't resist.'"[65]

When Dobrynin, apparently unaware that his government was installing strategic missiles in Cuba, was summoned by Rusk on 23 October, the Soviet ambassador knew something serious was afoot but was uncertain whether it concerned Cuba or West Berlin.[66] Dobrynin's uncertainty was exacerbated because the day before, fueled by White House publicity, the *New York Times* reported that Soviet crisis mongering had prompted senior administration officials to refine planning "for all contingencies in and around Berlin."[67] Curiously, the members of the Kremlin's Presidium, who did know of the missiles in Cuba, were also uncertain which crisis point Kennedy's speech would concern. Khrushchev called a special night meeting of the Presidium to discuss "further actions regarding Cuba and Berlin."[68] And Soviet intelligence apparently could not decide which of the two issues it would be. The letter Rusk handed to Dobrynin dispelled any uncertainty: the U.S. government regarded the removal of the Soviet strategic missiles in Cuba as nonnegotiable. Significantly, Kennedy's letter to Khrushchev deliberately reaffirmed the U.S.

commitment to West Berlin and stated that strategic missiles in Cuba, even if operational, did not change the United States' commitment to its rights in West Berlin "with all the power at its command."[69]

Kennedy developed this theme further in his television address that evening when he moved to preempt analogies between the quarantine of Cuba and the blockade of West Berlin. The Cuban quarantine, he said, would be selective: "We are not at this time . . . denying the necessities of life as the Soviets attempted to do in their Berlin blockade of 1948." And, as always, the United States would not discuss any issue under duress. "That is why," he continued,

> this latest Soviet threat—or any other threat which is made either independently or in response to our actions this week—must and will be met with determination. Any hostile move anywhere in the world against the safety and freedom of peoples to whom we are committed—including in particular the brave people of West Berlin—will be met by whatever action is needed.[70]

Meanwhile, Rusk warned U.S. officials in Europe to prepare for the worst.[71] Paul Nitze, deputy secretary of defense for international security affairs, told the allied military group in Washington that in raising the stakes so dramatically, Khrushchev was probably trying to push for the elimination of American foreign bases and the evacuation of allied forces from West Berlin, but Nitze regarded it as unlikely that the Soviets would respond to Kennedy's statement with an immediate blockade of West Berlin.[72] Dean Acheson, having flown to Paris as President Kennedy's personal representative to brief Charles de Gaulle, told the French president that it was likely that the Soviets were trying to provoke the Americans into striking the first military blow, freeing them up to answer elsewhere. "Berlin? Quemoy? Southeast Asia? Korea? or all these theatres at the same time?" Acheson wondered. De Gaulle reassured Acheson that if crisis erupted over Berlin, France would stand with its allies, especially if there was a war.[73]

In West Berlin, planned military training exercises were abruptly canceled and convoys along the autobahn reduced in both size and number in order to avoid actions that might be construed as provocative. The initial response of West Berlin's political leadership and press to the president's speech was encouraging. Just days before the crisis broke, Walt Rostow had conveyed a message from the president to the West Berliners saying that Americans would stand "firm and united" in determination that the city "shall remain free" by continuing the military protection "which the presence in Berlin of Western military forces alone can afford." After Kennedy's 22 October speech, West Berliners were aware that they might provoke the East Germans and Soviets, but they nevertheless emphatically and vocally endorsed the American action.[74]

In the heat of the crisis, Khrushchev apparently decided that his plan for forcing a resolution of the Berlin problem had become too dangerous, the risk of nuclear war too great.[75] When Vasily Kuznetsov, a senior official in the Foreign Ministry and Moscow's lead negotiator in the post–missile crisis settlement, suggested during the Caribbean crisis that the link could be made more explicit, Khrushchev snapped back, "We are here trying to get ourselves out of this *avantyura* [reckless gamble] and now you are pulling us into another one!"[76] In the so-called pen-pal series of communications between Kennedy and Khrushchev, the Soviet premier ignored the president's references to West Berlin. The Soviet ambassador to the United Nations, Valerian Zorin, his credibility in tatters, played down rumors of imminent action in Berlin by telling a group of neutral nation delegates, "The Americans are thoroughly mistaken if they think we shall fall into their trap. We shall undertake nothing in Berlin, for action against Berlin is just what the Americans would wish."[77] After Zorin's earlier statements denying that there were offensive weapons in Cuba, however, Washington was not inclined to take him seriously. The CIA's postcrisis assessment was that "Khrushchev's risky Cuban adventure was in large measure motivated by his desire to place the USSR in the strongest possible position for a diplomatic showdown on Berlin, planned to begin before the end of 1962. This decision seems to have been reached sometime during the closing weeks of April or in the first weeks of May 1962."[78]

It was not clear how the outcome of the Cuba crisis would influence Soviet policy, and Washington anticipated a long endgame.[79] The State Department's Policy Planning Staff tasked Henry Rowen with exploring the various tricks the Soviets might have up their sleeves, and Rowen and Jeffrey Kitchen were also to investigate what lessons might be drawn from the Cuban crisis for Berlin contingency planning.[80] Many officials considered it likely that the Soviets would try to find some way to compensate for their defeat in the Caribbean. It was still possible, and widely feared, that Khrushchev might lash out. If he did so, a move against Berlin would be even "closer to the jugular," as Paul Nitze put it, and therefore even more dangerous.[81]

Despite some halfhearted public hints to the contrary, Khrushchev had apparently privately decided that the time for pushing for final resolution of the Berlin problem had passed. He had played his hand and it had failed. The Cuban missile crisis had been a graphic reminder of the dangers of a nuclear crisis, and provoking another over West Berlin would be reckless.[82] When the East German leader Walter Ulbricht tried, in mid-January 1963, to prod the Soviet leader on the Berlin issue, Khrushchev insisted that he had exhausted the possibilities and that the Soviet bloc was in no position to push for any kind of settlement that would satisfy its minimum demands.[83] It was a message he had delivered to his East German allies before, but this time it carried extra weight in the context of Khrushchev's defeat in Cuba. With Ulbricht's pressure reduced and Khrushchev's political capital waning, there was little inclination to risk yet another acute crisis over West Berlin. In short, Khrushchev had decided that nuclear brinkmanship over West Berlin had reached a dead end.[84]

American insecurity regarding the commitment to West Berlin now dissipated, with remarkable suddenness. It was an unexpected, and extraordinarily important, byproduct of the Cuban missile crisis that became apparent only once the thirteen days had passed. By ordering the unusual military buildup in Cuba, Khrushchev had set out to change the strategic status quo—though to what specific ends is a question historians still debate—but his gambit did not just fail; rather, it backfired in a way that directly impacted the Berlin crisis. In effect, Khrushchev inadvertently forfeited one of the mainstays of Moscow's pressure on the Western alliance, and Washington knew it.

"I think we're not in bad shape with the Soviets now," Kennedy told congressional leaders in a private briefing on 8 January. The way in which the closing stages of the Cuban missile crisis had played out had fundamentally changed the cold war. "I think that China and Latin America are our two most dangerous areas right now," he continued. He singled out one change as particularly important: "I think if Berlin gets difficult we'd always—they have now given—Cuba's almost the same position Berlin was with us for a decade. Any action they take in Berlin we can take an action in Cuba."[85]

Kennedy talked of this Berlin-Cuba hostage scenario several times in private, but he never spoke of it publicly. Doing so would have been unnecessarily provocative to the Soviets and only invited its own diplomatic and political trouble. But it was a central element in the shifts of the cold war in 1963 that culminated in early moves toward détente. The neutralization of the Berlin problem was not the only development that made détente possible, but it was a crucial one. It cleared the way for initiatives that could make the cold war less dangerous, for reducing the threat of nuclear war, and for improving relations between East and West.

15

A Political Firefight

A poll conducted in March 1963 found that 67 percent of Americans expressed either strong or mild approval for the way in which Kennedy was conducting the country's foreign policy.[1] But in the days, weeks, and months after the crisis, a vocal and influential minority on the Hill refused to let that be the last word. They looked to redefine Kennedy's foreign policy record as weak and ineffective.

As George Reedy, one of Vice President Lyndon Johnson's closest and most astute advisers put it at the time, the bitter partisan domestic debate could be baffling: although the United States had actually scored a major success, "this success is being frittered away by partisan bickering and by efforts to make Cuba into a political issue." It was also confusing their Latin American allies: "They find that the United States has almost adopted a defeatist psychology on the heels of a victory."[2]

The ongoing controversy was fueled by deep partisan resentment and political opportunism as early contenders for the Republican nomination in the 1964 election jostled for position. It was, of course, in part also fueled by the administration's efforts to maintain pressure on the Soviets and the Cubans while at the same time projecting an image to a domestic audience that it was very much on the ball with regard to Cuba. Secretary of State Dean Rusk warned the Senate Foreign Relations Committee in January 1963, "The Cuban crisis is in no sense over. It continues to be a highly dangerous situation and could flare up in a number of contingencies."[3]

Critics agreed. The administration, they said, was guilty of flawed intelligence and poor decision making. As late as April 1963, some political critics cited the continued presence of Soviet troops and their nuclear-capable armaments in Cuba as evidence that the administration was appeasing the Soviets by allowing them to keep forces in Cuba that could visit Hiroshima-like devastation upon Florida. The administration was under fire from partisans, press frustration, and Cuban émigrés agitating for a U.S. invasion of Cuba to oust Fidel Castro. From November 1962 through February 1963, the Cuba problem was still very much alive in a day-to-day policy sense.

Kennedy's own performance during the crisis resonated well with the American people; a Gallup poll in the wake of the crisis measured the president's approval rating at an impressive 74 percent.[4] But the surprise with which the crisis broke was widely regarded as the result of a massive intelligence failure, and there was widespread public questioning of the abilities of U.S. intelligence services and, especially after the Bay of Pigs fiasco, about the competency of the Kennedy White House. Additional reports coming with increasing frequency of new and unidentified arms shipments to Cuba and indications of around-the-clock work on building up Cuban defenses were unsettling.

During the crisis itself, even the administration's harshest critics had rallied behind the flag. Kennedy "will have the 100 percent backing of every American regardless of party," Senator Kenneth Keating, Republican of New York, had said.[5] But behind that public national consensus, widespread resentment simmered. And having been robbed of what seemed like a national security trump card before voters went to the polls, critics ratcheted up the pressure following the election in part through a series of congressional inquiries that were originally scheduled to cover topics ranging from the Bay of Pigs episode to the defense appropriations bill for fiscal year

1964, but that were turned into investigations of a range of issues involving Cuba. Administration officials generally followed a tight, official script, and that script was notably candid about what forces remained on the island.[6] The accusations from critics varied, but their central theme was that the Kennedy administration was being too soft on Cuba.

One of the harshest accusations was that administration officials had distorted intelligence to fit an election-year political agenda. The White House, some critics charged, had deliberately created its own "October surprise" to steal the 6 November midterm elections, by providing misleading information about the nature of the Soviet buildup and by reducing aerial surveillance during September and early October. With a play on the analogies of the controversies first of a missile gap and then of a bomber gap, critics now accused the administration of having created a photo gap through what they claimed was negligent handling of aerial surveillance of Cuba in the fall.[7]

The accusations did not stop there. Charges flew that the administration was being duped by Khrushchev and Castro and that it was willfully ignoring that long-range missiles were being hidden in the myriad caves on the island of Cuba. Of these accusations, the last proved the most persistent, frustrating, and difficult to rebut largely because proving the negative—that missiles were not being hidden in caves—was impossible.

The controversy was enabled by a press corps still bristling at the administration's control of information. Refugee reports, many claiming eyewitness evidence, received considerable play in newspapers and television news. Many of the reports were false or mistaken, but they provided sensational copy. Fed by radical refugee émigré groups in Miami and encouraged by congressional critics such as Senators Barry Goldwater (Republican of Arizona), Kenneth Keating (Republican of New York), Strom Thurmond (Democrat of South Carolina), and Representative Donald Bruce (Republican of Indiana), rumors reached fever pitch that the Soviets had sent at least eighty long-range missiles to Cuba—not the forty-two the Soviets had claimed and a figure the administration had accepted—and that dozens of long-range nuclear missiles were being hidden underground in Cuban caves.[8] The difficulty the administration faced in swatting down the reports was a problem Kennedy had anticipated but nevertheless failed to prevent.

Newspapers published detailed maps identifying where the missiles were supposedly being hidden. They were accompanied by information attributed to "reliable sources recently arrived from Cuba." Despite the implication that it was firsthand evidence, it was often a euphemism for what Arthur M. Schlesinger Jr. later characterized as "anti-Castro zealots."[9] Proving beyond doubt that these refugee reports were wrong and that missiles were not in Cuba was an impossible task. Some senior officials, Kennedy among them, found it unlikely that the Soviets had anything to gain by lying about the number of missiles they had sent. But such confidence was particularly difficult to sell to the public, especially after recent dramatic demonstrations of Soviet duplicity that the administration had stressed for its own purposes. Even the CIA and DIA cautioned that Soviet statements on nuclear warheads "cannot be taken at face value."[10]

Some of the news stories proved remarkably accurate. As Khrushchev and Kennedy reached agreement on the withdrawal of the IL-28 bombers and the lifting of the quarantine on 20 November, the *New York Herald Tribune* published on its front page a story by the acclaimed correspondent Marguerite Higgins about the Lunas under the headline "More Cuba Missiles: We Reveal Castro Has A[tomic]-Artillery." In her article, Higgins described the capabilities of the Lunas and held that although the United States had no strong evidence of either the presence or absence of nuclear warheads in Cuba, "the presence of such missiles is taken to indicate that the warheads that give them their punch are probably on the island, too."[11] Higgins did not reveal her sources, but Russian documents confirm that her supposition on the presence of warheads was correct. At the time, however, the report was overshadowed by Kennedy's press conference later that day announcing the Soviet agreement to withdraw the IL-28s and the lifting of the U.S. naval quarantine.

There was also the matter of the thousands of Soviet troops in Cuba. In his press conference announcing the IL-28 deal, Kennedy pointed out that "Soviet ground combat units" were still in Cuba. He also stated that Khrushchev had said that those forces would be withdrawn "in due course," but the fact that they remained and the terms of their removal remained so vague gave further ammunition to the administration's critics.[12]

That Kennedy used the term "combat units" also seemed to confirm what some critics had been saying for some time. The distinction between "technicians" and combat troops had become more than a matter of semantics; it was now a politically sensitive point. Through the summer and fall, the White House had insisted that Soviets in Cuba were "technicians," while Republican critics called them "troops." The former implied that they their presence was benign. But as new information came in, the White House conceded that they were, in fact, heavily armed troops. Critics used that backtracking to charge that the White House had been blind to a threat that should have beeen taken seriously.

As the situation appeared on the verge of getting out of hand, besieged by partisan attacks and internal disagreements threatening to spill out into the open, Kennedy stole back the initiative by authorizing a publicity campaign that included the disclosure of an unprecedented amount of detailed intelligence information. This campaign was ultimately successful and had much to do with silencing the critics and rescuing the generally favorable impression of Kennedy's leadership that many people retained after the missile crisis.

IN EARLY FEBRUARY, word leaked out that Director of Central Intelligence John McCone, a Republican, had been warning since September that the Soviets might be installing medium-range ballistic missiles in Cuba. McCone based his warnings at the time on his belief that the Soviets would not install sophisticated SA-2 antiaircraft defenses in Cuba unless it was to protect long-range missile bases—a prediction the CIA had since concluded was wrong (more-recent revelations gleaned from former Soviet archives have also shown that that train of logic was flawed)—but Congressional Republicans jumped on apparent inconsistencies between what McCone's fall warnings and what other members of the administration with more dovish reputations had told Congress.

McCone posed an especially difficult problem for Kennedy. Despite his characteristically secret, ostensibly nonpartisan position, McCone remained active in Republican power circles, much more so than other nominal Republicans among Kennedy's advisers like Robert McNamara and McGeorge Bundy. A wealthy industrialist and former chairman of the Atomic Energy Commission in the Eisenhower administration, McCone came with useful political connections. In the wake of the disastrous Bay of Pigs episode, when Allen Dulles, a holdover from the Eisenhower administration (and former secretary of state John Foster Dulles's brother), was pushed out, McCone was brought in. Although he lacked intelligence experience, his appointment provided much-needed political cover against the inevitable criticism that the young, inexperienced Kennedy and his Democratic administration were jeopardizing the nation's security.

In the wake of the crisis, Kennedy, and especially his intensely loyal brother Robert, became suspicious that McCone did not have their best interests at heart. They suspected that the source of this particular leak, which implied that the Kennedys had turned a blind eye as the Soviets installed missiles in Cuba, was McCone himself.

On 5 February, the *Washington Post* ran the front-page headline "40 Missiles Reported Left in Cuba."[13] Reports also came through that one of the administration's most persistent critics on the Cuba issue, Senator Keating, was issuing statements that there were ten times the number of Soviet troops in Cuba. Semantically, Keating had a point. But Robert Kennedy worried that it created an unhelpful, and wrong, impression.

ROBERT KENNEDY: [Kenneth] Keating today said there are possibly ten times as many Russian troops in Cuba now than there were last July. Well, that's perhaps true but the dates really that he should be talking about are—

PRESIDENT KENNEDY: End of October.

ROBERT KENNEDY: —the end of October. And, I guess from your figures here that indicate that there were 22,000 troops, 15 to 22,000 troops on December 1 and now it's down to, February 1, to 17,000. So it indicates really that the troops are down rather than up—

MCNAMARA: That's right.

ROBERT KENNEDY: And yet he uses the first of July and, of course, that's misleading.

The president decided to end the speculation, rumor, and innuendo once and for all. To do so, he apparently drew lessons from the "missile gap" myth three years earlier, a controversy he and several senior members of the current administration had helped perpetuate and profited politically from. Even as the controversy built as the election neared, Eisenhower had flatly refused to confront the notion of a missile gap directly. Ample intelligence information, even photographs, was available that could dispel the idea completely. But Eisenhower was reluctant to divulge the source of that information: the new, highly classified U-2 surveillance plane. The result of Eisenhower's refusal to engage the topic in public was that Democrats had free rein to continue attacking the Eisenhower-Nixon record. Kennedy did not intend to make the same mistake. Whereas Eisenhower had prohibited the use of any intelligence information to quell the rumors, Kennedy was receptive to a proposal for transparency.

The proposal to do so came from McNamara. In an ExComm meeting on 5 February, he proposed a televised public briefing where he and General Joseph Carroll, the founding director of the Defense Intelligence Agency, would lay out in detail the intelligence information about what military forces had been in Cuba and what remained there. And, importantly, it could be prepared quickly because it could draw from the same pool of intelligence material that had been used by officials in their congressional briefings.

> There isn't very much that's classified in this material that we're telling the Congress. Some of it is very dramatic. The use of pictures and the description of some of the surveillance that was carrying on is quite gripping. I think both Mr. McCone's briefing and that of some of the Defense Intelligence Agency personnel could be used in either a news briefing or a TV program.[14]

McNamara, McCone, and other defense and intelligence officials had found their presentations in closed sessions before congressional committees to be very well received. It was likely, McNamara said, that a similar session would be very effective in a public setting.

> ROBERT MCNAMARA: We presented to the Armed Services Committee last week an hour long briefing that kept them on the edge of their chairs. It silenced them for several days at least.
>
> PRESIDENT KENNEDY: Yeah.
>
> MCNAMARA: And this was done by General [Joseph] Carroll and one of his photo interpreters, who I think does an absolutely magnificent job using color photographs and black and white photographs. It's nothing really very new but you leave with the impression that the surveillance effort has been extensive, and is extensive, and has disclosed all offensive weapons systems that might have existed on the island.[15]

In recent weeks, McNamara and other officials had delivered the core of the presentation several times to congressional committees. Much of it was already prepared and rehearsed, meaning that they could carry it out the next day. And it would be accompanied by a detailed, written statement by John McCone deemphasizing any apparent inconsistencies between his own statements and those of other government officials. Still, critics remained skeptical. Keating vowed to eat his hat in front of the Senate office building if the Pentagon claimed that all the missile sites had been bulldozed. He hoped Keating had a hat ready, McNamara joked.[16]

McNamara and John Hughes from the Defense Intelligence Agency, not Carroll, took the stage at the State Department Auditorium at 5 p.m. on 6 February. Television cameras were there to broadcast the special Cuba briefing nationally.

Armed with charts, facts and figures, and photographs, McNamara excelled at this kind of briefing. The two men projected dozens of surveillance photographs, most black-and-white but some color, on a large screen on the stage and provided detailed information about the capabilities of the military equipment and forces that had been in Cuba. To answer accusations that the administration had been negligent in its aerial surveillance of Cuba, McNamara revealed that since 1 July, U.S. military aircraft had conducted over four hundred reconnaissance flights over Cuba. Hughes showed before-and-after photographs of the missile sites. They showed photographs of the tactics the Soviets employed to hide equipment from the low-level surveillance flights, measures that included covering missiles with palm fronds or tarpaulins smeared with mud or paint to disguise the visual shape of the cylindrical object beneath. They showed photographs of weapons systems arriving in Cuba and later departing, construction crews building the concrete bunkers storing nuclear weapons, truck convoys transporting equipment away from the sites and toward the shipping docks, and cleanup crews bulldozing the former missile sites.

For two hours, McNamara and Hughes discussed, in detail, the issue of the Soviet combat forces that remained. They provided specific numbers of Soviet and Cuban weaponry along with high- and low-level surveillance photos. They showed photographs of Luna missile launchers, coastal defense missile installations, and most of the other weapons systems of which there were verifiable surveillance photographs. They answered reporters' questions. McNamara assured Americans that, "beyond any reasonable doubt," all Soviet offensive weapons has been removed from Cuba.[17] The reaction to the event was mostly positive. It had addressed many of the critics' core complaints with an avalanche of information and dispelled notions that the administration was trying to hide something. Criticism was muted. Tom Wicker of the *New York Times* saw the performance for what it was: a "hard sell" effort designed to head off domestic political criticism and to prevent Republican critics from hijacking the national security agenda.[18] John Norris, a columnist of the *Washington Post*, observed that McNamara "may have helped convince millions of Americans unversed in the complexities of the situation that there is a powerful Russian bastion 90 miles off the US coast."[19]

There was also some internal criticism. Some of the photographs and information had already appeared in various news accounts in recent weeks, but in the course of the briefing, McNamara and Hughes went into a level of detail that had previously been reserved for classified briefings. The CIA, piqued at the starring role being played by the Pentagon's new intelligence agency, criticized the DIA for disclosing too much about intelligence sources and methods and for being sloppy with factual information.[20] McNamara defended the disclosures. The public interest was so great, he argued, that he was compelled to disclose the information "even at the risk of degrading our intelligence collection capabilities."[21]

Kennedy followed up the next day by facing reporters himself. His press conference on 24 January had been less than effective in quieting the growing chorus of criticism. This time, coming on the heels of McNamara's briefing, his assurances that the administration had the situation well in hand were bolstered. But he still had to walk a fine line between confidence that all the offensive weapons had been removed and acknowledgment that some important matters remained to be resolved. "There still is a body of Soviet military equipment and technicians which I think is of serious concern to this Government and the hemisphere," he admitted, while pointing out that "there has not been an addition since the removal of the weapons, there has not been an addition and there has been the subtraction of that number of personnel." He said that he was still trying to draw from Khrushchev an assurance that these forces would be withdrawn "in due course." "We do not view that threat lightly," he warned. But he also expressed frustration with congressional and press critics who sounded increasingly shrill alarms. He urged members of those groups "to keep a sense of proportion about the size of the force we're talking about."[22]

Ultimately, the administration's new tactic of increased transparency proved remarkably successful, but not before critics mounted another attack. Keating backed away from his hat-eating vow by claiming that McNamara had "failed to answer satisfactorily any of the questions [he] challenged him to answer." Keating, along with four other leading congressional critics of the administration's Cuba policy—Thurmond, Representative William C. Cramer (Republican of Florida), Representative H. R. Gross (Republican of Iowa), and Representative Armistead Selden Jr. (Democrat of Alabama)—responded to McNamara's briefing by staging their own televised news conference on 8 February. They accused McNamara of deliberately playing down the implications of the continuing Soviet military presence in Cuba. They said that even the so-called defensive forces remaining could be a menace by enabling the Soviets to sneak in offensive weapons. Each carefully insisted, however, that he was not advocating direct military action.[23] Separately, the two early favorites for the Republican 1964 nomination also weighed in. Governor Nelson Rockefeller said that Cuba remained a serious threat to the United States, and Senator Barry Goldwater accused the administration of "a self-defeating policy of objecting only to 'offensive' weapons," a policy that left Cuba as too much of an ongoing threat.[24]

The administration faced two final political challenges. The first was to explain the apparent inconsistencies between the public statements of McNamara and McCone. One of the key points of contention was the significance of the remaining Soviet ground forces. McNamara tended toward optimism on the subject; McCone was more pessimistic. The CIA specifically identified McNamara's public implications that the deployment of Luna rockets was diminishing in size: "We think Mr. McNamara is basing his 'lessening' on a very slender reed," the CIA rebutted.[25] Bundy gathered McNamara, McCone, and Rusk together at the White House on 19 February to try to smooth over the differences and establish a set of guidelines for how to discuss the Cuba issue in public and in closed sessions on the Hill. At that meeting, according to Bundy's memorandum of the conversation, they agreed that the public line on apparent discrepancies on some of the most provocative of the military forces (MiGs, submarine bases, and Lunas) should be explained as differences in personal opinion rather than any fundamental disagreement.[26]

The second challenge was to defuse criticism emanating from Senator Keating and others. Keating had been a political thorn in the administration's side since the fall, when he started making sensational public claims that the Soviets were setting up nuclear missile bases in Cuba. The administration had tried, unsuccessfully, to refute those claims at the time by challenging Keating to reveal his sources and share whatever information he had with the CIA. In the details, Keating was probably mistaken; he was most likely basing his claims on reports by Cuban émigrés that they had seen SA-2 antiaircraft missiles, weapons that were large and advanced and looked to the untrained eye as if they might be nuclear missiles. But Keating's core contention proved correct—the Soviets were in fact installing missile bases in Cuba—and it bolstered his public credibility immensely. Kennedy and Bundy even joked about it. At one point in the post-crisis negotiations, before it was clear what Soviet intentions were, there seemed a very real risk that word might get out that the Soviets were installing a nuclear submarine base in Cuba, a rumor that would cause a major political headache for the administration.

THEODORE SORENSEN: Particularly since Keating asked us two weeks ago.

PRESIDENT KENNEDY: Why?

SORENSEN: He heard it was true and wanted to know if it was.

PRESIDENT KENNEDY: It probably is then. [*laughter*]

BUNDY: The advance guard of the [Central Intelligence] Agency rides again![27]

To convey to the public the impression that the administration took Keating seriously, even as its members continued to privately to treat him as a political nuisance and not a source of reliable information, John McCone agreed to meet with the senator so that Keating would have the opportunity to convey the information he claimed to have.[28] Keating asserted that more missiles and more troops remained in Cuba than the administration had acknowledged; rather than the 17,000 to 22,000 Soviet troops the administration claimed had been in Cuba, Keating said, there had been 35,000 to 40,000, a range that was remarkably accurate (the number is now known to have been over 42,000). But Keating also made claims that were off the mark or distorted: that the Soviets had actually sent eighty medium-range missiles, half of which remained; that the four armored units in Cuba each consisted of 4,000 men, rather than the 1,500 claimed by the administration; and that there were continued reports of radioactive material arriving in Cuba on Soviet ships.[29] Moreover, Keating told McCone that he had information that nuclear warheads for Lunas were being hidden in caves, a charge that government experts could only rebut by pointing out that storing such delicate equipment in caves would be "unduly hazardous and inconvenient" when more suitable storage bunkers were available.[30] But in the wake of McNamara's 6 February special press conference, Keating's accusations sounded increasingly desperate, and his charges failed to gain further traction.

Although the Cuba issue did not completely disappear, this wave of criticism proved to be the last serious, sustained congressional attack on the Kennedy administration's handling of the Cuban missile crisis.

Despite Armistead Selden's efforts to keep the Cuba debate alive by having the House Foreign Affairs Subcommittee on Latin America hold hearings, Congress generally moved on to other issues.[31] The Stennis committee, the most influential of the congressional groups investigating Cuba-related issues, issued its mildly critical report in early May before turning to the "What now?" question.[32] In April, with Soviet troops still in Cuba, Richard Nixon attacked the administration for allowing a "Soviet beachhead" in Cuba and giving the Soviets "squatters' rights in our own backyard," reviving Keating's precrisis charges that the White House had adopted a "look-the-other-way policy" to the military buildup in Cuba.[33] Keating himself even went so far as to propose a fourteen-point program of sanctions and economic pressure to compel the Soviets to remove the remaining weapons and troops from Cuba, a proposal that failed to gain traction.

The political crisis was finally defused, but the issue of Soviet troops in Cuba was never solved.

During a meeting with Rusk on 18 February, the Soviet ambassador to the United States, Anatoly Dobrynin, handed the secretary of state a missive from the Kremlin on the subject of the Soviet troops in Cuba. The document went out of its way to emphasize that Moscow was making special efforts to be responsive to Kennedy's requests and sensitive to the political difficulties that the troops were creating for him on Capitol Hill. As an act of good will, it said, the Soviet government "had decided to withdraw from Cuba the Soviet military personnel having to do with guarding the kinds of weapons which were removed from Cuba and also certain military specialists who were occupied in training Cuban military cadres. It is intended to recall from Cuba in the near future—before the middle of March—several thousand men." It did not say how many or what kinds of troops the Soviets were leaving there. Importantly, it also did not say how many would stay.[34]

If the issue became less urgent, it nevertheless did not disappear. The CIA kept close watch; through at least the end of March, the agency reported on the current status of Soviet troops in Cuba on an almost daily basis. At a meeting with Andrei Gromyko in the Oval Office on 10 October 1963, almost precisely a year since their last meeting there, when Gromyko had denied that the Soviets were deploying nuclear missiles in Cuba, Kennedy cited the removal of some troops as a reason to be encouraged about the prospects of East–West détente. "You've taken some of your troops out Cuba, so it's less of a problem for us here. That's some progress," Kennedy told the Soviet foreign minister. And on November 18, just days before his assassination, Kennedy spoke publicly of "unfinished business in Cuba."[35]

Had Kennedy decided to make the troops more of an issue in 1963, evidence suggests that he would have had the American people on his side. Asked in a September 1963 Harris poll whether "Kennedy should insist that the Russians remove their troops from Cuba or not," 77 percent of those surveyed responded that Kennedy should insist, 12 percent were unsure, and 11 percent said he should not insist. Those results were fairly predictable; more remarkable were the follow-up questions on what action the administration should take if the Soviet troops were not withdrawn. To the question "If the Russians do not remove their troops from Cuba, do you think we should put back the blockade on Cuba or not?" 67 percent responded that they should, 13 percent that they should not, and 20 percent that they were undecided. More striking still was the response to the question "If the Russians do not remove their troops from Cuba, do you think we should invade Cuba with American troops or not?" 34 percent called for invasion, 35 percent said should not invade, and 31 percent were undecided. Almost a year after the Cuban missile crisis, then, a significant portion of voters still supported military action in Cuba.[36]

After February 1963, the Cuba controversy cooled in the American domestic political debate, and U.S.-Soviet relations increasingly moved away from moments of crisis toward détente. International arms control measures, including the Partial Test Ban Treaty and, later, the Nuclear Non-Proliferation Treaty, were signed. American policymakers found more and more of their time devoted to the deteriorating situation in Southeast Asia, and the Soviets faced growing competition from China for leadership of the Communist world. But the Cuba issue never disappeared; debris from the missile crisis continued to clutter international relations for years. The missile crisis cast a long shadow over Soviet-Cuban relations, which were never the same again.[37] Cuba remained a persistent thorn in U.S.-Soviet relations, with periodic spikes in tension through the late 1960s and late 1970s as Fidel Castro's government sponsored and encouraged communist subversion in Africa and Latin America. There were scares in the United States from time to time, often sparked by domestic politics, that the Soviets were once again building up their military base in Cuba.

Those fears reached a climax again in October 1979, when President Jimmy Carter faced a full-fledged political crisis over the issue. News reports had picked up the story that the CIA had "dissevered" a brigade of about 2,600 Soviet combat troops in Cuba. The disclosure, first made by Senator Frank Church, a Democrat involved in a tough reelection fight, created a political firestorm for the Carter administration.[38] At the height of that crisis, McGeorge Bundy wrote an op-ed article in the *New York Times* claiming responsibility for the presence of Soviet troops in Cuba and explaining that the seeds of the controversy lay in decisions taken in the aftermath of the missile crisis. Bundy wrote that after the "offensive weapons" were removed, the ongoing presence of Soviet troops in Cuba ceased to be a priority for the administration and the intelligence community. He noted that the Kennedy and Johnson administrations had known about the remaining Soviet ground forces, debated the nature of the risk, and decided that a few thousand Soviet troops in Cuba posed no meaningful threat to the United States or other countries in the region.[39]

16

Shaping the Future

It was 10 June 1963, hot and sunny, ninety-six degrees in the shade. The graduates—991 of them—sweltered in their black robes, which soaked up the sun's rays. Some spectators sought relief under the trees on the field's periphery; as a result, thousands of seats that had been set out in the middle of the athletic field remained empty. But members of the Marine Corps Band in their dress uniforms, university officials and faculty in their academic robes, and President Kennedy, temporarily donning dark academic robes over his suit, had no respite from the broiling sun.

As Kennedy became the third president of the United States to receive an honorary degree from American University, in Washington, D.C., he called for that loftiest of goals: world peace.[1] "I speak of peace because of the new face of war," Kennedy said. Disavowing the notion of a Pax Americana, a peace enforced by military might, he drew implicitly on the recent nuclear scare over Cuba.

> Total war makes no sense in an age when great powers can maintain large and relatively invulnerable nuclear forces and refuse to surrender without resort to those forces. It makes no sense in an age when a single nuclear weapon contains almost ten times the

> explosive force delivered by all of the allied air forces in the Second World War. It makes no sense in an age when the deadly poisons produced by a nuclear exchange would be carried by wind and water and soil and seed to the far corners of the globe and to generations yet unborn.

He called on Americans to find common ground with the people of the Soviet Union. He spoke of the need for practical, achievable progress. He urged reallocating resources from developing ever more deadly weapons to solving humanity's common ills. "Peace need not be impracticable," he said, "and war need not be inevitable."

It was not the first time a statesman had called for world peace, but Kennedy's "peace speech," as it became known, proved pitch perfect and resonated unusually strongly. Even Khrushchev was impressed. It was, he said, "the greatest speech by any American President since [Franklin] Roosevelt."[2] The peace speech would be remembered along with Kennedy's inaugural address as one of the great speeches of the era. And it owed its resonance to the Cuban missile crisis.

It was an extraordinary period. The next day, 11 June, George Wallace, the governor of Alabama, stood in a schoolhouse door, symbolically trying to block the desegregation of Alabama schools. Kennedy's speech in response that night gave momentum to the passage of the nation's most comprehensive civil rights legislation, the core of what one historian notably called the "Second Reconstruction."[3] Just over a fortnight later, Kennedy delivered another oratory masterpiece in Berlin best remembered for his declaration, in halting German, "Ich bin ein Berliner." Not quite six weeks after that, the United States, the United Kingdom, and the Soviet Union signed in Moscow a long-sought treaty imposing limits on nuclear testing. Together, these moments demonstrated that the cold war was changing. Instead of being punctuated by nuclear crises over West Berlin and Cuba and territorial claims in East Asia, the nature of the confrontation was in the process of shifting. In its place came an increased emphasis on combating revolutionary and nationalist movements in Southeast

Asia and communist subversion in Latin America and Africa. Détente did not bring peace, exactly, but the threat of global thermonuclear annihilation came to dominate world affairs less. At least for a time.

Khrushchev himself became a casualty of this change. The Soviet leader who was so closely identified with shoe-banging tantrums and nuclear brinkmanship never escaped the humiliation he suffered from his great gamble gone awry. His performance during those weeks and months was used by his political enemies as a key piece of evidence in the Presidium's case against him. In October 1964, he was deposed and removed from power, forced into retirement with a modest pension.[4]

By the middle of summer 1963, it was finally looking more like the kind of presidency Kennedy had hoped for.

Kennedy did not intend to be a one-term president. If the New Frontier was to live up to his lofty and ambitious promises, he would need a second term and a more cooperative Congress. Having decided early in his political career that starting a campaign early was an important key to success, Kennedy was already looking ahead to the 1964 election. Through 1963, some difficult issues succumbed to "perhaps after the election" thinking. Most notable among these was the issue of Vietnam, where Kennedy's decision making was characterized by pragmatism and efforts to maintain maximum room to maneuver. Whether such an approach might ultimately have avoided the disaster that was to come is one of history's great "what if" questions.

It was clear in 1963 that the JFK in the 1964 campaign would be a formidable candidate. Many of Kennedy's rough edges had been painstakingly refined during 1959 and 1960, and by 1963 some had even been polished into benefits. In place of the uncharismatic, monotone speaker who had started his first national campaign in 1959 was someone who now appeared for all the world a naturally gifted speaker. His inaugural address had been a masterpiece and gone down in the annals of great oratory. Much of the reason for that was the stirring and lofty rhetoric penned mostly by his loyal and gifted speechwriter, Ted Sorensen. But the words were nothing without someone to deliver them convincingly. Kennedy had learned that art, had worked closely with Sorensen to develop not just the message but also the voice. And that, combined with the natural amplification afforded by being able to speak from a presidential podium, would be a valuable asset in '64. The campaigner who was looking ahead to '64 was now not just comfortable in public but also naturally witty, charming, and imbued with the confidence that came from having delivered some of the great speeches of the century. Instead of having constantly to fight to be heard—as in 1960—he now had his every word endlessly dissected and disseminated by the Washington press corps and spread through the nation's newspapers. That, of course, carried its own risks, especially after Kennedy's battles with the press.

Other weak spots had faded as well. The issue of his religion, which had caused his campaign team such concern in 1960, had largely dissipated, as Kennedy demonstrated that he was not, in fact, being directed by the Vatican, as some of his more extreme critics had initially suggested. Likewise, suspicions in the Democratic establishment about the machinations of Joe Kennedy were no longer a viable line of attack for challengers. The Kennedy family patriarch had been rendered largely incapacitated by a massive stroke in 1961 that left him speechless beyond monosyllabic responses. But even before that, as president, Kennedy had emerged from his father's shadow, had demonstrated to the doubters that he was not some puppet with his father as puppeteer.

Joe's money would again help, but as Kennedy had pointed out in the dictation recording he made before becoming president, money could both help and hinder. Through early 1963, Kennedy anticipated that Governor Nelson Rockefeller of New York would be the Republican nominee. If that was how it shaped up, vast amounts of money would likely be spent as the campaigns on both sides tapped into immense family fortunes. Instead, Rockefeller put his personal life ahead of his political life, opening the way for Senator Barry Goldwater of Arizona to emerge as the favorite.

No challenger could aim to decisively outspend the Kennedy campaign or count on missteps from the candidate himself. But the reelection campaign would by no means be easy. Having peaked in the wake of the Cuban missile crisis, Kennedy's poll numbers were again sliding. By November 1963, his approval rating remained high in comparison with that of other presidents, but had nevertheless fallen to the lowest level of his presidency. This decline came despite steady economic growth through the year that had defied the gloomy forecasts of pundits. For Kennedy to turn that slide in public support around, he would have to move the debate to his record and his policies. Because of that, Kennedy spent increasing amounts of time addressing both.

Just as Robert Kennedy intended to cite the Cuban missile crisis to bolster his credentials in the 1968 campaign, an intention manifested in the book *Thirteen Days*, it was likely that John Kennedy and his political team would use the episode in his 1964 campaign. Despite critics' charges, there is little evidence that Kennedy's decisions during the crisis were influenced by partisan concerns or, as even harsher critics sometimes asserted, that he cultivated the showdown for political gain. But with the crisis past, the episode spoke directly to his record as president.

Kennedy's handling of the Cuban missile crisis resonated favorably with voters. It was a lasting impression. Over a decade later, a Harris poll found that a majority of Americans saw his handling of that crisis as a "proud moment" in American history.[5] Abroad, Kennedy had confronted the Soviets and forced them to retreat. At home, he had thwarted efforts by critics to depict the crisis as a Kennedy failure. As he looked to 1964, the Cuban missile crisis appeared to provide a promising pivot point for his presidency.

ACKNOWLEDGMENTS

I owe an enormous debt to my colleagues at the Miller Center's Presidential Recordings Program, past and present. In particular, Tim Naftali and Philip Zelikow have been extraordinarily helpful and supportive in many, many ways over the years. Their historical curiosity and pioneering efforts, along with Ernest May, in working with the Kennedy tapes has been essential to my own efforts in trying to unravel the puzzles buried in this especially difficult medium of historical evidence. Marc Selverstone, Kent Germany, Guian McKee, Dave Shreve, Ken Hughes, Erin Mahan, Max Holland, Paul Pitman, and Frank Gavin have all contributed in some important way to aspects of this book and the underlying research and ideas from which it draws (although any errors, of course, remain my own). And our dedicated staff and interns make our work possible; I particularly want to thank Pat Dunn, Kerry O'Brien, Susan Dunham, and Keri Matthews.

Since 1998, the University of Virginia's Miller Center, under the leadership first of Philip Zelikow and then Gerald Baliles, has provided a remarkable institutional home for the kind of deep historical inquiry that working with the tapes requires. And being part of a community of first-rate scholars has made for an especially invigorating scholarly environment in which to research and write.

Over the course of my research I have had the pleasure of working in many archives here and abroad, and I thank the many archivists who have helped in one way or another. At the John F. Kennedy Library, Maura Porter has spent countless hours listening to the tapes, preparing them for public release. It is painstaking and difficult work, and important. Anyone working with the Kennedy tapes is in her debt. At the Johnson Library, where scholars can find much useful and unique material related to the Kennedy administration, Regina Greenwell has been especially helpful in identifying useful documents. The Reading Room, reference, and audio visual staff at both libraries, along with their colleagues in College Park, do the National Archives much credit.

I'm also thankful to the National Historical Publications and Records Commission for their essential work in funding historical documentary editing. The NHPRC did not fund work on this book directly, but it did fund work on transcription and annotation of the tapes, a treasure trove of new historical evidence; this book draws heavily from only a small portion of that material. Thanks in large part to funding provided by the NHPRC, those transcriptions will be published fully in forthcoming print volumes and digital editions.

Working with Drake McFeely and Jeff Shreve at W. W. Norton & Company has been an absolute pleasure, and I have very much appreciated their ideas, editing, encouragement, and, not least, patience.

Finally, I would like to thank Kate for her boundless support, patience, and good humor.

Notes

NOTE ON TRANSCRIPTS

This book makes extensive use of excerpts of published and unpublished transcripts of conversations on Kennedy's White House tapes. The following three volumes of transcripts, spanning the period 30 July through 28 October 1962, have been published:

The Presidential Recordings: John F. Kennedy: The Great Crises, vol. 1, *July 30–August 1962*, ed. Timothy Naftali (New York: W. W. Norton, 2001)

The Presidential Recordings: John F. Kennedy: The Great Crises, vol. 2, *September–October 21, 1962*, ed. Timothy Naftali and Philip Zelikow (New York: W. W. Norton, 2001)

The Presidential Recordings: John F. Kennedy: The Great Crises, vol. 3, *October 22–28, 1962*, ed. Philip Zelikow and Ernest May (New York: W. W. Norton, 2001)

Additional transcripts, identified in these notes by the conversation title and date, will appear in three forthcoming volumes:

The Presidential Recordings: John F. Kennedy: The Winds of Change, vol. 4, *October 29–November 7, 1962*, ed. David Coleman (New York: W. W. Norton, 2014)

The Presidential Recordings: John F. Kennedy: The Winds of Change, vol. 5, *November 8, 1962–November 29, 1962*, ed. David Coleman and Timothy Naftali (New York: W. W. Norton, 2014)

The Presidential Recordings: John F. Kennedy: The Winds of Change, vol. 6, *December 5, 1962–February 11, 1963*, ed. David Coleman and Marc Selverstone (New York: W. W. Norton, 2014)

ABBREVIATIONS

FRUS	*Foreign Relations of the United States*
JCS	Joint Chiefs of Staff
JFKL	John F. Kennedy Library and Museum, Boston, Massachusetts
LBJL	Lyndon Baines Johnson Library and Museum, Austin, Texas
Pres. Recordings: JFK	*The Presidential Recordings: John F. Kennedy: The Great Crises*, ed. Timothy Naftali, Philip Zelikow, and Ernest May, 3 vols. (New York: W. W. Norton, 2001)
Public Papers: JFK	*Public Papers of the Presidents: John F. Kennedy*, 3 vols. (Washington, D.C.: Government Printing Office, 1962–64)

PREFACE TO THE PAPERBACK EDITION

1 David M. Barrett and Max Holland, *Blind Over Cuba: The Photo Gap and the Missile Crisis* (College Station: Texas A&M Press, 2012).

2 Sergo Mikoyan, *The Soviet Cuban Missile Crisis: Castro, Mikoyan, Kennedy, Khrushchev, and the Missiles of November*, ed. Svetlana Savranskaya (Stanford: Stanford University Press, 2012). For an earlier, less detailed account, see Aleksandr Fursenko and Timothy Naftali, *"One Hell of a Gamble": Khrushchev, Castro, and Kennedy, 1958–1964* (New York: W. W. Norton, 1997), 290–315.

3 David R. Gibson, *Talk at the Brink: Deliberation and Decision During the Cuban Missile Crisis* (Princeton: Princeton University Press, 2012).

4 Sheldon Stern, *The Cuban Missile Crisis in American Memory: Myths Versus Reality* (Stanford: Stanford University Press, 2012).

5 National Security Archive, "Pentagon Estimated 18,500 U.S. Casualties in Cuba Invasion 1962, But If Nukes Launched, 'Heavy Losses' Expected," 16 Oct. 2012, http://www.gwu.edu/~nsarchiv/NSAEBB/NSAEBB397/.

6 "Minutes of Conversation between the Delegations of the CPCz and the CPSU at the Kremlin," 30 October 1962, in James G. Hershberg and Christian F. Osterman, eds., *Cold War International History Project Bulletin*, No. 17/18 (Fall 2012): 400–403.

7 Marjorie Connelly, "Americans are Still Voting for J.F.K.," *New York Times*, 16 Aug. 1996.

8 Harold Macmillan, "Queen's Speech," 30 Oct. 1962, Commons Sitting, Hansard, Series 5, Volume 666, c. 40.

PREFACE

1 Lydia Saad, "Kennedy Still Highest-Rated Modern President, Nixon Lowest," Gallup, 6 Dec. 2010, http://www.gallup.com/poll/145064/kennedy-highest-rated-modern-president-nixon-lowest.aspx; James D. King, "Looking Back at Chief Executives: Retrospective Presidential Approval," *Presidential Studies Quarterly* 29, no. 1 (March 1999): 166–74.

2 Robert F. Kennedy, *Thirteen Days* (New York: W. W. Norton, 1969); David Self, *Thirteen Days*, dir. Roger Donaldson (New Line Cinema, 2000).

3 Jeffrey M. Jones, "Despite Recent Lows, Bush Approval Average Is Midrange," Gallup, 5 Jan. 2009, http://www.gallup.com/poll/113641/despite-recent-lows-bush-approval-average-midrange.aspx.

4 Quoted in Hugh Sidey, *John F. Kennedy, President* (New York: Atheneum, 1963), 315.

5 Ibid., 321.

6 Philip Zelikow and Ernest May, preface to *Pres. Recordings: JFK*, 1:xvii–xxiv.

7 Dean Rusk, *As I Saw It*, ed. Daniel S. Papp (New York: W. W. Norton, 1990), 559.

8 Ernest May and Philip Zelikow, eds., *The Kennedy Tapes: Inside the White House during the Cuban Missile Crisis*, concise ed. (New York: W. W. Norton, 2001).

9 Meeting on the Defense Budget, 5 Dec. 1962.

10 Meeting on the NASA Budget, 21 Nov. 1962.

1: THE ULTIMATE SOURCE OF ACTION

1 Robert Dallek, "The Medical Ordeals of JFK," *Atlantic Monthly*, Dec. 2002, pp. 49–61.

2 Alexsandr Fursenko and Timothy Naftali, *"One Hell of a Gamble": Khrushchev, Castro, and Kennedy, 1958–1964* (New York: W. W. Norton, 1997).

3 Aleksandr Fursenko and Timothy Naftali, *Khrushchev's Cold War: The Inside Story of an American Adversary* (New York: W. W. Norton, 2006).

4 State Department, "Briefing Book for the President's Meeting with Khrushchev, Vienna, June 3–4, 1961," 25 May 1961, National Archives, box 27, Bohlen Papers, RG 59.

5 Aleksandr Fursenko and Timothy Naftali, *Khrushchev's Cold War: The Inside Story of an American Adversary* (New York: W. W. Norton, 2006).

6 Reproduced in *Pres. Recordings: JFK*, 2:80.

7 See Ernest May and Philip Zelikow, *The Kennedy Tapes: Inside the White House during the Cuban Missile Crisis*, concise ed. (New York: W. W. Norton, 2002).

8 "Radio and Television Report to the American People on the Soviet Arms Buildup in Cuba," 22 Oct. 1962, *Public Papers: JFK, 1962*, doc. 485.

9 Proclamation 3504 "Interdiction of the Delivery of Offensive Weapons to Cuba," 23 Oct. 1962, *Public Papers: JFK, 1962*, doc. 486.

10 For accounts of the thirteen days of the Cuban missile crisis, see Ernest May and Philip Zelikow, eds., *The Kennedy Tapes: Inside the White*

House During the Cuban Missile Crisis, concise edition (New York: W. W. Norton, 2001); Aleksandr Fursenko and Timothy Naftali, *"One Hell of a Gamble": Khrushchev, Castro, and Kennedy, 1958–1964* (New York: W. W. Norton, 1997); Michael Dobbs, *One Minute to Midnight: Kennedy, Khrushchev, and Castro on the Brink of Nuclear War* (New York: Alfred A. Knopf, 2008); and Robert F. Kennedy, *Thirteen Days: A Memoir of the Cuban Missile Crisis* (New York: W. W. Norton, 1969).

2: THE FOURTEENTH DAY

1 "Address and Question and Answer Period in Tampa before the Florida Chamber of Commerce," 18 Nov. 1963, *Public Papers: JFK, 1963*, doc. 465.

2 Khrushchev to Kennedy, 27 Oct. 1962, *FRUS, 1961–1963*, 11:258; Khrushchev to Kennedy, 28 Oct. 1962, ibid., 279.

3 Meeting of the ExComm, 29 Oct. 1962.

4 Meeting of the ExComm, 1 Nov. 1962.

5 Meeting with the JCS, 16 Nov. 1962.

6 Meeting of the ExComm, 29 Oct. 1962.

7 For "demonologists," see Meeting on the Soviet Union, 29 Sept. 1962, *Pres. Recordings: JFK*, 2:185; and Meeting on the Cuban Missile Crisis, 16 Oct. 1962, ibid., 459.

8 Meeting with Military Chiefs, 29 Oct. 1962.

9 Ibid.

10 Informal Conversation, 29 Oct. 1962.

11 Informal Discussion, 29 Oct. 1962.

12 Meeting of the ExComm, 29 Oct. 1962.

13 Ibid.

14 Ibid.

15 Ibid.

16 Khrushchev to Kennedy, 27 Oct. 1962, *FRUS, 1961–1963*, 11:258; Khrushchev to Kennedy, 28 Oct. 1962, ibid., 279.

3: EYES IN THE SKY

1 Meeting of the ExComm, 29 Oct. 1962.

2 Ibid.

3 Meeting of the ExComm, 2 Nov. 1962.

4 Aleksandr Fursenko and Timothy Naftali, *"One Hell of a Gamble": Khrushchev, Castro, and Kennedy, 1958–1964* (New York: W. W. Norton, 1997), 177–78; CIA/ORR, "Cuba 1962: Khrushchev's Miscalculated Risk," 13 Feb. 1964, LBJL, NSF, Country File, Cuba, box 35.

5 *Time*, 7 Dec. 1962, p. 14.

6 Meeting of the ExComm, 29 Oct. 1962; "Over Cuba: Flak at 11 o'clock," *Time*, 16 Nov. 1962.

7 Meeting of the ExComm, 29 Oct. 1962.

4: THE POSTMORTEM SEASON

1 Stewart Alsop and Charles Bartlett, "In Time of Crisis," *Saturday Evening Post*, 8 Dec. 1962, pp. 15–20.

2 Tom W. Smith, "The Cuban Missile Crisis and U.S. Public Opinion," *Public Opinion Quarterly* 67, no. 2 (Summer 2003): 280.

3 Fletcher Knebel, "Washington in Crisis: 154 Hours on the Brink of War," *Look*, 18 Dec. 1962, pp. 42–44, 49–50, 52, 54; Alsop and Bartlett, "In Time of Crisis," 15–20.

4 Max Frankel, "Air Attack on Cuban Bases Was Seriously Considered," *New York Times*, 30 Oct. 1962, p. 1.

5 Hanson W. Baldwin, "An Intelligence Gap," *New York Times*, 31 Oct. 1962, p. 19.

6 Ibid.

7 *New York Herald Tribune*, 2 Nov. 1962; Meeting of the ExComm, 2 Nov. 1962.

8 Meeting of the ExComm, 30 Oct. 1962.

9 Ibid.

5: MOCKINGBIRD DON'T SING

1 Benjamin C. Bradlee, *Conversations with Kennedy* (New York: W. W. Norton, 1975).

2 Evelyn Lincoln, *My Twelve Years with John F. Kennedy* (New York: David McKay, 1965), 6.

3 Fletcher Knebel, "Kennedy vs. the Press," *Look*, 28 Aug. 1962, pp. 17–21.

4 Ibid., p. 18.

5 Pierre Salinger, *With Kennedy* (Garden City, N.Y.: Doubleday, 1966), 117; Lincoln, *My Twelve Years with John F. Kennedy*, 6.

6 Knebel, "Kennedy vs. the Press," 20. See also Chalmers Roberts, "Image and Reality," in *The Kennedy Presidency: Seventeen Intimate Perspectives of John F. Kennedy*, ed. Kenneth W. Thompson (Lanham, Md.: University Press of America, 1985), 181–83.

7 Bradlee, *Conversations with Kennedy*. 23.

8 James N. Giglio, *The Presidency of John F. Kennedy*, 2nd ed., rev. (Lawrence: University Press of Kansas, 2006), 278.

9 Robert Dallek, *An Unfinished Life: John F. Kennedy, 1917–1963* (New York: Little, Brown, 2003), 498–99.

10 Hanson Baldwin Oral History, interviewed by John T. Mason, U.S. Naval Institute, 1976, 750–51.

11 Ibid.

12 Associated Press, "Political Use of the FBI Dates Back to the 1940s," *Chicago Tribune*, 4 Dec. 1975, p. 3; Nicholas M. Horrock, "F.B.I. Is Accused of Political Attacks for 6 Presidents," *New York Times*, 4 Dec. 1975, p. 85; Laurence Stern, "FBI Misuse since '30s Is Outlined," *Washington Post*, 4 Dec. 1975, p. A1.

13 Ronald Ostrow, "FBI Data Challenged by Katzenbach, Ramsey Clark," *Los Angeles Times*, 4 Dec. 1975, p. B1.

14 George E. Sokolsky, "Leaks and Censorship," *Washington Post*, 8 Nov. 1962, p. A25.

15 *Pres. Recordings: JFK*, 1:187; Knebel, "Kennedy vs. the Press," 20.

16 Hanson W. Baldwin, "Soviet Missiles Protected in 'Hardened' Positions," *New York Times*, 26 July 1962, p. 1.

17 Ibid., 1–2.

18 President Eisenhower's Topics, undated, Eisenhower Library, Ann Whitman File, Transition Series, box 1, President Eisenhower's Copies & Topics Suggested by Mr. Kennedy; Tim Weiner, *Legacy of Ashes: The History of the CIA* (New York: Doubleday, 2007), 167.

19 PFIAB's full roster during Kennedy's presidency consisted of Dr. James Killian, Clark Gifford, Benjamin Fairless, Adm. Richard Connolly, Lt. Gen. James Doolittle, Gen. John Hull, Robert Lovett, Edward Ryerson, Colgate Darden, William Baker, William Langer, Robert Murphy, Edwin Land, Gen. Maxwell Taylor, Gordon Gray, and Franklin Pace.

20 Clark Clifford, with Richard Holbrooke, *Counsel to the President* (New York: Random House, 1991), 352.

21 *Pres. Recordings: JFK*, 1:189.

22 Ibid., 192.

23 Baldwin Oral History, 750.

24 *Pres. Recordings: JFK*, 1:192.

25 Ibid., 196.

26 Timothy Naftali's research led to this finding. Ibid., 444 n. 2. It was a suspicion also voiced by Robert Kennedy in a 1964 oral history interview.

27 Ibid., 597.

28 Ibid., 197.

29 Ibid., 598.

30 Ibid., 598–99.

31 Howard J. [excised] to Executive Secretary, CIA Management Committee, "Family Jewels," 16 May 1973, CIA FOIA Electronic Reading Room, http://www.foia.cia.gov.

32 In his memorandum, Elder put the date at 7 March 1962. It is likely that he was referring to the March 1963 operations against Scott and Allen,

but it is possible that he was referring to another, undisclosed operation. Walter Elder to William E. Colby, "Special Activities," 1 June 1973, "Family Jewels," CIA FOIA Electronic Reading Room, http://www.foia.cia.gov.

33 Robert S. Allen and Paul Scott, "McNamara Admits New Policies Will Create Missile Gap by 1966," *Los Angeles Times*, 26 Feb. 1962, p. 2; idem, "President Weighs Plan to Carry War to Reds in South-Vietnam," ibid., 1 Feb. 1963, p. A5; idem, "U.S. Navy Patrol Planes Reported 'Buzzed' by Cuban-Based Aircraft," ibid., 1 March 1963, p. A5; idem, "Castro Uses Ransom on Subversion," ibid., 26 Feb. 1963, p. A5.

6: THE BOMBER PROBLEM

1 Meeting of the ExComm, 2 Nov. 1962.

2 Meeting of the ExComm, 6 Nov. 1962.

3 Meeting of the ExComm, 1 Nov. 1962.

4 "Castro's Broadcast, 31 October 1962," 1 Nov. 1962, UN Archives, DAG-1/5/2/2/6/1–3, Office of the Secretary-General; Bromley Smith, Summary Record of the 16th Meeting of the Executive Committee of the National Security Council, 1 Nov. 1962, *FRUS, 1961–63*, 11:339–41.

5 See, e.g., Khrushchev to Kennedy, 26 Oct. 1962, *FRUS, 1961–1963*, 11:235–36. Privately, Khrushchev himself had referred to those same weapons as "offensive." Aleksandr Fursenko and Timothy Naftali, *Khrushchev's Cold War: The Inside Story of an American Adversary* (New York: W. W. Norton, 2006), 477.

6 See, e.g., Khrushchev to Kennedy, undated, *FRUS, 1961–1963*, 11:199–200; Khrushchev to Kennedy, undated, ibid., 206–7; Roberts to Foreign Office, 12 Nov. 1962, National Archives (London), PREM 11/3996: 83827, PRO; Roberts to Foreign Office, 13 Nov. 1962, ibid.

7 INR Morning Briefing, "Cuba: Reported offloadings of military equipment," 3 Oct. 1962, JFKL, NSF, box 61, Cuba, Subjects, Testimony, 5/7/62–2/27/63.

8 Arthur M. Schlesinger Jr., *Robert Kennedy and His Times* (Boston: Mariner, 2002), 510–11.

9 Meeting of the ExComm, 6 Nov. 1962.

10 Memcon of 10th ExComm Meeting, 28 Oct. 1962, *FRUS, 1961–1963*, 11:284.

11 Meeting of the ExComm, 2 Nov. 1962.

12 "Radio and Television Remarks on the Dismantling of Soviet Missile Bases in Cuba," 2 Nov. 1962, *Public Papers: JFK, 1962*, doc. 501.

13 Meeting of the ExComm, 1 Nov. 1962.

14 Ibid.

15 Meeting of the ExComm, 3 Nov. 1962.

16 Ibid.

17 Meeting of the ExComm, 2 Nov. 1962.

18 McGeorge Bundy, "NSC ExComm Record of Action," 2 Nov. 1962, JFKL, NSF, box 316, "ExComm Minutes."

19 Meeting of the ExComm, 1 Nov. 1962.

20 Meeting of the ExComm, 2 Nov. 1962.

21 Meeting of the ExComm, 7 Nov. 1962.

22 McCloy to Rusk, 4 Nov. 1962, *FRUS, 1961–1963*, 11:366–70.

23 Statement on Cuba by Director of Central Intelligence, 6 Feb. 1963, National Archives, RG 200, McNamara Papers, box 36, Cuba, 1962–63.

24 See, e.g., Khrushchev to Kennedy, undated, *FRUS, 1961–1963*, 11:199–200; Khrushchev to Kennedy, undated, ibid., 206–7; Roberts to Foreign Office, 12 Nov. 1962, National Archives (London), PREM 11/3996: 83827, PRO; Roberts to Foreign Office, 13 Nov. 1962, ibid.

25 Informal Office Discussion, 5 Nov. 1962.

26 Conversation on the Surveillance Plane Incident, 5 Nov. 1962.

27 Meeting of the ExComm, 6 Nov. 1962.

28 Conversation on the Surveillance Plane Incident, 5 Nov. 1962.

29 Meeting of the ExComm, 3 Nov. 1962.

30 Ibid.

31 Meeting with the JCS, 16 Nov. 1962.

32 Meeting of the ExComm, 7 Nov. 1962.

33 Ibid.

34 Yuri Zhukov was the foreign editor of *Pravda* and had recently been meeting with high-level U.S. officials to discuss the Cuban crisis.

7: STANDING IN JUDGMENT

1 "Debate over Cuba," *New York Times*, 23 Sept. 1962, p. 187.

2 President's News Conference, *New York Times*, 30 Aug. 1962, p. 10.

3 Bill Becker, "Cuba Quarantine Is Urged by Nixon," *New York Times*, 19 Sept. 1962, p. 1; Carl Greenberg, "Nixon Wants Kennedy to Quarantine Cuba," *Los Angeles Times*, 19 Sept. 1962, p. 2.

4 Chalmers M. Roberts, "Rockefeller Image and How It Grows," *Washington Post*, 21 Sept. 1962, p. A4; Joseph Alsop, "Kennedy's Off-Year Campaign," ibid., 26 Sept. 1962, p. A17.

5 Quoted in Thomas G. Paterson and William J. Brophy, "October Missiles and November Elections: The Cuban Missile Crisis and American Politics, 1962," *Journal of American History* 73, no. 1 (June 1986): 96.

6 Hugh Sidey, *John F. Kennedy, President* (New York: Atheneum, 1963), 301.

7 Walter Trohan, "Big Unknown in Election," *Chicago Tribune*, 6 Nov. 1962, p. 1.

8 Lawrence F. O'Brien, *No Final Victories: A Life in Politics—From John F. Kennedy to Watergate* (Garden City, N.Y.: Doubleday, 1974), 142.

9 Paterson and Brophy, "October Missiles and November Elections," 90–91.

10 Sidey, *John F. Kennedy, President*, 293.

11 Ibid.

12 Paterson and Brophy, "October Missiles and November Elections," 91–92; Sidey, *John F. Kennedy, President*, 293.

13 Paterson and Brophy, "October Missiles and November Elections," 92.

14 Walter Trohan, "Reaction to Cuba Big Unknown in Election," *Chicago Daily Tribune*, 6 Nov. 1962, p. 1.

15 Drew Pearson, "Faked Photos in Golden State—The Washington Merry-Go-Round," *Washington Post*, 2 Nov. 1962, p. D11; "Brown Charges Smear in Photos," ibid., 8 Nov. 1962.

16 "Brown, Nixon Battle for Every Last Vote," *Washington Post*, 6 Nov. 1962, p. A2.

17 "Nixon Scraps Schedule, Plans Election Eve Talk," *Washington Post*, 5 Nov. 1962, p. A2; Bill Becker, "Nixon Shifts Plans; Will Rebut 'Attacks,'" *New York Times*, 5 Nov. 1962, p. 1.

18 Kenneth P. O'Donnell and David F. Powers, *"Johnny, We Hardly Knew Ye": Memories of John Fitzgerald Kennedy* (Boston: Little, Brown, 1972), 307.

19 Joseph Alsop, "Kennedy's Off-Year Campaign," *Washington Post*, 26 Sept. 1962, p. A17.

20 President's News Conference, 23 July 1962, *Public Papers: JFK, 1962*, doc. 302.

21 Thomas C. Reeves, *A Question of Character: A Life of John F. Kennedy* (New York: Free Press, 1991), 166.

22 Sidey, *John F. Kennedy, President*, 294.

23 Quoted ibid., 297.

24 Quoted ibid., 298.

25 For a discussion of political arguments about the Kennedy administration's handling of the crisis, see Richard Ned Lebow, "Domestic Politics and the Cuban Missile Crisis: The Traditional and Revisionist Interpretations Reevaluated," *Journal of Diplomatic History* 14 (Fall 1990): 471–92.

26 "Statement by the President Urging Citizens to Vote on Election Day," 3 Nov. 1962, *Public Papers: JFK, 1962*. doc. 502; "The President's News Conference," 20 Nov. 1962, ibid., doc. 515.

27 When Alaska and Hawaii became states, the number of House seats was temporarily increased to 437. In the Nov. 1962 election, the number

dropped back to the normal 435; Walter Trohan, "Big Unknown in Election," *Chicago Tribune*, 6 Nov. 1962, p. 1.

28 Paterson and Brophy, "October Missiles and November Elections," 118; ibid., 92.

29 Conversation between President Kennedy and William Guy, 9 Nov. 1962; Conversation between President Kennedy and John Reynolds, 9 Nov. 1962. Kennedy also called his younger brother Edward Kennedy, but the bulk of that recording remains closed by the JFKL.

30 Carroll Kilpatrick, "Kennedy 'Heartened,' Aides Jubilant; 'Clear Net Gain' for Program Hailed," *New York Times*, 8 Nov. 1962, p. A8.

31 Conversation between President Kennedy, Pat Brown, and Jerry Brown, 9 Nov. 1962.

32 Conversation between President Kennedy and John Connally, 9 Nov. 1962.

33 Harold Martin, *Saturday Evening Post*, 7 Sept. 1957, quoted in Drew Pearson, "Washington Merry-Go-Round," 9 Dec. 1962, *Washington Post*.

34 Statement by the President on the Death of Mrs. Roosevelt, 7 Nov. 1962, *Public Papers: JFK, 1963*, doc. 505.

8: A TUB OF BUTTER

1 Dean Rusk, *As I Saw It*, ed. Daniel S. Papp (New York: W. W. Norton, 1990), 294; author interview with Carl Kaysen, 12 Oct. 2005.

2 Informal Discussion on the Foreign Service, 30 July 1962, in *Pres. Recordings: JFK*, 1:48–50.

3 Rusk, *As I Saw It*, 296.

4 Ibid., 198.

5 Ibid., 204.

6 Ibid., 207.

7 Ibid., 296.

8 Meeting on Foreign Policy, 5 Nov. 1962.

9 Ibid.

10 Ibid..

11 Rusk, *As I Saw It*, 277.

9: THE MILITARY PROBLEM

1 John A. McCone, Memorandum of conversation between President Kennedy and Former President Eisenhower, 17 Nov. 1962, *FRUS, 1961–1963*, 11:479. There were also submarine-launched missiles included in the ANADYR buildup. See William Burr and Thomas Blanton, eds., "The Submarines of October: U.S. and Soviet Naval Encounters during the Cuban Missile Crisis," National Security Archive Electronic Briefing Book no. 75, 31 Oct. 2002; and Peter A. Huchthausen, *October Fury* (Hoboken, N.J.: Wiley, 2002).

2 This accusatory phrase comes from Senator Kenneth Keating's (Republican, New York) 31 Aug. 1962 statement in the Senate. *Congressional Record* (31 Aug. 1962): 18361.

3 "Department of Defense Appropriations for Fiscal Year 1964," *Hearings before a Subcommittee of the Committee on Appropriations,* House of Representatives, 88th Cong., 1st sess., pt. 1 (Washington, D.C.: Government Printing Office, 1963), 86.

4 Dale R. Herspring, *The Pentagon and the Presidency: Civil-Military Relations from FDR to George W. Bush* (Lawrence: University Press of Kansas, 2005), 147.

5 Meeting with the JCS, 16 Nov. 1962.

6 Herspring, *The Pentagon and the Presidency*, 123–34.

7 Quoted in Peter Wyden, *Bay of Pigs: The Untold Story* (New York: Simon and Schuster, 1979), 307.

8 Robert F. Kennedy, *Thirteen Days: A Memoir of the Cuban Missile Crisis* (New York: W. W. Norton, 1969), 97.

9 Lyndon Johnson to Sargent Shriver, 1 Feb. 1964, in *The Presidential Recordings of Lyndon B. Johnson*, vol. 4, ed. Kent B. Germany (New York: W. W. Norton, 2006), 67–70.

10 Meeting of Berlin Group on Crisis Planning, 22 Oct. 1962, *Pres. Recordings: JFK*, 3:34–35; Stanley Kubrick, Terry Southern, and Peter George, *Dr. Strangelove or: How I Learned to Stop Worrying and Love the Bomb*, dir. Stanley Kubrick (Columbia Pictures, 1964).

11 Anatoli I. Gribkov and William Y. Smith, *Operation ANADYR: U.S. and Soviet Generals Recount the Cuban Missile Crisis* (Chicago: Edition Q, 1994); Aleksandr Fursenko and Timothy Naftali, *"One Hell of a Gamble": Khrushchev, Castro, and Kennedy, 1958–1964* (New York: W. W. Norton, 1997), 166–67; SNIE 85-3-62 "The Military Buildup in Cuba," 19 Sept. 1962, LBJL, NSF, Country, Cuba, box 37, Cuba—Intelligence Reports 1962–63, vol. 2; CIA, Intelligence Handbook on Cuba, 1 Jan. 1965, LBJL, NSF, Country, Cuba, box 24, Intelligence, vol. 2, 1/65–4/65.

12 Department of State Press Release No. 651, 18 Nov. 1960, LBJL, NSF, box 22, Country Files: Latin America: Cuba, Fact Sheet 12/63; NIE 85-62: Situation and Prospects in Cuba, 21 March 1962, LBJL, NSF, box 9, NIEs, 85: Cuba; CFP-DCSOPS-6, "Cuba-Threat and Army Plans," 7 Dec. 1962, U.S. Army Center for Military History, 228.01, Geog G Cuba 370.2 US Forces. Castro's comment is quoted in Theodore Draper, *Castro's Revolution: Myths and Realities* (New York: Praeger, 1962), 82.

13 Meeting with the JCS, 16 Nov. 1962.

14 SNIE 95-4-62: Castro's Subversive Capabilities in Latin America, 9 Nov. 1962, LBJL, NSF, box 9, NIEs, 85: Cuba. The Stennis committee identified this late identification of the Soviet ground combat forces as an intelligence flaw. Interim Report by Preparedness Investigating Subcommittee of the Senate Committee on Armed Services, "The Cuban Military Buildup," 9 May 1963, 2.

15 NIE 11-14-62, "Capabilities of the Soviet Theater Forces," 5 Dec. 1962, LBJL, NSF-NIEs, box 2, 11-62 USSR.

16 CIA, Phasing of the Soviet Military Deployment to Cuba, 28 Nov. 1962, JFKL, NSF, box 46A, Cuba, Subjects, CIA Memos, 11/20/62–11/29/62; CIA, "The Crisis: U.S.S.R./Cuba," 29 Nov. 1962, ibid.; CIA, Soviet Presence in Cuba, 7 Dec. 1962, JFKL, NSF, box 47, Cuba, Subjects, CIA Memoranda, 12/1/62–3/26/63; CIA, "The U.S.S.R.'s Intentions with Respect to its Military Presence in Cuba," 13 Dec. 1962, ibid.; and CIA, The Cuban Situation, 16 Dec. 1962, ibid.; CIA, "The Cuban Situation," 18 Dec. 1962,

ibid. This assessment continued through the 1960s, on the basis of such evidence as the arrival in Cuba of some wives of Soviet personnel. CIA, Weekly Cuban Summary, 3 Feb. 1965, LBJL, NSF, Country, Cuba, box 36, CIA Daily and Weekly Summaries, vol. 1, 12/64–2/65.

17 Meeting of the ExComm, 1 Nov. 1962.

18 Meeting on the Military Situation in Cuba, 29 Oct. 1962.

19 Meeting on the Military Situation in Cuba, 16 Nov. 1962.

20 Ibid.

21 OPLAN 312–62 was the designation of the contingency plan for a graduated series of air attacks on Cuba to remove threats. See *FRUS, 1961–1963*, 11:473 n.1; Gribkov and Smith, *Operation ANADYR*, 224–26; Meeting with the JCS, 16 Nov. 1962.

22 Gribkov and Smith, *Operation ANADYR*, 4; Fursenko and Naftali, *"One Hell of a Gamble,"* 188; Aleksandr Fursenko and Timothy Naftali, "The Pitsunda Decision: Khrushchev and Nuclear Weapons," CWIHP *Bulletin* 10 (March 1998): 223–25; Raymond Garthoff, "New Evidence on the Cuban Missile Crisis: Khrushchev, Nuclear Weapons, and the Cuban Missile Crisis," CWIHP *Bulletin* 11 (Winter 1998): 251–54.

23 Meeting on the Military Situation in Cuba, 29 Oct. 1962.

24 Meeting with the JCS, 16 Nov. 1962.

10: MISSILES OF NOVEMBER

1 Soviet Forces in Cuba, Annex A, 5 Feb. 1963, JFKL, NSF, box 51, Cuba, Subjects, Intelligence Materials, 2/63; DIA, "Round-up of Significant World Events," 23 Nov. 1962, National Security Archives, Cuban Missile Crisis Collection, Item No. CC02562; Office of Naval Intelligence, "Intelligence Briefs," *ONI Review* 18, no. 1 (Jan. 1963): 557.

2 Meeting with the JCS, 16 Nov. 1962.

3 Raymond L. Garthoff, "U.S. Intelligence in the Cuban Missile Crisis," in James G. Blight and David A. Welch, eds., *Intelligence and the Cuban Missile Crisis* (London: Frank Cass, 1998), 29.

4 CIA/DIA, "Cuba 1962: Khrushchev's Miscalculated Risk," 13 Feb. 1964, LBJL, NSF, box 35; Roger Hilsman to Dean Rusk, "Review of Recent Developments in Cuba," 23 Jan. 1963, JFKL, NSF, box 51, Cuba, Subjects, Intelligence Materials 1/63.

5 See below for further discussion of this issue.

6 Anatoli I. Gribkov and William Y. Smith, *Operation ANADYR: U.S. and Soviet Generals Recount the Cuban Missile Crisis* (Chicago: Edition Q, 1994), 4; Aleksandr Fursenko and Timothy Naftali, *"One Hell of a Gamble": Khrushchev, Castro, and Kennedy, 1958–1964* (New York: W. W. Norton, 1997), 188; Aleksandr Fursenko and Timothy Naftali, "The Pitsunda Decision: Khrushchev and Nuclear Weapons," CWIHP *Bulletin* 10 (March 1998): 223–25; Raymond Garthoff, "New Evidence on the Cuban Missile Crisis: Khrushchev, Nuclear Weapons, and the Cuban Missile Crisis," CWIHP *Bulletin* 11 (Winter 1998): 251–54.

7 CIA, "The Crisis: U.S.S.R./Cuba," 3 Nov. 1962, JFKL, NSF, box 46, Countries: Cuba, CIA Memoranda, 11/1/62–11/3/62.

8 *New York Times*, 9 Nov. 1964, pp. 32, 17.

9 Meeting of the ExComm, 2 Nov. 1962. For a detailed discussion of the SA-2 system's specifications and capabilities, see CIA/DIA, "Cuba 1962: Khrushchev's Miscalculated Risk," 13 Feb. 1964, LBJL, NSF, box 35.

10 "The Trend toward Modernization in the Soviet Navy," *ONI Review* 17, no. 2 (Feb. 1962): 39–52, box 1292; folder: ONI Review vols. 17–18, Naval Historical Office, Washington Navy Yard; CIA/DIA, "Cuba 1962: Khrushchev's Miscalculated Risk," 13 Feb. 1964, LBJL, NSF, box 35.

11 Trevor Cliffe, *Military Technology and the European Balance*, Adelphi Papers 89 (London: International Institute for Strategic Studies, 1972) 46; CIA/DIA, "Cuba 1962: Khrushchev's Miscalculated Risk," 13 Feb. 1964, LBJL, NSF, box 35.

12 *Pres. Recordings: JFK*, 2:21.

13 Ibid., 3:327.

14 Fursenko and Naftali, *"One Hell of a Gamble,"* 242.

15 Quoted in ibid.

16 Maxwell Taylor, "The Cuban Crisis: Operational Aspects," 26 Dec. 1962, National Defense University, Maxwell Taylor Papers, box 16, folder G: Compilation of High-Level Exchange in Cuban Crisis.

17 Marine Corps Emergency Actions Center, "Summary of Items of Significant Interest," 29 Oct. 1962, National Security Archive, Cuban Missile Crisis Collection, Item no. CC01664; "Chronology of JCS Decisions Concerning the Cuban Crisis," p. 52, 21 Dec. 1962, National Defense University, Maxwell Taylor Papers, box 16, Compilation of High Level Exchanges in Cuba Crisis.

18 Quoted in John A. Heintges to Special Assistant to the Assistant to the Secretary, 29 Dec. 1962, National Security Archive, Cuban Missile Crisis Collection, Item no. CC02795.

19 Briefing Report for General Taylor, 10 Nov. 1962, National Archives, RG 218, box 6; Briefing Report for General Taylor, 11 Nov. 1962, ibid.

20 Dino A. Brugioni, *Eyeball to Eyeball: The Inside Story of the Cuban Missile Crisis* (New York: Random House, 1990), 296–97.

21 John A. Heintges to Special Assistant to the Secretary of Defense, 29 Dec. 1962, National Security Archive, Cuban Missile Crisis Collection, Item no. CC02795. There is no record of the JCS meeting. If a record of this meeting existed, it would likely have been destroyed in Aug. 1974. See http://www.gwu.edu/~nsarchiv/nsa/DOCUMENT/940228.htm.

22 Robert S. McNamara, with Brian VanDeMark, *In Retrospect: The Tragedy and Lessons of Vietnam* (New York: Vintage Books, 1996), 341.

23 Smith quoted in James G. Blight, Bruce J. Allyn, and David A. Welch, *Cuba on the Brink: Castro, the Missile Crisis, and the Soviet Collapse* (New York: Pantheon Books, 1993), 261.

24 Memorandum for the Chairman, JCS, "Rules of Engagement," undated, National Archives, RG 218, Maxwell Taylor Papers, box 6.

25 Michael C. Desch, "'That Deep Mud in Cuba,' The Strategic Threat and U.S. Planning for a Conventional Response during the Cuban Missile Crisis," *Security Studies* 1, no. 2 (Winter 1991): 333; JCS, "Chronology of JCS Decisions Concerning the Cuban Crisis," p. 65, National Defense University, Maxwell Taylor Papers, box 16, Compilation of High Level Exchange in Cuba Crisis.

26 Off-the-record Meeting on the Military Situation in Cuba, 29 Oct. 1962.

27 U.S. intelligence had only ever had photographic confirmation of thirty-three MRBMs in Cuba and could find no compelling reason not to believe the Soviets and Cubans when they said that there had been only forty-two MRBMs in Cuba and that all had been removed. Office of Naval Intelligence, "The Missiles Leave Cuba," *ONI Review* 17, no. 12 (Dec. 1962): 511; Office of Naval Intelligence, "Intelligence Briefs," *ONI Review* 18, no. 1 (Jan. 1963): 557; Meeting of the ExComm, 3 Nov. 1962.

28 Khrushchev to Kennedy, 28 Oct. 1962, *FRUS, 1961–1963*, 11:279.

29 Colonel A.B. Parsons (USAF), "Talking Paper for the Chairman, JCS, for the JCS Meeting, 30 Oct," 30 Oct. 1962, National Archives, RG 218, Maxwell Taylor Papers, box 6.

30 Meeting of the ExComm, 3 Nov. 1962.

31 Kennedy and his advisers explicitly discussed the possibility that the Soviets could reintroduce nuclear warheads to Cuba quickly and secretly. One possibility they considered was that the Soviets might deliver the warheads by submarine. Another was that they might send them by air, especially after the Soviet airline Aeroflot began on 7 Jan. 1963 a regular weekly civilian service from Moscow to Havana via Murmansk. Roger Hilsman to Dean Rusk, "Review of Recent Developments in Cuba," 23 Jan. 1963, JFKL, NSF, Cuba, Subjects, Intelligence Materials, 1/63.

32 The full list included in the proclamation was the following: "Surface-to-surface missiles; bomber aircraft; bombs, air-to-surface rockets and guided missiles; warheads for any of the above weapons; mechanical or electronic equipment to support or operate the above items; and any other classes of materiel hereafter designated by the Secretary of Defense for the purpose of effectuating this Proclamation." Proclamation 3504: Interdiction of the Delivery of Offensive Weapons to Cuba, 23 Oct. 1962, *Public Papers: JFK, 1962*, doc. 486.

33 Meeting of the ExComm, 7 Nov. 1962. See also Meeting of the ExComm, 31 Oct. 1962.

34 Harlan Cleveland's meeting notes, 7 Nov. 1962, JFKL, Harlan Cleveland Papers, box 76, Cuba 11/7/62.

35 Harlan Cleveland, Draft telegram to Stevenson and McCloy, 8 Nov. 1962,

JFKL, Harlan Cleveland Papers, box 78, Cuba-Cuban Crisis-"H.C.'s Book"—Top Secret, 11/62. According to Cleveland's handwritten note on the draft, he conveyed the message by telephone.

11: A DEAL

1 "The President's News Conference," 20 Nov. 1962, *Public Papers: JFK, 1962*, doc. 515.

2 Meeting of the ExComm, 7 Nov. 1962.

3 Ibid.

4 Meeting of the ExComm, 8 Nov. 1962.

5 Ibid.

6 Meeting of the ExComm, 12 Nov. 1962.

7 Kennedy to Khrushchev, 15 Nov. 1962, *FRUS, 1961–1963*, 11:460–62.

8 Khrushchev to Kennedy, 20 Nov. 1962, *FRUS, 1961–1963*, 11:495–501.

9 Meeting of the ExComm, 12 Nov. 1962.

12: WITH ONE VOICE

1 Marquis Childs, "How Much Should the Public Know," *Washington Post*, 19 Nov. 1962, p. A16.

2 *Congressional Quarterly Almanac* (1962): 1003–11.

3 Salinger, *With Kennedy*, 290–91.

4 Ibid., 286–87.

5 Fletcher Knebel, "Kennedy vs. the Press," *Look*, 28 Aug. 1962, p. 21.

6 Richard Fryklund, "Control of News Seen as U.S. 'Weapon,'" *Evening Star* (Washington, D.C.), 29 Oct. 1962; Nick B. Williams, "The Danger of 'News Management,'" *Los Angeles Times*, 20 Jan. 1963, p. F6. These quotations were rereported with minor variations in some outlets. See, e.g., Jack Raymond, "Pentagon Imposes Restraints on News Coverage," *New York Times*, 1 Nov. 1962, p. 17; Salinger, *With Kennedy*, 285.

7 Rephrasing the question, however, led to a different result. When asked, "Do you think the press should have the right to print anything it wants to about situations, such as Cuba and Laos, or not?," 63 percent said it should have the right, 28 percent that it should not, and 10 percent were undecided. Gallup Poll (AIPO), May 1961, Roper Center Public Opinion Archive.

8 James Reston, "How to Make Things Worse Than They Really Are," *New York Times*, 2 Nov. 1962, p. 30.

9 See, e.g., "'Managed News' Plan Rapped by I.A.P.A. Heads," *Chicago Daily Tribune*, 5 Feb. 1963, p. 7; "Morton Rips Managed News Policy of U.S.," *Chicago Tribune*, 22 Feb. 1963, p. C9; "Security News Is Held Back, Salinger Says," ibid., 28 Feb. 1963, p. A6.

10 Editorial, *Washington Star*, 30 Oct. 1962.

11 Editorial, *New York Times*, 31 Oct. 1962, p. 36.

12 Editorial, "News as Weapon," *Washington Post*, 1 Nov. 1962, p. A24.

13 Editorial, "'When Spoken To,'" *Chicago Daily Tribune*, 23 Nov. 1962, p. 20.

14 UPI, "Pentagon Policy Decried," *New York Times*, 1 Nov. 1962, p. 17.

15 "News Management by Administration Scored," *Los Angeles Times*, 13 Jan. 1963, p. A3.

16 Arthur Krock, "Mr. Kennedy's Management of the News," *Fortune*, March 1963, pp. 82, 199.

17 Editorial, "We Do Not Know," *Chicago Daily Tribune*, 8 Jan. 1963, p. 20.

18 Rockefeller quoted in Robert Thompson, "Right to Know vs. Privacy," *Los Angeles Times*, 3 Feb. 1963, p. K1.

19 George E. Sokolsky, "The Arrogance of Ignorance," *Washington Post*, 30 Nov. 1962, p. A19.

20 "Pentagon Ruling on News Scored," *New York Times*, 5 Nov. 1962, p. 28; Editorial, "News as a Weapon," *Chicago Daily Tribune*, 2 Nov. 1962, p. 16; George E. Sokolsky, "Leaks and Censorship," *Washington Post*, 8 Nov. 1962, p. A25.

21 Editorial, "News as a Weapon," *Chicago Daily Tribune*, 2 Nov. 1962, p. 16.

22 Reston, "How to Make Things Worse Than They Really Are," 30.

23 Williams, "The Danger of 'News Management,'" F6.

24 Dorothy McCardle, "Notables Ribbed at Gridiron Club Roast," *Los Angeles Times*, 10 March 1963, p. G3; Harold Brayman, *The President Speaks Off the Record* (Princeton, N.J.: Dow Jones, 1976), 653.

25 Benjamin C. Bradlee, *Conversations with Kennedy* (New York: W. W. Norton, 1975), 164.

26 Meeting of the ExComm, 2 Nov. 1962.

27 Theodore C. Sorensen, *Kennedy* (New York: Harper & Row, 1965), 321.

28 "Pentagon Denies Distorting News in Havana Crisis," *New York Times*, 3 Nov. 1962, p. 8.

29 Quoted in "News Curtailment Denied by Pentagon," *New York Times*, 30 Nov. 1962, p. 21.

30 "U.S. Aide Defends Lying to Nation," *New York Times*, 7 Dec. 1962, p. 5.

31 Associated Press, "News Block at Pentagon Is Denied," *Washington Post*, 30 Nov. 1962, p. A4.

32 Quoted in "News Manipulation by Administration Scored," *Los Angeles Times*, 13 Jan. 1963, p. A3.

33 Pierre Salinger, *With Kennedy* (Garden City, N.Y.: Doubleday, 1966), 286; "Rusk Aides Told to Report Talks," *New York Times*, 2 Nov. 1962, p. 15; Daniel Rapoport, "Crisis News Policy to Be Hearing Topic," *Washington Post*, 14 Jan. 1963, p. A6.

34 "Rusk Aides Told to Report Talks," *New York Times*, 2 Nov. 1962, p. 15.

35 Ibid.

36 Robert Thompson, "Kennedy to Tell Policy on Cuba," *Los Angeles Times*, 20 Nov. 1962, p. 1.

37 Quoted in Editorial, "'When Spoken To,'" *Chicago Daily Tribune*, 23 Nov. 1962, p. 20.

38 *Pres. Recordings: JFK*, 1:599.

39 William Moore, "Kennedy News Curbs Upheld by Sylvester," *Chicago Daily Tribune*, 4 Dec. 1962, p. A4.

40 Carroll Kilpatrick, "Kennedy Tells Top Policy Aides First Duty Is to U.S. Interests," *Washington Post*, 23 Jan. 1963, p. A2; Tom Wicker, "Kennedy Sums Up Foreign Policies," *New York Times*, 23 Jan. 1963, p. 3.

41 Summary Record of the Meeting of the ExComm, 25 Jan. 1963, *FRUS, 1961–1963*, 11:683.

42 Meeting of the ExComm, 25 Jan. 1963.

43 Bradlee, *Conversations with Kennedy*, 154.

44 Ibid., 161–62.

45 Quoted in Thompson, "Right to Know vs. Security," K1.

46 "White House to Argue News with News Media," *New York Times*, 23 Feb. 1963, p. 5.

47 Bradlee, *Conversations with Kennedy*, 162.

13: THE MISSILES WE'VE HAD ON OUR MINDS

1 Meeting of the ExComm, 29 Nov. 1962.

2 Thomas K. Finletter to Rusk, 26 Nov. 1962, JFKL, NSF, box 42, Cuba-Cables–11/24/62–11/28/62.

3 The official memorandum of this conversation recorded, "The President commented that the Russians won't take out their ground forces until we give a no-invasion assurance. It is better for us to have the Soviet units in Cuban than to give a formal no-invasion assurance." *FRUS, 1961–1963*, 11:541. See also Allan Evans to Roger Hilsman, 29 Nov. 1962, JFKL, Roger Hilsman Papers, box 1, Cuba—ExComm Notes 10/62–12/62.

4 JCS to Kennedy, 16 Nov. 1962, *FRUS*, 1961–63, 11:472–74.

5 Raymond L. Garthoff, "New Evidence on the Cuban Missile Crisis: Khrushchev, Nuclear Weapons, and the Cuban Missile Crisis," CWIHP *Bulletin* 11 (Winter 1998): 252; "Talking Paper for the Joint Chiefs of Staff,

for the Meeting with the President," 16 Nov. 1962, National Archives, RG 218, Maxwell Taylor Papers, box 6, 091 Cuba (1962) Cuba Crisis—Misc.—Gen. Taylor File.

6 Talking Paper for the JCS, for the Meeting with the President, 16 Nov. 1962, National Archives, RG 218, Maxwell Taylor Papers, box 6; Meeting with the JCS, 16 Nov. 1962; Meeting with the JCS, 15 Jan. 1962.

7 Meeting with the JCS, 15 Jan. 1963.

8 Roberts to Foreign Office, 12 Nov. 1962, in National Archives (London), PREM 11/3996: 83827.

9 A. Akalovksy to Brubeck, Memorandum of conversation between Stevenson, McCloy, and Kuznetsov, 13 Nov. 1962, in JFKL, Cleveland papers, box 77, Cuba 11/14/62; *FRUS, 1961–1963*, 11:486; Stevenson to Rusk, 15 Nov. 1962, ibid., 464; Bundy to ExComm, 16 Nov. 1962, ibid., 468; McCloy to Rusk, 19 Nov. 1962, ibid., 486–87.

10 Khrushchev to Kennedy, 20 Nov. 1962, *FRUS, 1961–1963*, 11:496; *Public Papers: JFK, 1962*, 830–38.

11 Aleksandr Fursenko and Timothy Naftali, *Khrushchev's Cold War: The Inside Story of an American Adversary* (New York: W. W. Norton, 2006), 503.

12 Matthias Uhl, "Nuclear Warhead Delivery Systems for the Warsaw Pact, 1961–65: Documents from the Russian State Archives of Economics and the German Federal Military Archives of the Reorganization and Modernization of the Armed Services of the Soviet Bloc," Parallel History Project on NATO and the Warsaw Pact Paper, Sept. 2002; idem, "Storming on to Paris: The 1961 *Buria* Exercise and the Planned Solution of the Berlin Crisis," in Vojtech Mastny, Sven G. Holtsmark, and Andreas Wenger, eds., *War Plans and Alliances in the Cold War: Threat Perceptions in the East and West* (London: Routledge, 2006), 58–62; Fursenko and Naftali, *Khrushchev's Cold War*, 472; Malinovskii to Pliev, early Nov. 1962, trans. and reprod. in Savranskaya, "Tactical Nuclear Weapons in Cuba," 385–98.

13 United Press International, "'Would Have Boxed K's Ears,' Castro Says," *Washington Post*, 22 March 1963, p. A14; James G. Blight and Philip Brenner, *Sad and Luminous Days: Cuba's Struggle with the Superpowers after the Missile Crisis* (Lanham, Md.: Rowman & Littlefield, 2002), 80. See also Vladislav M. Zubok, "'Dismayed by the Actions of the Soviet

Union': Mikoyan's Talks with Castro and the Cuban Leadership, November 1962," CWIHP *Bulletin* 5 (Spring 1995): 59, 89–92; "Mikoyan's Mission to Havana: Cuba-Soviet Negotiations, November 1962," ibid., 93–109, 159; JCS Situation Report 7633, 30 Nov. 1962, in JFKL, Cuba, Cables, 11/30/62–12/31/62 [Folder 2 of 2], NSF, box 43; Fursenko and Naftali, *Khrushchev's Cold War,* 503; Fursenko and Naftali, *"One Hell of a Gamble,"* 311; James G. Blight, Bruce J. Allyn, and David A. Welch, *Cuba on the Brink: Castro, the Missile Crisis, and the Soviet Collapse* (New York: Pantheon Books, 1993), 249.

14 Fursenko and Naftali, *"One Hell of a Gamble,"* 315.

15 Garthoff, "U.S. Intelligence in the Cuban Missile Crisis," p. 61 n. 52; A. I. Gribkov, ed., *On the Brink of the Nuclear Abyss,* trans. Svetlana Savranskaya (Moscow: Gregory Page, 1998).

16 Strom Thurmond, "Weekly Newsletter," 1 Feb. 1963, in JFKL, Background Materials III 2/7/63, POF, box 58; Senate Committee on Foreign Relations, Hearing, 16 Jan. 1963, in *Executive Sessions of the Senate Foreign Relations Committee* (Historical Series), vol. 15, 88th Cong., 1st sess., 1963, p. 66.

14: REMOVING THE STRAITJACKET

1 "Outline for Talk to NSC, January 18, 1962," 17 Jan. 1962, *FRUS, 1961–1963*, 8:238.

2 Record of the 508th Meeting of the National Security Council, 22 Jan. 1963, *FRUS, 1961–1963*, 8:458 n. 3; "Roger Hilsman's Remarks at Director's Meeting," 22 Jan. 1963, JFKL, Roger Hilsman Papers, box 5, National Security-Hilsman Summary of President's Views 1/22/63.

3 Ernest R. May, "America's Berlin: Heart of the Cold War," *Foreign Affairs* 77, no. 4 (July/Aug. 1998): 148–60. Kennedy's words are from Meeting on the Military Situation in Cuba, 29 Oct. 1962.

4 Donald P. Steury, *On the Front Lines of the Cold War: Documents on the Intelligence War in Berlin, 1946–1961* (Washington, D.C.: CIA History Staff, Center for the Study of Intelligence, 1991), xi.

5 Memorandum of conversations between John Foster Dulles and Dwight Eisenhower, 30 Nov. 1958, *FRUS, 1958–1960*, 8:142–43; Memorandum of conversation, Dulles and Eisenhower, 18 Nov. 1958, ibid., 84–85.

6 *FRUS, 1961–1963*, 14:705 n. 1.

7 Foy Kohler's comments are recorded in Memorandum of conversation, Ambassadorial Group on Berlin and Germany, 11 July 1962, JFKL, NSF, box 84; Memorandum of conversation, Policy Planning Council Meeting of 28 Aug. 1962, 31 Aug. 1962, National Archives, RG 59, box 212, PPS Staff 196.

8 "Rusk's Testimony to the Senate Committee on Foreign Relations, 16 June 1961," Senate Committee on Foreign Relations, *Executive Sessions of the Senate Foreign Relations Committee* (Historical Series), vol. 13, pt. 2, 87th Cong., 1961, p. 181.

9 Pierre Salinger, *With Kennedy* (New York: Doubleday, 1966), 225–37; Aleksandr Fursenko and Timothy Naftali, *"One Hell of a Gamble": Khrushchev, Castro, and Kennedy, 1958–1964* (New York: W. W. Norton, 1997), 176–77.

10 *New York Times*, 31 Aug. 1962. Valerian Zorin to U Thant, 10 Aug. 1962, UN Archives (New York), ser. 291, box 8, file 5, Countries-Germany-Berlin-Mar 59–Dec 63. UN Press Release SG/1313, 4 Sept. 1962, Record of U Thant's press conference in Vienna, Austria, ser. 0889, box 5, file 5, UN Archives; Transcript of U Thant's press conference, 17 Sept. 1962, Note No. 2662, UN Archives, ser. 0883, box 2, file 4. UN Press Release SG/1305, 30 Aug. 1962, Record of U Thant's press conference in Moscow, UN Archives, ser. 0889, box 5, file 6, Press Conferences, vol. 1.

11 *Pres. Recordings: JFK*, 3:411.

12 Aleksandr Fursenko and Timothy Naftali, *Khrushchev's Cold War: The Inside Story of an American Adversary* (New York: W. W. Norton, 2006), 441–44.

13 Thompson to Rusk, 25 July 1962, *FRUS, 1961–63*, 15:252–53. Khrushchev had asked Thompson to convey his message directly to the White House and bypass regular State Department channels. Nevertheless, Thompson upheld protocol and sent the telegram through normal State Department channels.

14 Thompson to Rusk, 26 July 1962, *FRUS, 1961–1963*, 15:253–54; Thompson to Rusk, 28 July 1962, ibid., 255.

15 Fursenko and Naftali, *"One Hell of a Gamble,"* 194; idem. *Khrushchev's Cold War*, 441–44.

16 Thomas G. Paterson and William J. Brophy, "October Missiles and November Elections: The Cuban Missile Crisis and American Politics, 1962," *Journal of American History* 73, no. 1 (June 1986): 94; Lawrence Freedman, *Kennedy's Wars: Berlin, Cuba, Laos, and Vietnam* (New York: Oxford University Press, 2000), 161.

17 Frank A. Mayer, *Adenauer and Kennedy: A Study in German-American Relations, 1961–1963* (New York: St. Martin's, 1996), 68; Fursenko and Naftali, *Khrushchev's Cold War*, 522–23.

18 Hans Kroll, *Lebenserinnerungen eines Botschafters* (Berlin: Kiepenheuer & Witsch, 1967), 571–75; "Endkampf um Berlin in 4 Wochen," *Deutsche Soldaten Zeitung*, 28 Sept. 1962; Fursenko and Naftali, *Khrushchev's Cold War*, 441–44.

19 Marc Trachtenberg, "The Influence of Nuclear Weapons in the Cuban Missile Crisis," *International Security* 10, no. 1 (Summer 1985): 137–63.

20 Kroll, *Lebenserinnerungen eines Botschafters*, 571–75; "Endkampf um Berlin in 4 Wochen."

21 Aleksandr Fursenko and Timothy Naftali, "The Pitsunda Decision: Khrushchev and Nuclear Weapons," CWIHP *Bulletin* 10 (March 1998): 223–25; Raymond Garthoff, "New Evidence on the Cuban Missile Crisis: Khrushchev, Nuclear Weapons, and the Cuban Missile Crisis," CWIHP *Bulletin* 11 (Winter 1998): 251–54.

22 Memorandum of conversation between Khrushchev and Udall, 6 Sept. 1962, *FRUS, 1961–1963*, 15:308–10, based on a transcript of the meeting prepared by the U.S. interpreter. See also Fursenko and Naftali, *"One Hell of a Gamble,"* 208–9.

23 Richard Reeves, *President Kennedy: Profile of Power* (New York: Simon and Schuster, 1993), 351; Frederick B. Adams Jr., *To Russia with Frost* (Boston: Club of Odd Volumes, 1963).

24 Memorandum for the Prime Minister, 11 Sept. 1962, National Archives (London), PREM 11/3806, 83827.

25 State Bureau of Intelligence and Research, "Soviet Intentions on Berlin in the Light of Their Recent Statements and Moves," 6 Sept. 1962; Hilsman to Rusk, "Soviet Intentions on Berlin the Light of Recent Private Remarks by Khrushchev," 20 Sept. 1962, JFKL, NSF, box 85.

26 Bundy to Sorensen, 23 Aug. 1962, *FRUS, 1961–1963*, 15:284–85; Anatoly Dobrynin, *In Confidence: Moscow's Ambassador to America's Six Cold War Presidents (1962–1986)* (New York: Times Books, 1995), 68.

27 Meeting with Congressional Leadership on Cuba, 4 Sept. 1962, *Pres. Recordings: JFK*, 2:62–63; Meeting on Soviet Arms Shipments to Cuba, 4 Sept. 1962, ibid., 22.

28 Theodore C. Sorensen, *Kennedy* (London: Hodder and Stoughton, 1965), 673.

29 *Department of State Bulletin* 47 (15 Oct. 1962): 559.

30 "Rusk's testimony before a joint sitting of the Senate Committee on Foreign Relations and the Senate Committee on Armed Services, September 5, 1962," in *Executive Sessions of the Senate Foreign Relations Committee Together with Joint Sessions with the Senate Armed Services Committee* (Historical Series), vol. 14, 87th Cong., 2nd sess., 1962), 70.

31 Sorensen, *Kennedy*, 669.

32 Seymour Topping, "Soviet Expected to Act on Berlin before End of '62," *New York Times*, 17 Sept. 1962.

33 Rusk interview with John Scali broadcast by the American Broadcasting Corporation, 29 Sept. 1962, *Department of State Bulletin* 47 (22 Oct. 1962): 598. In another television interview the same day, the assistant secretary of state for inter-American affairs, Edwin Martin, carefully distinguished between U.S. intermediate-range Jupiter missiles in Turkey and hypothetical Soviet intermediate-range missiles in Cuba. They would not be analogous, he said, and they could not be traded. Donald May, "Won't Make Deals with Russians on Cuba, Rusk Says," *Washington Post*, 1 Oct. 1962.

34 Willy Brandt, *Begegnungen mit Kennedy* (Munich: Kindler, 1964), 163–64; MemCon, Kennedy and Brandt, 5 Oct. 1962, *FRUS, 1961–1963*, 15:347.

35 *Washington Post*, 9 Oct. 1962.

36 Robert F. Kennedy's address to the American Legion Convention, 9 Oct. 1962, JFKL.

37 Bowles, MemCon of conversation with Dobrynin, 13 Oct. 1962, *FRUS, 1961–1963*, 11:27.

38 *New York Times*, 15 Oct. 1962.

39 Khrushchev to Kennedy, 9 Nov. 1961, *FRUS, 1961–1963*, 7:57.

40 *Washington Post*, 16 Oct. 1962.

41 *Pres. Recordings: JFK*, 2:411.

42 Ibid., 451.

43 MemCon, McNamara, Bundy, Taylor, Robert Kennedy, George Ball, et al., 17 Oct. 1962, *FRUS, 1961–1963*, 11:95.

44 For the transcript of the president's remarks and the question and answer period following, see Kennedy's address to the National Foreign Policy Conference for Editors and Radio-TV Affairs Broadcasters, 16 Oct. 1962, JFKL, box 135, Pierre Salinger Papers, White House Staff Files.

45 Dobrynin to Gromyko, 19 Oct. 1962, in CWIHP *Bulletin* 8–9 (Winter 1996–97): 278–79.

46 *Pres. Recordings: JFK*, 2:473–74; Memorandum of conversation between Kennedy and Schroeder, 17 Oct. 1962, *FRUS, 1961–1963*, 15:362–70.

47 MemCon, Kennedy and Gromyko, 18 Oct. 1962, *FRUS, 1961–1963*, 15:370–76.

48 MemCon, Rusk and Gromyko, 18 Oct. 1962, *FRUS, 1961–1963*, 15:376–87.

49 *Pres. Recordings: JFK*, 3:581.

50 Ibid., 2:578–99; MemCon, Kennedy and Gromyko, 18 Oct. 1962, *FRUS, 1961–1963*, 15:370–76; Arthur M. Schlesinger Jr., *A Thousand Days: John F. Kennedy in the White House* (Boston: Houghton Mifflin, 1965), 805. Gromyko's detailed report on the meeting, sent two days before Kennedy made public the news of the missile sites, places overwhelming emphasis on the Cuba issue. "Cable from Soviet Foreign Minister Gromyko on October 18, 1962 Meeting with President Kennedy," 20 Oct. 1962, in CWIHP *Bulletin* 8–9 (Winter 1996–97): 279–82. The emphasis is the same in the recollections of the two senior Soviet participants. Dobrynin, *In Confidence*, 76–77; Andrei Gromyko, *Memories*, trans. Harold Shukman (London: Hutchinson, 1989), 175.

51 Lord Harlech (Ormsby-Gore) recorded interview by Richard Neustadt, 12 March 1965, Oral History Collection, JFKL.

52 Minutes of NSC Meeting, 21 Oct. 1962, *FRUS, 1961–1963*, 11:141–49; Schlesinger, *A Thousand Days*, 803.

53 Telephone call between Macmillan and Kennedy, 26 Oct. 1962.

54 Robert F. Kennedy, *Thirteen Days: A Memoir of the Cuban Missile Crisis* (New York: W. W. Norton, 1969), 9.

55 Nikita Khrushchev, *Khrushchev Remembers: The Glasnost Tapes*, trans. and ed. Jerrold L. Schecter (Boston: Little, Brown, 1990), 182.

56 *Pres. Recordings: JFK*, 2:581.

57 David Coleman, "Eisenhower and the Berlin Problem, 1953–54," *Journal of Cold War Studies* 2, no. 1 (Winter 2000): 3–34.

58 Klein, "The Defense of Berlin if Cuba is Blockaded," 19 Oct. 1962, JFKL, NSF, box 85; Klein to Bundy, "Immediate Military Measures for Berlin," 19 Oct. 1962, ibid.

59 Ibid.

60 Abbot Smith to John McCone, "Survivability of West Berlin," 23 Oct. 1962, JFKL, NSF, box 85.

61 *Pres. Recordings: JFK*, 2:552. See also Sorensen, "Possible Consequences of Military Action," 19 Oct. 1962, JFKL, Sorensen Papers, box 49.

62 *Pres. Recordings: JFK*, 2:412.

63 See, e.g., Report on the conversation between de Gaulle and Dean Acheson, 22 Oct. 1962, in Ministère des Affaires Étrangères (Commission de Publication des Documents Diplomatiques Français), *Documents Diplomatiques Français, 1962,* vol. 2, *1er Juillet–31 Décembre* (Paris: Imprimerie Nationale, 1999), 318; Couve de Murville to the French embassies in Bonn, Rome, The Hague, Brussels, Luxemburg, Washington, and London, 25 Oct. 1962, ibid., 327; Roger Seydoux to Couve de Murville, 22 Oct. 1962, ibid., 311; Erin R. Mahan, *Kennedy, de Gaulle, and Western Europe* (New York: Palgrave Macmillan, 2002), 135; *Pres. Recordings: JFK*, 2:318; Jill Kastner, "The Berlin Crisis and the FRG, 1958–62," in *The Berlin Wall Crisis: Perspectives on Cold War Alliances*, ed. John P. S. Gearson and Kori Schake (New York: Palgrave Macmillan, 2002), 142.

64 Meeting with the JCS on the Cuban Missile Crisis, 19 Oct 1962, *Pres. Recordings: JFK*, 2:583. Emphasis in transcript.

65 *Pres. Recordings: JFK*, 3:14.

66 Dobrynin, *In Confidence*, 75, 78; Dean Rusk, *As I Saw It*, ed. Daniel S. Papp (New York: W. W. Norton, 1990), 235; Fursenko and Naftali, "*One Hell of a Gamble,*" 240.

67 *New York Times*, 21 Oct. 1962.

68 Malin's notes, quoted in Fursenko and Naftali, *Khrushchev's Cold War.*

69 Kennedy to Khrushchev, 22 Oct. 1962, *FRUS, 1961–1963*, 6:165.

70 Kennedy, "Radio and Television Report to the American People on the Soviet Arms Buildup in Cuba," 22 Oct. 1962, *Public Papers: JFK, 1962*, 806–9.

71 Rusk to the American Embassy in Paris, "Cuba and Berlin," 26 Oct. 1962, JFKL, NSF, box 98.

72 Alphand to Couve de Murville, 22 Oct. 1962, *Documents Diplomatiques Français, 1962*, 2:314.

73 Report of meeting between Charles de Gaulle and Dean Acheson, 22 Oct. 1962, *Documents Diplomatiques Français, 1962*, 2:316, 318.

74 Lightner to Rusk, 23 Oct. 1962, JFKL, NSF, box 98.

75 Vladislav Zubok and Constantine Pleshakov, *Inside the Kremlin's Cold War: From Stalin to Khrushchev* (Cambridge: Harvard University Press, 1996), 260–61.

76 Ibid.

77 Rusk to U.S. NATO Mission, "Assessment of Current Soviet Intentions," 7 Nov. 1962, *FRUS, 1961–1963*, 15:420. MemCon, Kennedy, Adenauer, Rusk, and Schroeder, 14 Nov. 1962, ibid., 443. Zorin quoted in Lightner to Rusk, 26 Oct. 1962, NSF, box 98, JFKL. See also Schlesinger, *A Thousand Days*, 823.

78 CIA Office of Current Intelligence, Berlin Handbook, April 1963, JFKL, NSF, box 91, Countries: Berlin Handbook April 1963.

79 Thomas L. Hughes to Rusk, "Khrushchev Prepares for a Long End Game in Cuban Crisis," 7 Nov. 1962, LBJL, NSF, box 8, Policy Papers and Background Studies in Cuba Affair (II).

80 Rostow to Bundy, 29 Oct. 1962, *FRUS, 1961–1963*, 11:294.

81 NSC Subcommittee on Berlin, "Berlin in Light of Cuba," undated, *FRUS, 1961–1963*, 15:417.

82 Hosting a reception for foreign journalists at the Kremlin, the Soviet premier was vague on the Berlin problem, but did state that the Berlin problem was "assuming greater acuteness," the first time he said anything that might have been interpreted as an indication of further trouble since the end of the missile crisis. Thomas L. Hughes to Rusk, "Khrushchev Prepares for a Long End Game in Cuban Crisis," 7 Nov. 1962, LBJL, NSF, box 8, Policy Papers and Background Studies in Cuba Affair (II).

83 Ulbricht quoted in CIA, Berlin Handbook, April 1963, JFKL, NSF, box 91, Countries: Berlin Handbook April 1963.

84 Fursenko and Naftali, *Khrushchev's Cold War.*

85 Briefing on Foreign Policy for Legislative Leaders, 8 Jan. 1963.

15: A POLITICAL FIREFIGHT

1 Voters Appraise Dimensions of Kennedy Leadership Survey, March 1963.

2 George Reedy, Memorandum for Vice President Lyndon Johnson, undated, LBJL, Vice Presidential Aide's Files of George Reedy, box 3, Cuba [1 of 8].

3 Senate Committee on Foreign Relations, *Executive Sessions of the Senate Foreign Relations Committee* (Historical Series), vol. 15, 88th Cong., 1st sess., 1963, 15.

4 *Time*, 14 Dec. 1962, p. 20.

5 Quoted in *Time*, 2 Nov. 1962, p. 16.

6 See, e.g., CFP-DCSOPS–6, "Cuba-Threat and Army Plans," 7 Dec. 1962, in U.S. Army Center for Military History, 228.01, GEOG G Cuba 370.2 US Forces.

7 On the "photo gap," see Max Holland, "The 'Photo Gap' That Delayed

Discovery of Missiles in Cuba," *Studies in Intelligence* 49, no. 4 (2005): 15–30.

8 See, e.g., *Evening Star*, 6 Nov. 1962, p. 1.

9 Arthur M. Schlesinger Jr., *Robert Kennedy and His Times* (Boston: Mariner, 2002), 539.

10 CIA/DIA, "Cuba 1962: Khrushchev's Miscalculated Risk," LBJL, NSF, box 35.

11 Marguerite Higgins, "More Cuba Missiles: We Reveal Castro Has A-Artillery," *New York Herald Tribune*, 20 Nov. 1962, p. 1.

12 "The President's News Conference," 20 Nov. 1962, *Public Papers: JFK, 1962*, doc. 515.

13 "40 Missiles Reported Left in Cuba," *Washington Post*, 5 Feb. 1963, p. A1.

14 Meeting of the ExComm, 5 Feb. 1963.

15 Ibid.

16 Statement on Cuba by Director of Central Intelligence, 6 Feb. 1963, National Archives, RG 200, McNamara Papers, box 36, Cuba, 1962–63.

17 Tom Wicker, "McNamara Insists Offensive Arms Are Out of Cuba," *New York Times*, 7 Feb. 1963, p. 1.

18 Ibid., p. 2.

19 John G. Norris, "Administration Case on Cuba not Air-Tight," *Washington Post*, 8 Feb. 1963, p. A11.

20 CIA, "Disclosures of U.S. Intelligence Methodology," 29 March 1963, JFKL, NSF, Cuba, Subjects, Intelligence Materials 3/63; CIA, "Additional Points in Secretary McNamara's Presentation not Directly Discussed by Mr. McCone," undated, JFKL, NSF, box 61, Cuba, Subjects, Testimony, 5/7/62–2/27/63.

21 *New York Times*, 7 Feb. 1963.

22 The President's News Conference, 7 Feb. 1963, *Public Papers: JFK, 1963*.

23 *Washington Post*, 9 Feb. 1963, p. A1.

24 Quoted in *Congressional Quarterly Almanac* (1963): 316; Willard Edwards, "Leaders in Congress Challenge His Story," *Chicago Daily Tribune*, 7 Feb.1963, p. 1

25 CIA, "Removal of FROGs," undated, JFKL, NSF, box 61, Cuba, Subjects, Testimony, 5/7/62–2/27/63.

26 Bundy to Rusk, McNamara, and McCone, 19 Feb. 1963, *FRUS, 1961–1963*, 11:705

27 Meeting of the ExComm, 3 Nov. 1962.

28 *New York Times*, 9 Feb. 1963; William Moore, "CIA Gets Cuba Briefing," *Chicago Daily Tribune*, 9 Feb. 1963.

29 U.S. intelligence had confirmed through radio intercepts that a shipment containing a small amount of radioactive isotopes had arrived in Cuba aboard the *Michurinsk* in mid-January. CIA, "Comments on Statements Made by Senator Keating on 8 February," 20 Feb. 1963, JFKL, NSF, Cuba, Subjects, Senator Kenneth B. Keating, Statements, 11/62–4/63.

30 Ibid.

31 Frederick G. Dutton to McGeorge Bundy and Larry O'Brien, 12 Feb. 1962, JFKL, NSF, box 61, Cuba, Subjects, Testimony, 5/7/62–2/27/62.

32 Memorandum of telephone conversation between George Ball and Cong. Mahon, 11 Feb. 1963, 10 a.m., JFKL, George Ball Papers, box 3, Cuba 1/5/63–10/31/63; Interim Report by Preparedness Investigating Subcommittee of the Senate Committee on Armed Services, "The Cuban Military Buildup," 9 May 1963.

33 *New York Times*, 21 April 1963, pp. 1, 62; Schlesinger, *Robert Kennedy and His Times*, 539–40.

34 MemCon, Rusk and Dobrynin, 18 Feb. 1963, JFKL, Bundy Papers, box 33, Daily Memoranda for the Record, July 1963–Dec. 1962.

35 JFKL, NSF, box 47; Meeting with Andrei Gromyko, 10 Oct. 1963; "Address and Question and Answer Period in Tampa before the Florida Chamber of Commerce," 18 Nov. 1963, *Public Papers: JFK, 1963*, doc. 465.

36 Harris survey, Sept. 1963, Roper Center Public Opinion Archive.

37 James G. Blight and Philip Brenner, *Sad and Luminous Days: Cuba's Struggle with the Superpowers after the Missile Crisis*, 2nd ed. (Lanham, Md.: Rowman & Littlefield, 2007).

38 David Newsom, *The Soviet Brigade in Cuba: A Study in Political Diplomacy* (Bloomington: Indiana University Press, 1987).

39 McGeorge Bundy, "The Brigade's My Fault," *New York Times*, 23 Oct. 1979, p. A23.

16: SHAPING THE FUTURE

1 *Lodestar* (American University), spring pictorial issue, June 1963.

2 Arthur M. Schlesinger Jr., *A Thousand Days: John F. Kennedy in the White House* (Boston: Houghton Mifflin, 1965), 904

3 Carl M. Brauer, *John F. Kennedy and the Second Reconstruction* (New York: Columbia University Press, 1977).

4 Aleksandr Fursenko and Timothy Naftali, *Khrushchev's Cold War: The Inside Story of an American Adversary* (New York: W. W. Norton, 2006); and William Taubman, *Khrushchev: The Man and His Era* (New York: W. W. Norton, 2003), 578–79.

5 Harris/CCFR Survey of American Public Opinion and U.S. Foreign Policy 1974, Dec. 1974.

Index